In Search
of a
Northern Soul

A journey of discovery in north east England

Stephen Wood

Orwell House

In Search
of a
Northern Soul

Permissions

I acknowledge with thanks the consent of the following:

Simon Evans, for his kind permission to reproduce observations from his stage show

Michael Palin and his publishers *Orion Publishing Group* for permission to reference his book "*Sahara*"

Robson Green for his permission to quote his lines on Northumberland

Bill Bryson and his publishers *Transworld Publishing* for permission to reference and quote from his book "*The Road to Little Dribbling*"

Eland Publishing for permission to quote from **Winston Churchill** in his book "*My Early Life*"

Pascal Mercier and his publishers *Atlantic Books* for permission to quote from his book *Night Train to Lisbon.*

I am particularly indebted to the representatives of the late **Pete McCarthy** and his publishers *Hodder & Stoughton* for their kind permission to reference his influences and to quote from his book "*McCarthy's Bar*"

In Search
of a
Northern Soul

Acknowledgements

From the very seed of the idea to pressing the "*publish*" button, there have been many points at which I have faltered, regarded my pen with despair and withdrawn to the pub. And so I owe a deep debt of gratitude to those who have helped, cajoled, inspired and encouraged me, without whom no doubt this book would never have been completed. The following are singled out for particular thanks, whether they like it or not.

Nick Herrmann of *Cornerstones Literary Agency* for his incisive mentoring throughout the whole writing process, **Doug Hermann** *(curiously no relation)* who was brave enough to follow my efforts as the paragraphs arose and offered me invaluable advice from his uniquely American and personal perspective, and **Andrew Croome** who followed my pen with a keen eye on the syntax and my wandering grammar.

And although they may be surprised to see themselves mentioned here, the management and staff of **The Park Hotel, Tynemouth** for their assistance, company and encouraging interest in someone who was, after all, just a customer passing through.

And not least my long-suffering wife **Gillian**, who had the unenviable task of line-editing, a burden she discharged with commendable and heroic diligence, as well as being sensible and facing me in the right direction when my scribblings wandered off-target.

Finally, to all those I met on my journey, strangers all of them. Thank you for your company, your anecdotes, your inspiration and for the little glimpses into your personal lives that you allowed me. Your names, in some cases, may have been changed but where you do recognise yourselves I hope that you will look back and remember our meeting with a smile. I do.

Contents

for my father

In Search

of a

Northern Soul

A journey of discovery in north east England

Orwell House

ONE

A Night in Newcastle, 1969

When I tell people I'm a Geordie, born and bred on the north banks of the Tyne, they tend not to believe me. That's because I don't sound like one. I used to, many years ago when the north east still had a shipbuilding industry and County Durham was littered with pits. I scampered around Tynemouth and Whitley Bay then and my voice had the natural music of the north. But not anymore, not since I moved away when my schooldays came to an end and I finished up in the south. But we'll come to all that.

What I do have are memories. Memories of the north east which sing to me sometimes. They catch me unawares and I find myself imagining I'm back there. I'll tell you one, just to get started.

***

I remember a cold, dark evening in December 1969. I'm 16 years old and I'm standing on the wide, concrete platform at Tynemouth station with 3 of my pals. The high Victorian ironwork of the concourse channels a chill breeze but I don't feel it much, not because I'm a Geordie, but because tonight The Who are playing at Newcastle City Hall, and we Tyneside teenagers have tickets. I am far too excited to be worried about the weather.

I am worried though about the group of lads hanging around not far down the platform, loud and sweary. They probably mean no harm, but they might do, and we try not to attract their attention.

We stand together, blue jeans over Chelsea boots, a jacket over an open shirt with a fashionable pointed collar, we are dressed beyond our years. Will The Who be loud? Of course they will. Will they play Pictures of Lily? Of course they will. Will there be any trouble? Probably.

The two-carriage diesel clanks into the station. Heavy handles on heavy doors let us into the first, and to my relief the hooligans get in the other. Inside it's inhospitable, cold, and the metal framed seats are hard. The fabric is bare, and stained. There is no toilet, unless you count the draughty space between the carriages.

A banging of doors and the train jolts forward. The lights of the town and the darkness of cuttings and tunnels pass by as I peer out of the wet, streaked window. I am conscious of the occasional shout and laughter from the rear carriage, but otherwise there is little chatter between the dozen or so passengers around us. Single men reading newspapers in the dim carriage lights, too old for The Who. Couples talk in low tones. A few lads in twos and threes.

The train rumbles through the stations of the North Tyneside line to Newcastle, through North Shields, Percy Main, Wallsend, and Byker to Manors in the city. It takes about half an hour, which we pass by discussing our favourite band member, and whether he will behave outrageously on stage. We conclude that he will, because he always does.

The arched, glazed entrance doors of Newcastle City Hall on Northumberland Street are swarming with concert goers, noisy with the roar of a teenage, mainly long-haired, crowd. We jostle and are jostled as we make our way in. It is smoky, hot, and slightly terrifying. Banks of Marshall amplifiers, speakers and a huge drum kit are set up on the stage. Leather jacketed people wander about it plugging and unplugging things. We wait.

They are late, of course, which adds to the excitement as it is intended to do. Or perhaps Keith Moon has got lost or can't be roused. But eventually to roars and cheers they appear and without ado or introduction release a wall of sound so loud I can't tell if it's Pictures of Lily or if something has gone wrong.

For a couple of hours it is deafening, flashing chaos. People around me jump about, arms flailing, hair flailing, banging heads to John Entwhistle's thumping bass. Pete Townsend's arms windmill at his guitar, and Keith Moon is a blur of whatever Keith Moon is made of. It is the first time I have been to a place where such energy emanates from the stage, and from the crowd towards it. I am either not confident enough, or too reserved or just too young to express myself in physical contortions, and can only watch mesmerised as it all happens around me.

In the end, a thumping rendition of I Can See For Miles is the grand finale. Roger Daltry swings the microphone on its wire, Pete Townsend does more arm flailing, John Entwhistle stands at the back, and Keith Moon jumps up and down on his drum kit, kicks it, and throws it about until it is in many more pieces than it was when it started out today. It is pandemonium. It is anarchy. It is just what the crowd came to see.

And then the lights come up. It is strangely quiet. The crowd has lost its wild impetus and people begin moving towards the exits. They are more sedate now, and it's almost an anti-climax as we find ourselves outside the hall, the throng dissipating into the Newcastle night.

It is getting late. It's pub closing time and shouting can be heard from nearby streets. It's a few minutes' walk back to Manors station, and we are nervous. A small group of lads passes nearby, staggering arm in arm, laughing and drinking from bottles. They pay us no attention. Glass smashes somewhere, followed by angry shouts. We walk a little quicker. The sound of a police siren pierces the air not too far away, changing tone as it passes.

A girl, the worse for wear, shouts something at us from a group across the road. It's broad Geordie, and I can't make out what she said. She shouts again and the group she is with laughs. We walk on quickly, heads down, hoping they will get bored with us.

A girl's scream cuts through the night. It's impossible to tell whether it is a cry of fear, or of delight. More glass shatters somewhere. More shouting.

Manors station is no escape. It's the late train down from Newcastle to the coast and the various stops along the way, and for those who have spent the night drinking in the pubs and clubs of the city it's the last opportunity to get home. They are full of beer and belligerence. We avoid catching their eyes, in fear of hearing the words "*Are you looking at me?*" It is a question to which there is no acceptable response.

We survive to the platform at Tynemouth, where the station is quiet, and the streets a little safer. My parents will be waiting up and will hear the front door with relief. They know where I have been.

***

You would be forgiven for thinking that memories such as that would leave an uncomfortable taste, or at the least a mixed one. You might even question why I am writing this if not to cast aspersion on the land of my birth. You might even wonder at my premise, this Search for a Northern Soul as I have titled this book, if memories such as that night in Newcastle are anything to go by. Why would I want to? But my memories are a kaleidoscope which derive from a wide spectrum of experiences. Like all memories they encompass a whole landscape of events, times and emotions. Just like yours do, I'm sure.

And if I can burrow deeper into the more remote recesses of my mind, beyond the memories I laid there myself, into the genetic memories installed in my DNA by the experiences of my ancestors, I will see more clearly those people, those lives, my heritage, all of which has made me what I am.

When my memories arise, when I see the north east of England in my mind's eye, do I see my soul?

TWO

Premise, Inspiration, Why

This story is about a journey, a journey back to my roots in the North East of England, and back in time to the people and places of my heritage. I am going back to explore the land of my birth, my childhood, and my ancestors. I'm going to dig deep into the lives of those who went before me, into the mines and the black gold of coal, the oil and dust of shipbuilding and mining, and the riches of the culture and the character of the North East.

But what of that memory of late-night Newcastle in 1969? It was over 50 years ago that I went to see The Who, and at that distance memory can be hazy. But we *did* see them at Newcastle City Hall, and they *were* louder than anything I had ever heard before. I honestly can't remember whether Keith Moon destroyed his drum kit that night, but he nearly always did and so I think I'm safe in saying that he did so. And Newcastle *was* an intimidating place at night. I *was* genuinely often scared. The belligerent and sometimes hostile atmosphere of the city at that time is something that has stayed with me over all those years.

When Dick Clement and Ian la Frenais wrote the character of Oz for Jimmy Nail in the 1980s television comedy series Auf Wiedersehen Pet, Oz was portrayed as a loud, abrasive, drunken Geordie lout. His major passions in life were drinking and supporting Newcastle United. Yet, Oz could be likeable, in a way. He was a Geordie. But fill him full of beer and stand well back. Dick and Ian were themselves Northerners and they knew what they were talking about. Oz was authentic, he was real, and he drank in Newcastle on Friday nights.

There is, of course, more to this than fearsome nights in Newcastle in the 1960s and 1970s. There's mining for a start. The arrival of the industrial revolution in the North East in the 18th and 19th centuries gave rise to a great upsurge in coal mining, particularly in north Durham to the south of the river. In 1850 The Times described the county of Durham as being "*little more than one huge colliery*". In 1869 there were 157 collieries and pits in the Durham coalfield alone. Entire villages were forged in the countryside for no other purpose than to serve those pits. The lives of the men who then worked both above and below ground in the drifts and pit shafts that littered the region from one horizon to the other were relentlessly harsh and dirty, yet undertaken with a pride and stoicism which is difficult, today, to imagine. There was no NHS, no benefits for the unemployed or the simply idle, or, as was so frequently the case, for those incapacitated by injuries sustained far underground in an age when health and safety had yet to be invented.

In 1851, 525 men were killed in the Durham coalfields, and in 1909 in the worst of them all, at Stanley, 168 men died in one single disaster, an explosion underground.

And then there's shipbuilding. On the banks of the river Tyne itself the burgeoning shipbuilding industry drew workers from far and wide to the noise, clamour and heat of the shipyards. They too laboured for small reward to the benefit of unseen masters. Great fortunes were made by pit and shipyard owners, but those fortunes did not much enrich those who wielded the picks or the rivet hammers.

And again, much further North away from the commotion of the mines and shipyards, where the industrial revolution went largely unnoticed, in small, remote and muddy villages folks worked the land, the farms and the estates, and they fished the coastal waters with little more reward than subsistence.

On these coasts others fell to helping themselves, the smugglers and black-marketeers. The deserted shorelines witnessed constant conflict between these profiteers and the men in red determined to arrest their activities – the men of the Coastguard Service. My three-times great grandfather was one of them.

My heritage may touch upon the likes of Oz, but he is just one part of the story. The north east is rich in culture and its industrial legacies are strong. But there is also a legacy of decay when those industries declined and died. My ancestors were concerned in both. With the passing of time successive generations have witnessed rebirth and regeneration as a new world arises from the ashes and shadows of the past.

These places and people are the roots of my heritage. It is because of them that I am here.

***

I was born within sight of the Tyne, in the Tynemouth Victoria Jubilee Infirmary on the north banks of the river on Tuesday 6th October 1953. This makes me a true Geordie. I grew up with my parents and younger brother in Tynemouth where I spent my childhood and teenage years on the coast around the seaside resort of Whitley Bay and the industry of the river. Before that, both my mother's and my father's immediate ancestries are in the mining communities of County Durham and the small, scruffy villages which arose around the coalfields and pits. Many still exist, but the dominating infrastructure of the mines and shipyards does not.

Further back in time, before the grime and illusions of the industrial revolution attracted them to the clamour of industrial Tyneside, they came from far north Northumberland, Alnwick with its Castle and Harry Potter and places like Embleton, Craster and Low Newton, villages which today are almost exactly as they were 200 years ago.

And yet further on to Bamburgh, Lindisfarne and Berwick, where the Border lies and the Northumbrian accent begins to meld with the Scottish. The river Tweed runs from the southern uplands of Scotland to the North Sea dividing two nations which have historically beat the living daylights out of each other every few years. All these places are tributaries of the blood which now runs in my veins.

***

Born amidst the mining communities of County Durham, by education and determination my father hauled himself away from the coalfields. He brought my mother north over the river to the relative refinement of Whitley Bay and pursued his career as a naval architect. He became a Director of a respected, internationally renowned company, and as a consequence I had a comfortable, middle-class upbringing. I managed modest academic achievement and embarked on a career in law which eventually took me to East Anglia where I have remained, now with my career behind me in the autumnal environment of retirement.

From an early age I was conscious that my grandparents on both sides were different. They seemed to have less money, their houses were not as nice and their clothes smelled of mothballs and boiled cabbage. They were from the mining communities my father had left behind, south across the river in County Durham. Yet I was close to them, especially my grandmother on my mother's side. I looked forward to her visits when she would play board games with my brother and me on the dining-room table, and when we caught her cheating she laughed until her bronchitis made her wheezy and breathless. As a small child I held a silent curiosity about their lives, where they came from, and who came before them.

As I grew older I started to research my family history. In the slightly uncomfortable knowledge that no one would be around for ever, I asked lots of questions and noted the answers. In the days before the internet research was gruellingly slow, but nevertheless I started to draw up a family tree which expanded over the years onto a long piece of wallpaper. Then my career and all the distractions of life got in the way and the roll of wallpaper was forgotten, pushed off into some corner of the attic to gather dust. Visits to my parents on Tyneside involved planning and long, arduous drives. My connection with the north east seemed to be slipping away.

About 15 years ago my father died, and not long afterwards my mother was brought away from Tyneside to be close to me and my brother in East Anglia. Most of my ties with the north east were severed then, and I found myself wistfully wondering what had become of my northern heritage. I more frequently called to mind distant childhood memories. Then I re-discovered the roll of wallpaper, and I took a close look at the names on that family tree. They were real people, people but for whose industry and procreation I would never have existed at all. I wanted to discover them, their lives, and I wanted to find my own connection with the landscape of the north east.

I have lived in Norfolk now for more than 40 years. Norwich is a fine city. It is a comfortable place to live. I have built a life here, a family, a career and now a retirement. I have favourite pubs, places to walk in quiet countryside, agreeable friends with whom to drink beer and discuss the wrongs of the world. I even have a delightful wife to keep me on the straight and narrow as my life becomes ever more irascible and hair grows from places it never used to do. I can sit and do simply nothing, should I want to. I like it here.

But do I have a sense that I belong in this place? Some time ago I read an account by Pete McCarthy who set off to wander around the west of Ireland where his immediate family had come from in search of his own heritage, his own sense of belonging, and an explanation for his curious affection for Guinness. He talked of a "*genetic memory*", a latent memory of somewhere he had never lived but where his ancestors had, and which he thought would help him in his quest, if he could find it. Pete titled his book "*McCarthy's Bar*", and his journey of discovery was an inspiration for me to follow, metaphorically, in his footsteps and to see if this feeling, this sense of belonging and home, might be found in the land where I was born and where those with my blood lived many years before.

"It's what you feel inside" Pete burbled to an Irish barman in a McCarthy's bar in Budapest before he embarked on his journey. Or was it just the drink talking?

And so, just as Pete had to go to Ireland, I have to go North to the land of Oz, to look for my childhood on the coast, for my heritage in the old mining villages of north Durham and the shipyards of Tyneside, and to wild north east Northumberland, in the search for my Northern Soul, and a place which says "*this feels like home*".

Sadly, Pete died in 2004 at the early age of 52, so I can't go with him. But I shall take his book.

PART ONE

TYNESIDE

Tynemouth, North Shields, Whitley Bay and Newcastle

"We leave something of ourselves behind when we leave a place, we stay there, even though we go away. And there are things in us that we can find again only by going back there."

Pascal Mercier

THREE

North Shields, Tynemouth

For a journey that has been preceded by a great deal of eager anticipation, weeks of planning and research, the road north from East Anglia is a tribulation. It's a full 107 miles of mainly single carriageway from Norwich to Newark where one picks up the A1. Why the major, indeed pretty much only, road serving the north and west of the country from East Anglia is a mere single ribbon of tarmac is beyond me, jammed as it is with every agricultural implement known to mankind, sugarbeet and turnip lorries and heavy juggernauts slogging to and from the east coast ports of Great Yarmouth, Harwich and Felixstowe.

And then when you do eventually reach Newark, the A1 stretches north to Newcastle for another 150 miles of roadworks, cones and contraflows. Chris Rea had obviously never been on the A17 or the A1 otherwise he would have relocated his "Road to Hell".

But I knew this would happen as I've done it countless times before. I did it many years ago when my father was terminally ill, and then again for my mother not long afterwards, when she had to be rescued from the dangers of living alone in her eighties, physically and mentally frail and brought south to care and compassion. I haven't been back since.

***

As the A1 rolls on northwards, the counties change. The flatlands and cabbages of Lincolnshire give way to the rolling aspect of Nottinghamshire, then on into the Yorkshires where the higher land of the Dales and The Pennines to the west and the North York moors to the east encompass the Vale of York and the Great North Road.

At Scotch Corner the A1 intersects with the A66 which would take me east to Teesside or west to Cumbria, Carlisle and the Lake District. Feelings of familiarity begin here, growing stronger with each landmark as I watch the journey north advancing. I remember Scotch Corner for its bizarrely situated inter-war hotel, standing grandly in the midst of pretty much nothing. There was once a roundabout here, but now the A1 hurtles uninterrupted beneath a flyover.

Past Durham, the columns of Penshaw monument appear silhouetted on a horizon hilltop, a replica of the Temple of Hephaestus dedicated to John Lambton, first Earl of Durham. Its sight has always been a sign I am getting close to home. The road dips and by-passes Chester-le-Street, and then divides, the A1 to pass Newcastle to the west by The Angel of the North, and the other fork to the Tyne Tunnel, then east on the coast road down to Tynemouth and Whitley Bay.

As I approach the coast I remember the shops, the pubs, the filling station on the roundabout. It all seems to slow down around me. The years roll away. It is strangely calming. I know this place.

***

I've taken the risk of booking myself into The Park Hotel for the night of my arrival. It's a risk because I don't hold particularly fond memories of The Park. It's a large, low and sprawling Art Deco building, built in 1939, white with nautical curved lines. Location-wise, you can't fault it. It's almost on the beach, the great sweeping Longsands which connect Tynemouth and Whitley Bay, with only the road between the hotel and the sea. The view, it has to be said, is stupendous, which is more than could be said for the hotel itself.

The Park was originally designed in an indulgent, classically art deco style. It was built to cater for the new tourism brought by the railways in the 1920s and 1930s, and it enticed the inter-war well-to-do with cocktails and dancing. But over the years the paint peeled, investment dwindled, and by the 1970s it had become depressingly shabby. Coach parties and pensioners' excursions moved in. Champagne was exchanged for bottles of Brown Ale and Carlsberg, the corrugated cardboard bar front had all but fallen off, and the high heels had given way to trainers and jogging pants. Although only some 500 yards from the house I was brought up in and one of the nearest bars by far, it was never a destination for me.

My last encounter with The Park was when my father passed away and I made the journey north for his funeral. My wife and I booked into The Park, for no other reason that it was so close at hand. It was dismal.

But it is perfectly located for my exploration of the coast and the river, and I have read that it has undergone a multi-million pound renovation. Hence the risk.

***

From the spacious car park at the front of the hotel, The Park still looks white with its nautical lines, and worryingly familiar. Nothing betrays whether it has, as advertised, been totally refurbished. But through the cleaned up brass and glazed entrance doors it's like opening Alice's wardrobe onto an unexpected world. The recent renovations have seen a wall or two knocked down and it's a much bigger space than I remember. A mix of high and low dark wood tables with chairs and stools are widely spaced on a varnished floor. The bare brickwork with exposed ducting and cables gives it an industrial feel. It's minimalist, but the low, amber lighting and sparkling backdrop behind the long, mahogany bar is warm and welcoming. This is a bar in which I will be pleased to linger awhile.

Which is a Good Thing as I can avoid having to walk into Tynemouth for my dinner. It's freezing outside, as it often is. The comedian Simon Evans, when performing in Newcastle one evening, commented, *"The first time I came up here it was the middle of winter. Had been for years."*

The first night in the bar of a hotel where you're staying for a few days is important. It's an opportunity to get one's bearings, assess the ambience, the bar staff and the regulars, and to check the location of the exits in case Oz turns up.

It's quiet, either because it's well out of the tourist season or because The Park is still struggling to cast off its former reputation, and I'm the only one at the bar as I take a high stool and introduce myself to the barman and a pint.

Ben is a young man, smartly dressed in hotel bar uniform of black trousers and white shirt. He welcomes me with a genuine ease and a soft Geordie accent as he asks me how I am and what I'm doing here. It's my first encounter on this journey with the musical speech of my childhood, and I'm quite surprised at myself when my response unexpectedly takes on a similar, long forgotten cadence.

I was engrossed in talking to Ben, telling him about my journey and the start of it here not a few hundred yards from where I was born, and I didn't notice the gentleman come in until he was standing next to me. Mid 60's, small in stature, bespectacled, round and a little paunchy with economic strands of hair, in his coat he looked like John Le Carré's enigmatic George Smiley. But the beaming smile which creased his fleshy face belied his trade and when he had relieved Ben of a large glass of Merlot he turned to me and introduced himself to me. Brendan, at my service.

He, too, offers his greeting in an easy, northern accent. "Are you local?" I ask him.

Brendan waves his arm towards the door, "Aye, just out the back." I know that the Metro line runs at the back of the hotel, then there is a post war housing estate where I used to run around a very long time ago.

"Links Avenue?" I suggest.

"Yes." Brendan looks surprised. "Are you from round here, then?"

I tell Brendan that I used to be, that I lived across the road from him on The Broadway, and although I suspect it is in Brendan's nature to be friends with everybody, we are soon comrades. Of course, I tell him about my journey and my book and my search for memories, and Ben moves off to wipe some glasses as he's just heard it all anyway.

Brendan is on his second Merlot when I get to ask him about himself. He's not a spy, but he has survived cancer (what sort he doesn't tell me and I don't ask), he's got one leg shorter than the other, and he lives alone since he lost his wife, how he doesn't say, and again I don't enquire. But what is extraordinary about this rotund little man is that some years ago he actually walked the Camino Way, all the way from his front doorstep in Links Avenue just behind us. He walked to the ferry at Wallsend accompanied by his friends and family, no doubt with flags, bunting and packets of sandwiches, and that in itself, he says, took all day. Then from the Hook of Holland on foot all the way through Holland, Belgium, the full length of France, and across northern Spain to Santiago de Compostela on the west coast. I'm guessing, but that's at least 1,500 miles, maybe more. He tells me this as a matter of fact, without triumph or boast. I'm astonished.

"The Way of the Apostle St James, the pilgrimage to his shrine" I tell him, partly so that he doesn't have to explain it but mainly so as not to appear ignorant. "That's astonishing. I'm amazed. How long did it take you?"

"Weeks. I didn't hurry." Brendan grins widely. "I'm not the shape for hurrying."

"What a journey!"

"It was brilliant. Wonderful people on the way, people on bikes, some on donkeys. Pretty basic lodgings to stay in but that didn't matter. I rested a day or two here and there and took it easy. I stayed a few days in Santiago and got the train home."

17

I've never met anyone who has done the Camino Way, for religious reasons, personal fulfilment or even accidentally, and I think Brendan deserves another Merlot in belated recognition of this tremendous accomplishment. Glasses are raised and the joviality increases with every passing anecdote.

As a first night it's immediately settled me in. Brendan eventually eases himself into his coat, downs the last dregs of his glass and shakes me warmly by the hand. "I won't be in for a couple of nights," he tells me, "but I'm sure we'll meet up again. Enjoy your travels." He leaves with the softness of his northern music lingering, and as Ben goes about his clearing up behind the bar I find myself alone on my stool, my eyes unfocused as I gaze into the prospect of the journey ahead of me. I'm looking forward to tomorrow, when my story can properly begin.

***

The place to begin, obviously, is at the beginning, and so I find myself on a pleasant morning on Hawkey's Road, North Shields, in a car park. This is where the grand, Victorian pile of The Tynemouth Victoria Jubilee Hospital once stood. It's a largely residential road with a mix of 19th century Victorian terraces, post war semi-detached housing, and where the hospital itself once stood there is now a low, modern health centre, the car park and an ambulance station. The hospital was demolished in the 1970s, and the only original piece that remains is an ornate memorial to the two world wars, preserved rather incongruously amid the offices of progress.

My mother told me that she was in hospital for 10 days when giving birth to me. That seems like a long time today when childbirth is little more than a day procedure, but it was apparently the norm back then. White-aproned nurses with black stockings and Oxford shoes would have fondly cradled me. It is a disappointment to have no memory of that.

Walking in the grounds of the health centre I could be standing on the very spot I emerged into the world. Certainly very close to it. I do feel it a shame that the grand old building had to be pulled down, even if only to be turned into an arts centre or offices or some civic amenity. I've seen photos of it taken in the early part of the 20th century and I'm sure that if it had managed to survive until today, a D Notice or some sort of Listing would have been put on it to preserve the architecture and history of the place, if not to commemorate the occasion of my birth. I look around, but there is no blue plaque that I can see.

And so it was from the walls of the building that once stood here, I emerged into the world no doubt wrapped in swaddling clothes, wheeled in a huge pram, red-faced and bewildered over 66 years ago. I'm out of the pram now, but still red-faced and frequently bewildered. I wonder if I bawled in Geordie.

And that's it. People come and go about their business, quite unaware of the staggeringly important event that took place on this very spot all those years ago.

***

From Hawkey's Road it's a couple of miles walk through North Shields, east to the small town of Tynemouth which sits, unsurprisingly, at the mouth of the river. Terraces of Victorian houses mix with modern shop fronts, betting shops, charity shops, fast food outlets and mini-markets. It's actually less run down than I had expected, but far from affluent, and although it is a weekday there is but a scattering of pedestrians.

Reaching Tynemouth itself, turning into Front Street, there is a more prosperous air to the place. Across the road is the solid Victorian terrace of Kings School where I went until the age of 9, uniformed in blazer and cap like 100 other boys. I can remember the classroom chalk and the warm milk. Founded in 1860 it has now re-branded itself as The Kings Priory Academy, which I suppose must be progress of some sort, although I expect it is to do with the way in which it is funded.

Front Street is wide with parking down the middle where in years gone by it thronged with carriages, carts, horses and Victorians in bonnets and tall hats. It runs past an eclectic mix of shops, pubs and cafes for only a few hundred yards to the headland where the craggy ruins of the Priory preside over the estuary of the Tyne and the road sweeps northwards up the coast. It is all very familiar as I amble slowly down the street, although the shops of the 1950s that then existed as drapers, butchers and grocers are now boutiques, antique shops, coffee shops and high end restaurants. Marshall's fish and chips, said by some even today to be the finest in the north east, emits a tempting salt and vinegar bouquet into the street. The Turks Head, an early venue for experimenting with Newcastle Brown Ale, still looks like a public toilet from the outside. Inside I remember it as dark, smoky and mysterious, populated by much older men huddled together over beer talking in low tones, their eyes darting suspiciously at newcomers. I never discovered what secrets they might have been protecting.

At the end of the street I am met with something I did not expect to see. Set in a rather grand building on the corner and with a modern but tasteful ground floor façade, the sign over the café bar declares "Woods". This wasn't here when I was a youngster. I know there is a Woods café in the former pub only a few doors from where I lived on the road between Tynemouth and Whitley Bay, but I had no idea this place was here. I wonder if they are related.

Woods is bright and airy, and is obviously new. There is a lot of glass and there is a grand view of the ruined castle and priory over the road. As we are quite high above the river here I can see the south bank and the buildings of South Shields a mile or so away across the water. It's very nice, which is good as it (almost) bears my name.

I order a coffee. The café is populated by an older clientele, lots of anoraks, walking sticks and stout boots, ideal for the beaches and coast paths around here.

The gentleman sitting next to me at the window counter has the sort of beard grown only by people who have a receding chin. I think they believe it disguises it, but really it stands out like a bush on a bare hillside. He's also wearing a metallic blue multi-pocketed cagoule over a heavy Arran sweater, and on the counter top are gloves, a pair of goggles, a tea cosy shaped woollen hat, a map and a small but powerful looking pair of binoculars. His boots are big and heavy with seafarer's socks rolled down over the ankles. He looks as if he is prepared for the sort of expedition that would be accompanied by a team of huskies or crampons and an ice pick, rather than that which might be encountered in the benign, if breezy, conditions currently prevailing in Tynemouth Front Street.

I offer him a cordial "Hello", to which he responds with unexpected enthusiasm, as if glad to have something to take his mind off the fruit tea he's experimentally ordered. He is Peter, and not from the British Antarctic Survey, but a metallurgist from Nuneaton walking the East Coast Path from Scarborough to Berwick-on-Tweed. That's a gruelling 150 miles or so and, as he confirms, he's about half way through it.

"Did you know," he asks me, "there will soon be nearly 3,000 miles of paths around the coast of England?" I did, actually, but I feign surprise out of courtesy. He plans to walk it all, and has already completed several hundred from the Cornish coast to North Wales.

I spend a pleasant while with Peter as he tells me about his walking, where he gets his socks from and the best hats for different sorts of rain. Eventually he gathers up his kit, and I ask him to take special notice of Low Newton and the coastguard cottage to which we will be coming in due course, when he staggers past in however many days' time.

Then I sit alone again with my coffee, the gentle chatter around me and the clink of crockery from behind the counter. I'm already drawn to the comfortably familiar aspect of Front Street and the distant river through the windows of the café.

I'm conscious that no genetic memories are going to form here. My ancestors never lived in Tynemouth, or in North Shields, Whitley Bay or Newcastle so far as I'm aware. For now, and until I cross the river over to the land of the coalfields, personal memories are what I am looking for, and the changes I might find between those memories and the modern landscape.

***

From Woods bar, just across the road, the grand mouth of the Tyne unfolds. The wide river is guarded by two piers, north and south. The north pier, straight as a die, stretches out almost a mile into the North Sea, a massive, grey granite structure which has withstood every element the North Sea could throw at it for more than 120 years since its completion in 1895. At the end there is a tall, heavy lighthouse. At the root of the pier on the river side is a small sandy bay which accommodates Tynemouth Sailing Club, and on the other side, to the north, the headland rises above the mouth of the river where the craggy ruins of Tynemouth Castle and Priory stand, amid more recent wartime structures and manicured green lawns with signs telling you to keep off it.

It's a long walk down that pier. The tugging of the cold wind at my coat takes me back at least 50 years to when my father walked me down here when I was a child, his wool coat buttoned tightly over a navy blue tartan scarf and a flat, peaked cap, my little hooded anorak tied under the chin over as many pullovers as my mother could get on me. It might have felt a mild day in the shelter of the town today, but out here it's anything but and it's a struggle against the stinging salt spray from the sea crashing against the buttresses.

The overwhelming feeling about this pier is its sheer weight. It's built on two levels, the higher pedestrian level to the north, seaward, side being about 10 feet wide with a chest high sea wall below which the sea heaves and swells with unimaginable power. It's built of massive stone blocks, granite I assume, and no less than 3 *million* tons of it were used in the construction of the two piers. The lower level on the harbour side, about 15 feet below me and separated by iron railings, is wider and I notice the old rusty rail tracks set in the concrete. There is no railing or protection to the crashing waves in the harbour about 20 feet below and the public are not allowed down there. There is also a rusty old rail running along the top of the sea wall next to me, and something in my memory tells me that once, when I was a child here clinging onto my father's arm, there was a great crane that ran on those rails. There's no sign of it now, and the tracks have clearly not been used for many years.

At the end there is a group of 3 or 4 people huddled in the lee of the wind under the lighthouse. A gentleman who appears to be wearing four sets of weatherproofs all at the same time, tells me "*it's allers cad n windy oot here, ye nah*", which, with my Geordie training, I know to mean that the weather is frequently inclement at the end of the pier. I confirm that indeed it is, but either he didn't hear me or doesn't speak my language because he just stood there rather stoically with his shoulders hunched in a way that said clearly, "*What in the name of God am I doing out here?*" Although the reward for the effort of struggling out here is the magnificent panorama of the coastline. On the way back I swear a seagull aimed its business at me, as is their custom, but it might have been the spray in the wind.

There's an information board at the foot of the pier which I hadn't noticed on my way in, which tells me about the history of the pier and the crane I had remembered. The original huge, steam-driven crane named "Mamoth" (sic) was installed in 1883 and used in the further construction of the pier, hauling the enormous blocks of stone. The crane was washed off the pier during a storm in 1893, but replaced within a couple years. In 1969 a diesel crane was installed, then dismantled in 1988.

Relating how the mouth of the Tyne was exposed to the full force of the North Sea, the board also tells us that "*many ships were frequently wrecked*", which suggests

23

considerable ill-fortune or a persistent lack of judgment on the part of some ship captains.

From the pier it's only a couple of hundred yards to the headland on which sits Collingwood's Monument, and which commands a spectacular, unbroken view of the river, across to the south where lie South Shields and County Durham, the land of the coalfields and my deeper heritage.

The monument, a memorial to Nelson's second in command at the battle of Trafalgar, stands 23 feet tall and flanked at its base by 4 cannon from the Royal Sovereign, Collingwood's ship in the battle. It commands an impressive view across the river to the lands in the South. Erected in 1845, it gazes regally and with authority across at County Durham where, at that very time not more than a few miles away and in the very direction of Collingwood's gaze, men toiled in treacherous conditions deep underground to mine the coal which the industries of the time, and Collingwood himself, depended upon.

Standing here beneath it, I am struck by the sheer wealth of history that surrounds this spot. From my own childhood days playing and bicycling around the headland in the 1950s and 1960s, it is easy to imagine the shipping which has travelled this river over centuries, from sail barges, colliers and bulk tankers to the plush cruise ships of the 21st century. I recall John Masefield's lines in his poem "Cargoes":

Dirty British coaster with a salt-caked smoke stack
Butting thought the Channel in the mad March days
With a cargo of Tyne coal
Road-rail, pig lead
Firewood, ironware and cheap tin trays

Masefield wrote those lines in 1902, drawing on his own experiences of life at sea, and at a time when the Durham coalfields and the industries of the North were supplying just the ships that would have plied this river, past where I stand and out beyond the shelter of the pier to the challenging turbulence of the North Sea.

To my left, that great pier reaches out into the grey waters of the river-mouth, and above it stand the ruins of the castle and the priory, founded in the 7th century but much changed over time. Over all those years, men have stood here, where I am now. They saw the same dark clouds passing through the sky as I do, the same lands rising far in the south, and the same dark greyness of the North Sea, white flecked in the gusty wind. What were the thoughts of those who made their footprints in this very grass, I wonder. Were they thoughts of ships and trade? Or of God? Or of War?

***

The banks of the river here at its mouth are not, and so far as I am aware never were, crowded with docks and warehouses. Those will arise a little further up-river, but here the bank is bordered by a low sea wall and promenade, and then slopes down only a few yards to where the water laps on the rocks, stones and mud flats. It's deep, black, clingy mud which sucks and squelches at anyone foolish enough to venture into it, which as a schoolboy I was, searching with a little trowel for lugworms and ragworms with which to bait my fishing hook.

We would have had Wellies on, of course, as demanded by our long suffering mothers, and a khaki sackcloth rucksack which was crammed with tangled nylon line, lead weights, broken floats, and a smell of rotting fish that would fell a horse. Three or four little boys bent over prodding the clutching mud and occasionally pulling out some unfortunate creature which was slung, loose, into the rucksack to await being slung out again, on a hook, back into the water a few hundred yards up river. We might have felt like Ransome's Swallows and Amazons, but Dickens' mudlarks was probably what the casual observer would have seen.

Just beyond the mud, treacherously hidden at high tide, are the Black Middens. These rocky outcrops reaching out into the river have claimed many ships and dozens of lives over the years. Especially before the piers were constructed, but even afterwards too, they were a trap set to ensnare any vessel which ventured too close. By reason of weather, wind, poor navigation or even a skipper too full of gin, the backs of ships were broken and sailors died, just yards from the shoreline. I knew about the Black Middens as a youngster, but as we combed the slimy mud for bait their significance was lost on us.

Then, when we had enough worms, we trudged up the riverbank to the fish quay at North Shields, the beginning of the Tyne's industry, and where we hoped for a catch of cod, whiting or dabs. The promenade stretches all the way up to what is known as Low Lights, where the fish quay and the industry of the Tyne properly begins. Today there are a number of people enjoying a walk by the river. One never tires of the views, the smell of the salt air, even the slightly pongy wafts from the mud flats.

The fish quay is less than half a mile up from the river mouth. A concrete and wooden pier is constructed to form a small harbour, the pier and the quayside about 15 feet of green slimy wooden piles above the water. And on the land side, over the scruffy road, the warehouses with garage sized doors open to the quay through which, in days gone by, men in aprons could be seen doing things, very, very quickly, to fish. The fishing boats were tied up two or three deep against the quayside and the pier. Plastic and wooden crates were stacked around, some empty, some full of fish or crabs. Ropes lay about, nets hung from poles to dry or be repaired, and the persistent smell of fish hung heavily in the air. There was a constant clamour of Geordie voices, shouting, laughing, lots of swearing. There was always a great clattering of seagulls.

We got to know those men on the quayside quite well. They were hard Geordie men, with a hard, Geordie attitude to life, and a relentlessly physical job to do, but they teased us in a friendly, matey way, and gave us tea from their chipped enamel mugs. Looking back, I think they probably felt quite protective of us, and I have no doubt they would have looked out for us if anything untoward had happened. Looking around now, I don't see them.

We would set up on the edge of the quay, squatting on an iron bollard or an upturned crate, and hurl our lines out into the water in any space we could find between the boats and mooring ropes. Then we would wait. It was a futile exercise, for there was no chance of catching a fish, at least not one to eat. I suppose we enjoyed the bustle of the fishing trade around us, and the opportunity to learn new swear words. Today, The Tyne is clean and sea trout and salmon can be caught from its banks, but then it was a dirty brownish green colour with a rainbow film of oil, and unpleasant looking things floated on the surface. The only fish which took our bait back then were spiny, toothy things, and eels.

But one day my brother and I caught a coley, a small haddock like creature which caused us enormous excitement and we dashed home straight away. The poor thing was only about 9 inches long, but to us it was a prize of great value, and we expected adulation and congratulations from mother and father which were, of course, duly forthcoming when it was pulled from the fishy depths of the rucksack and laid reverently on the kitchen table.

A Coley may look a bit like a small cod, or a haddock, and today they are considered a decent, cheap alternative, but when they lived in the brown soup that was the river Tyne of the 1950's, the flesh had a distinctly toiletty quality.

I'm sure my father knew this as he stood doubtfully by while my mother took a knife to its meagre grey belly. The stink which immediately pervaded the room persisted long after the remains had been removed by my father to a smell-proof bin. Our disappointment was considerable, but it was quickly forgotten and my brother and I were soon back at the quayside in our wellies and woolly bobble hats.

***

At the edge of the river a cast figure sits on a bollard staring out into the mouth of the Tyne, his hands resting on his knees. It is a statue commissioned to commemorate the fishermen who lost their lives at sea. Its inscription reads:

*"Until you have the courage to lose sight of the shore,
you will not know the terror of being forever lost at sea".*

There is also a small Heritage Centre, which I thought would be promising, but it turned out that it was currently concentrating on the activities of slavery on Tyneside which, so far as I am aware, is not a feature of my heritage and so I decline the £3 entrance fee and move on up river.

I am surprised to find that there is still some fishing activity from the quay. In fact, as I walked the promenade from Tynemouth, I saw a couple of inbound fishing boats enveloped in clouds of seagulls, shrieking with excitement. At the quayside I count only half a dozen boats, all originating from elsewhere than North Shields.

I drop in for coffee at The Quay Bar which is a pleasantly modernised former warehouse looking out onto the river. It's surprisingly small and cosy inside with a lot of fishing related paraphernalia about the place - coils of rope, crab cages, netting slung from the ceiling, that sort of thing. The Geordie barman, for who I'm the only customer this morning, tells me that most of the boats are from Northern Ireland and Scotland, but there are still fish markets held on the quayside, and I notice a few wet fish retail outlets and boxes, pallets, lines and nets strewn about here and there.

The old, timber fish sheds have been replaced by a low modern structure, and the rough old quay is smooth concrete with a parking pay and display machine. Across the newly tarmacked road where the fish were gutted and layered in ice, there are no longer the fish processing businesses where lines of women would clean and fillet fish to be thrown into rows of wooden buckets. Mostly the hospitality industry has taken over. Walking down the road, the quay and the river on my left, I pass mostly restaurants, bars and cafes, all nice looking and all very new. There's even an Italian bistro. Above some of the old warehouses, the upper floors are now smart apartments, many with balconies, and obviously a stupendous view across the river.

Walking further west, up river, the bars and cafes give way to some of the old industrial structures. The North East Rubber Company building is in the process of demolition. A developer's board announces yet more new apartments. The occasional riverside business seems to be still ongoing, but there is much that looks as if it is in its last throes, and soon I am walking behind modern, smart riverside apartment blocks built right on the old quaysides. There are dozens of them for hundreds of yards, where I remember there being ramshackle timber sheds and muddy slipways where the oily, grey water lapped on slippery stones and concrete.

***

And so it continues until I am about half a mile from the fish quay, upriver, and face to face with what I think was probably the most dangerous pub I have ever been in. Dark, small and, I'm sure, full of pirates, The Chain Locker was the sort of dockside pub that would have frightened the life out of Henry Morgan himself. Why we went there I honestly have no idea. But you didn't have to show ID back then, and I don't suppose that Blackbeard or whatever the landlord's name was, would have cared one way or the other whether we were old enough to buy a pint, although why we should forsake the safety of a merely dodgy pub for the perils of The Locker, where we would not dare to catch anyone's eye, is beyond me.

There were actually three pubs here in this one hundred yard stretch of the quayside, all perilous. The Porthole, The Locker, and the Northumberland Arms otherwise known as The Jungle. The Jungle had such a fearsome reputation that we didn't even dare venture in there. Men with arms the size of tar barrels tattooed with an anchor, or "I love Mum" were its patrons, or so we were led to believe. Hook nosed Fagins bent over pewter tankards, and ladies of doubtful repute, concealed in corners waiting for the moment to arrive when enough ale had been consumed for their services to be required.

There was no jukebox at The Locker, not even in those days of 1960s rock and roll. There was no dartboard, no shove-halfpenny, and no skittles. This was not a place to socialise or be entertained, but to sit darkly and grimly and harbour nefarious thoughts. I don't remember "What Shall We Do With a Drunken Sailor" being sung in low tones, but it would have been fitting if it were.

A Heritage signboard on a wall nearby gives an uncompromising indication of what this area was like. It records a report in the Shields Daily News of 1855. It states:

"Who can estimate the amount of immoral conversation that passes,
the unlawful schemes plotted, or the low,
filthy literature read in common lodging houses
and the intemperance that prevails in this nest of vice."

We survived it though, and I am anxious to re-discover its delights and take a pint or two in old, familiar surroundings.

But, perhaps inevitably, what I see is not the open door of a welcoming pub, or any sort of pub at all. The façade of the old building still stands preserved for posterity in its brown, glazed tile, but behind lies no bar, no dark sailors' sanctuary, only the clean, square glazing of a modern apartment. In its declining years the pub became known as The Crane House, and that name has been restored above the doorway. Standing there for a moment or two before the entrance door I recall that the last time I stood here as a nervous teenager it was to summon the courage to go in, from which memory forms an unusual mix of amusement and nostalgia.

This is, in fact, the farthest point on the north bank one used to be able to walk more or less next to the river, before encountering the dockyards and slipways which barred the way, lining the Tyne much of the way up to the city of Newcastle past Willington Quay and Wallsend, almost on the route of Hadrian's Wall itself. Just beyond the pub were the gates of Smith's Dock, and the first of the high cranes which dominated the Tyneside skyline for many years. I expect that the pub was named The Crane House after that fact.

Smiths Dock was a big place, a lively hive of shipbuilding activity. There were three massive dry docks, with all the infrastructure that went with this huge industry. I can remember standing before those gates as men in caps, grimy overalls and the ubiquitous Woodbines continually passed to and from the gates with the banging and clattering of rivetters, fitters and welders coming from behind piles of heavy chains, steel drums, stacked steel plates and other tools and materials for building ships.

Smiths was a very successful yard. Established at North Shields in 1851 it went on to build ships of great repute, and in the war built corvettes, armed trawlers and anti-submarine vessels for the Admiralty's war effort, and later container ships and tankers. In the 1960s Smiths merged with one of the largest Dock companies on the Tyne, Swan Hunter, until in the 1980s the collapse of the shipbuilding industry resulted in closure. It didn't happen overnight, and had been a long time coming. The shift to the Far East and the economics of the industry drew the life from the North East, and eventually the gates were padlocked, the riveting machines fell silent, and the men went away, mostly to the dole office. It was a sad and often a very angry time.

I can remember the consequences. Groups of shabbily dressed men on street corners, grim faces set with resentment, nothing else to do. They would have preferred to return to the oil and sweat of the shipyard than stand there, unemployed. There is a pride among Geordies, a dignity which had been hard won and yet so discouragingly lost. There was a strong mood of abandonment. The scrapheap of the shipyard translated into the scrapheap of humanity. I cycled past the scrapheaps trying to avoid their eyes. Even as a boy, I was aware of the pervading atmosphere of discontent, and that it could so easily be ignited into fierce hostility.

Nevertheless, there were many who refused to discard the Geordie resilience. Pete McCarthy wrote of the Irish diaspora driven by political conflict and famine. The collapse of the shipbuilding industry, and the coalmines which I will come to, was the cause of a Tyneside diaspora too. Many abandoned the North East and sought fortune, or at least a living, elsewhere. And they went far and wide. When Michael Palin stopped off in Gibraltar at the beginning of his journey into the Sahara, he found himself in a café on one of the main streets, where he asked for some tea. He was surprised to hear the waiter's response in full-on Geordie *"Coop or moog?"*

Like most others, Smiths Dock quickly fell into dilapidation. What had been left on site when those gates finally closed was left to rust and decay, but eventually salvation came in the form it has for nearly all of the Tyne riverside. Development. Standing now outside of what used to be The Chain Locker, instead of padlocked steel gates and fencing and a barren wasteland of broken concrete and rusty steel before me, there is a brand new residential apartment complex. There is a glass walled high-end restaurant looking over the river on the ground floor, and 8 or so storeys of apartments above. The rest of the land formerly occupied by the dock has been cleared and made ready for the imminent arrival of the developers. A steel grey stockade surrounds it, spindly weeds growing at the base of the fences.

As I wander about the huge site, I can see that the three great bays, the docks themselves, have been preserved. I expect that those who will be able to afford a residence in this place will also be able to afford the yacht or cruiser which will be moored there. Glass fibre and aluminium replacing the steel and iron. But a boat nevertheless.

Stylish, balconied and with an impressive view to the South over and beyond the river, this is the fate of nearly all the former dockland. If not apartments, then restaurants, bars and leisure clubs. Dry docks and slipways have been converted into marinas, new jetties the home for luxury yachts and cruisers.

Once there was money here, then there wasn't, and now there is again. Not money gained from the sweat and toil of shipbuilding, but from the profits of finance, law, banking and information technology.

The Chain Locker and all that surrounds it, the renovated quays and strikingly the lack of high cranes dominating the skyline, are so remarkably different to how I remember them. Yet, I cannot help feeling this morning that there is a familiarity about the place, the atmosphere, the sound of a Geordie accent somewhere, or a familiar building still standing amid the development and regeneration. Is this, I wonder, what a sense of belonging feels like? I stand for a while in such thought, waiting for something to tell me.

***

But I am not going to get a pint here, standing in front of the old ex-pub, and so, disappointed, I head across the road to the Ferry landing and a ride on the Tyne.

Although a pedestrian and cycle tunnel has existed since 1951, until the Tyne Tunnel for vehicles was opened in 1967 there was nowhere to cross the river east of Newcastle, some 8 miles upstream at the iconic Tyne Bridge, or before that bridge was built in 1928 even further. So for the inhabitants of the area at the mouth of the river, it was an extensive trek to get over the water by bridge if you ever had the need to do so.

But a ferry has existed to connect the north and south banks since time immemorial, and it now operates as part of the Metropolitan Borough's transport system. It's a diesel boat now, of course, and since the tunnel took away the vehicular traffic it takes foot passengers only, but the ferry landing from which it embarks and disembarks its customers is in the same location as it was when my father would take me for a joy ride, in the 1950s and 1960s.

Just across the road from the late Chain Locker is a narrow alleyway between the gable ends of two riverside buildings leading to the landing. The approach and the landing itself are smaller than you would expect, and certainly smaller than I remember. Or perhaps I just got bigger.

The diesel boats were introduced in 1972, following the retirement of the steam ferry, the Northumbrian. I can still smell the oil and the smoke, and hear the booming hooter as we traversed the river, skilfully avoiding all sorts of heavier traffic plying the Tyne. The Northumbrian had a crew of 8 or so, from a real captain with a hat to deckhands with flat caps and a Woodbine permanently hanging from their mouths.

The Northumbrian's last voyage was on 25th April 1972, and a local amateur film maker, Lilian Wincote, recorded the occasion on Super 8 or whatever the technology of the time was. It is an extraordinary record of the day. The old boat was quite a big vessel with a fat, tall funnel and she looked heavy in the water, like an oily tugboat. It was crowded with workers and vehicles. A shot in the film shows the ticket price for a private car was 3 shillings and sixpence, about 17.5p today. A passenger in the car would cost an extra sixpence. There were also prices for cattle, pigs and sheep.

There's a pub on the other side, right by the South Shields terminal, called the Alum Ale House. I've never been in it, and I have no idea why it should be named after a salt of aluminium which was mined extensively from shale deposits up to the mid-19th century some 100 miles or so south of here on the North Yorkshire coast. Alum, now mostly produced synthetically, was used in a wide variety of industrial processes including as a dye fixative. Before synthetic alternatives were available this was a complicated manufacturing process which involved, amongst other things, copious amounts of human urine. At the peak of alum production the industry required 200 tonnes of it every year, equivalent to the produce of 1,000 people. The demand was such that it was imported from

London and Newcastle, buckets were left on street corners for collection and reportedly public toilets were built in Hull in order to supply the alum works there. Perhaps South Shields was some sort of a urine collection point, in which case I hope the pub has moved on with the times.

***

There are two vessels which ferry passengers to and fro across the river these days, the Pride of the Tyne built in 1993 and the newer Spirit of the Tyne which came into service in 2007, both replacing earlier diesels which followed the retirement of the heavy old tub The Northumbrian. Both The Pride and The Spirit are rather odd, top heavy looking vessels, and surprisingly large, the Pride having a capacity of more than 300 passengers and the Spirit 200. Only one ferry usually operates at a time except at peak periods, and the crossing takes 7 minutes.

One surprising and encouraging fact is that the Pride of the Tyne is equipped with a bar. It's not that it is, in itself, remarkable to find a bar on a ferry, but I did not expect to find one on a crossing that takes only 7 minutes. I suppose that if you can't get your drink ordered and downed in 7 minutes you would simply refuse to disembark at the other side and remain on board, crossing backwards and forwards across the river while you finish up, or get another one in. For all I know there may be a whole community of Geordie drinkers who gather on-board with day saver tickets.

As my ferry pulls up to the quayside I am disappointed to see that it is the teetotal Spirit of the Tyne. Still, it's only 7 minutes to the pub on the other side and I think I can wait.

Although I could sit comfortably inside the spacious, heated cabin area, I decide to stand out on deck, leaning on the railings to watch the river go by, and the far bank of South Shields drawing nearer. It's a wide, exposed view of the river, and very chilly in the salty wind.

Unlike the terminal on the north bank at North Shields, squeezed by waterside paraphernalia, the south terminal is a wide, clear quayside with a new riverside promenade and unobstructed views both down the river to the mouth and the piers, and up towards Newcastle. I am struck by the many areas of bare riverside, cleared of the shipyards and docks, oases of new apartment complexes sprouting here and there, no doubt with many more to come. Back across the river I have a grand view of Smiths Dock from whence I have come, now just a vacant lot with more fences and weeds. Upriver from there what was once the grandest shipyard of them all, Swan Hunter, which built the Titanic's rescue ship Carpathia among other renowned vessels. All gone.

There is, if not a forest certainly a substantial copse, of cranes silhouetted on the skyline. These are not the great cranes of shipbuilding, hauliers of steel plate and buckets of rivets, but the cranes for loading and unloading containers. The Port of Tyne Authority possesses a substantial complex of bonded warehouses and container parks, just upriver from where I stand at the south ferry terminal. The Tyne has become an important hub for inbound and outbound commerce, but as I look up and down the river today I can see only two ships of any substance, a DFDS roll-on roll-off ferry, and some cargo vessel unloading at the Port of Tyne quay. Not many years ago the ships would have been docked two or three deep along the vast quaysides. Those quays are empty today.

A few yards from the ferry terminal across clean, new, paving, I am greeted by an unwelcome event. The Alum Ale House is closed. I can find no sign, no notice with opening hours displayed. I wander around the building for a few minutes hoping to find some back door entrance reserved, perhaps, for those in the know or the simply determined, but there is none. I wonder if potential customers have been seduced by the Bar on the Boat, but it seems unlikely. Sadly, the pleasures within its walls shall remain a mystery.

I wander around the small cluster of well-maintained buildings close by the terminal. The Customs House which once oversaw the comings and goings of ships and trade is now a nice looking café. The Word, the National Centre for the Written Word is a modern, circular glass building set next to the stone flagged market area and which hosts an impressive library, technology displays and all sorts of hugely interesting stuff. But The Word is not part of my memory, and the return ferry is in just 15 minutes, so I don't go in.

The loosely uniformed man I accost on the return ferry tells me that it is thought the old Northumbrian now resides in Brussels, a floating restaurant.

***

It would be fitting, I think, to have a look in the old Turks Head on Tynemouth Front Street, after getting back from the ferry and before retiring to The Park this afternoon. If for no other reason than to see if it is still as murky as it was 50 odd years ago.

I don't know what the matter with me was that day, but I must have been off my guard, as the 3 fruit machines and five – five! – big sports screens should have been reason enough to retreat, not to mention the "Dogs Welcome" sign on the door. But by the time I had retaken my senses I was seated with a pint next to a table where two young women were fawning over a yapping spaniel, feeding it crisps and, unbelievably, pieces of lemon. When it got up onto the lap of the owner, paws on the table and knocked over a drink I could stand it no more, made a mental note never again to trouble The Turks Head with my custom, and went home to The Park.

FOUR

Whitley Bay

The Park Hotel stands about halfway along Longsands beach, a wide sweeping bay which runs between Tynemouth and Cullercoats towards Whitley Bay. I've walked out of the hotel this morning, stepped across the road, and have found myself on the grassy banks, dunes crisscrossed with pathways, which lead down to the sand.

To my right, the sands stretch up to The Lido, or the Tynemouth Outdoor Pool as it is now known, then the rocky cove of King Edwards Bay underneath the headland where the Castle and Priory preside over Tynemouth village. It's about 20 minutes' walk up from the hotel, and this is where I'm going to start the day, before exploring north up the coast past the enchanting cove at Cullercoats and the front at Whitely Bay where amusement arcades and the funfair at the famously white domed Spanish City provided entertainment for tourists, visitors and me, and also, I'm sad to recall, a confrontation zone for those with nothing better to do, the troublemakers of the 1960s. Then I'll head on to the lighthouse at St Mary's Island. I'm looking forward to this. All of these places are etched in my memories of over 60 years ago.

The road is high above the cliffs of King Edwards Bay. A path zig-zaggs down to the small promenade and the little crescent of sand far below. Although the weather is actually quite good today, the sea is boiling in the bay, crashing against the rocks in clouds of spray. I had forgotten how treacherous it is here, and how as children we would splash about in it, oblivious to its dangers. Now there are numerous signs warning of the hazardous swells and currents.

Although it's a long way down to the bay from here, and I have a feeling that it will seem even further on the way back up, I am going to have to brave the steps because down there, set into the cliff perched on the end of the bay, is a small wooden shack with smoke billowing from various apertures and a shaky looking narrow balcony at the front. This is Riley's Fish Shack, famously mentioned in several influential reviews, and not to be missed. It wasn't here the last time I visited, and judging by its precarious position might not be in the near future should the wind turn. Now is a good time.

The Shack is a welcome relief from the spray and biting wind swirling in the bay. I am relieved to find that the wooden plank floor doesn't sag under my footsteps, and in fact it's more substantial than it appeared when I looked down on it. It's also packed with proper catering paraphernalia, stainless steel, a huge wood fired grill pit, and astonishingly, draught beer. The entrance door is a flimsy frame of wood and plastic sheet, and I am greeted by a young Geordie lass dressed in lifeboat kit. I ask her how they get the beer barrels down to here. She frowns and tells me she's not sure. She thinks it might be on a rope. Or perhaps by boat.

Inside it's tiny with stool seating for about 6. Outside on the veranda, supported by wooden stilts, there are about a dozen more for those who are prepared to brave both the weather and the possibility of falling off. A few hardy souls are tucking into plates of seafood of various sorts. I go for the langoustines which are large, juicy and extremely messy.

And I was right. The climb back up to the road is much further than it was down, which may be due to the langoustines or beer (yes, it is a bit early but they'd taken the trouble to get it down there). Once at the top, a few steps down the road takes me to the cliff top above the Tynemouth Lido.

***

The Lido was built in 1925, a rectangular, concrete salt water pool set below the rocks of Tynemouth against the sandy beach. It was bright, white and blue, and surrounded by changing rooms and tiered seating. In the summer the pool attracted throngs of holidaymakers and locals, like me, to splash about in the unheated seawater, and build castles in the sand beside it.

The day trippers who sought out The Lido, the ice cream stalls and the candy floss which surrounded it, were mostly down from Newcastle, Gateshead, Wallsend and all the metropolitan suburbs of Tyneside. It was a day out, an escape from the weekday work in the shipyards to take in the ozone filled sea air. Flat caps, baggy trousers and Woodbines mingled comfortably with children, families and open shirts displaying medallions. Geordie voices chattering, hollering, laughing.

And it got packed. Beauty contests were held there, amateur swimming competitions and probably knobbly knees competitions, although at that age I was more interested in splashing about or searching for crabs in rock pools than I was in anyone's knees, even the more shapely legs of the beauty contestants. And even though the weather in summer in the North East was at best unreliable, I remember it as always sunny, and there were never too many unidentified things floating in the water to worry about.

It would be at a weekend, or a holiday, or one of Dad's rare days off from work that we would all get ready for a day at the beach or The Lido. It was just a little way down the road to the sands and then on up to the pool, so we didn't need to take the car. Mother and father would gather together the paraphernalia we needed for our day while we fidgeted about wondering why on earth we needed so much *stuff*. There were towels and flannels, hats, bathing suits, bags of sun cream and mother's requisites. An inflatable lilo, a beach umbrella and a canvass windbreak with its awkward, spindly wooden frame, and of course a picnic of crisps, sandwiches and bottles of pop.

And then, with mother in charge of a wicker basket and we boys in charge of nothing but our urgent enthusiasm, Dad wobbled into the road under a pile of everything else. And so we set off, mother, father, myself and my brother, Little John.

The naming of my brother has always been a mystery. Neither he nor I were given middle names, which would have gone some way to avoiding the problem, and when it came to naming him, 3 years after me, my parents suffered a breath-taking imagination failure, naming him John, after my father, who had no middle name either.

I suppose it just didn't occur to them that this might cause some confusion, although why not I cannot conceive as they were both usually sensible people. I don't know at what point it became apparent that shouting "*John!*" up the stairs or down the garden was inadequately specific, but clearly there came a time when a solution had to be found, and with yet further originality father became Big John, and my brother became Little John, to his eternal irritation.

When we arrived at The Lido or the beach as the case may be, it was my mother who wandered the area to pick out a suitable spot. She rambled around inspecting the sand and the people about while Little John and I traipsed after her becoming more and more irritated and Dad trudged behind under his burden of beach equipment, like a patient mule. Eventually, mother would declare herself satisfied with a plot and Dad would collapse onto it, the contents of his ramshackle load released haphazardly onto the ground.

My mother had quite a strong sense of modesty, which I imagine came from her Grandmother who we will meet later. It wasn't a stern, matriarchal chastity, and she wasn't prim or prissy, but she had a bashful shyness about public propriety, table manners, passing wind – the sort of things that my brother and I took easily in our stride. Thus, once we were settled and Dad had extricated himself from the clutches of the windbreak, getting changed out of our walking shorts into our bathing costume, in public, was something mother was careful to supervise.

Heaven forbid that any member of the public should observe a little boy without his pants on. First a long towel was wrapped around the waist and secured. Then, in what can only be described as a blind fumble under the towel, the shorts were released and slipped down the leg. Mother's anxiety at this point was high, for obvious reasons. Then, with more awkward pulling and tugging the bathing costume was hiked up beneath the towel, which could then be released and we would scamper off down the sand to the sea. Or, if we were at The Lido, rush to the side of the pool and jump straight in, knees up to form a bomb and create as much of a splash as our little bodies could deliver.

When we were done in the water we trudged back up the sand, or to the terrace, shivering as the breeze caught the wetness of our skin. Mother would towel our hair and bodies, to get the circulation going so she said, and then we sat down with a fresh towel around our shoulders and a bag of crisps. I remember savouring the taste as it mingled with the dry saltiness of the seawater in my mouth. And then, when the warmth of the sun had dispensed the shivers, we would be up again, dashing down the beach to the rocks where sea urchins and starfish were to be found, and poked with a stick.

My mother didn't enter the water, at least not that I remember, and although my father did on occasion in baggy swimming shorts to paddle at the water's edge, both took their pleasure in watching us cavorting about, building castles and dams in the sand and splashing about in the shallows. My mother sat demurely by the windbreak or under the parasol if it was sunny, in a light floral dress, a wide brimmed hat and dark sunglasses, and as often as not a very silly looking reflective silver thing which she held under her chin to ensure her neck received an equal tan. My father, in baggy trousers, a loose fitting shirt and a cap, was content to sit and watch the world go by, relieved for a time from his work with ships, engineering, and the business of the Tyne.

But inevitably, a combination of shipyard redundancies and cheap package holidays to Benidorm in the 1970s drew The Lido's customers away, and without its patrons the pool started to decay. Without the money and with dwindling local enthusiasm the concrete greyed and crumbled, the paint on the ironwork of the railings peeled and rusted into streaky brown. It simply fell apart, and as it did so and as our childhoods advanced, our days there diminished, and then were no more.

Eventually the abandoned pool became such an eyesore that the local authority filled it with rocks with the intention of creating something natural looking, but it was a feeble attempt and only made it worse. And so it remained deserted, a stark reminder of different times, and a sad memory for me of truly happy, childhood moments.

But I had been delighted to discover that some years ago a group of local people got together with an idea to renovate the pool, and great plans were drawn up. It was to be totally re-born, with a modern, heated pool, glass fronted restaurant, terraces for sunbathing and relaxing, and all sorts of fabulous facilities to attract visitors and breathe life back into it again. An internet website displays astonishing images of what it would be like. Plans were submitted to the local authority who were enthusiastic about the idea, but less so at the £8 million price tag.

I have been looking forward to discovering how they have been getting on with the project, and today it is with dismay that I stand looking down from the bank above at still decaying concrete and ironwork. The paint has gone and the pool itself is silted with sand. The open sea crashes over its low sides. It is much worse than it was when I last saw it many years ago. Not a digger, not a spade or a trowel seems to have been lifted towards its renovation. It looks to me as if it has been left to rot, to be reclaimed by the sea.

In the 5 years or so since the renovation group looked at the costings and set up the fundraising to get it up and running, of the £8 million budget it has raised £100,000 at the time I last checked in February 2020. At that rate the pool will have been reclaimed by the sea long before the target is reached. It is such a shame. In an area where so far I have seen so much that has been restored or tastefully redeveloped, such as the new life breathed into the North Shields quaysides, this place will have to remain just a memory of childhood, happy times. Now it's been reclaimed, not by developers or investors, but by corrosion, decay, and the unrelenting power of the elements.

***

Set back from The Lido across the promenade and the road, the coast is lined with seaward facing, large Victorian terraces, many with 4 storeys and clearly affluent. Tynemouth is, and was, abundant with this type of housing and the prosperity of the residents is striking, especially compared to the dock workers' dingy terraces a short distance away in North Shields, or the working class playground of Whitley Bay less than a mile north. Tynemouth was a uniquely Conservative constituency for nearly 50 years between 1950 and 1997, amid an overwhelmingly staunch Labour populace. It is an oasis of affluence in a region which for many lacks such material comforts.

Perhaps the most prominent example is the crescent of Percy Gardens just in front of me as I stand above The Lido. It's a fine example of Victorian urban architecture of which even the likes of Bath or Harrogate would be proud. About 40 or so grand four storey terraces curve elegantly around manicured gardens, beds, yuccas, immaculate low hedges and a green lawn facing the sea with majestic views of the coast. Unlike much of the inferior 19th century two-up two-down terraced housing built for the Tyneside workforce and which has typically been demolished to make way for car parks, supermarkets, social housing and flats, these have been immaculately preserved. They stand nobly and expensively, a reminder that the North East had its wealth as well as its poverty.

A look at the Census for 1901 tells us who lived here in the days when the majority of the population, including my own ancestors, were down a pit or a greasy slipway. A random selection of residents in that year includes Shipbrokers, Steamship Owners, Ships Stores Dealers, Wine & Spirit Merchants, a Solicitor and a Chartered Accountant. These were people who had done well from the profits of industry. There were no flat caps or Woodbines here, save the ones they both physically and metaphorically looked down to in The Lido.

It is also striking that the census discloses that every household had at least one servant, and most often three or four. At No. 26 lived a family headed by Charles H. T. Hopkins, a Major (Ret'd), Ship-owner, who had no less than seven servants, including a cook, a parlour maid, a scullery maid, a nursery maid, and a sick nurse. Charles Hopkins was aged only 42. He had 2 very young children aged just 1 and 3 years old, but no wife is listed here. Without genealogical research one can only speculate, but life could be harsh, even for the well-heeled.

Indeed, it is also notable that there are number of houses where the head is listed as a Widow, "*living off own means*". Some are below the age of 50. Wealthy perhaps, but not necessarily without misfortune.

The road which serves the crescent of houses is private now, and great iron gates on stone pillars guard the electronically controlled entrance. A stone gatekeeper's lodge squats next to them. Pedestrians can enter the crescent through a side gate, otherwise the residents wouldn't get any post or Amazon deliveries, and I take a walk down the arc of imposing houses. Nearly all of the doorways have multiple doorbells or entry systems, which speaks loudly of what has become of them. A 2 bedroom flat will cost upwards of £400,000 here, and a 6 bedroom house, if one could be found, over 1.5 million. Nice view, though.

***

From here, the coastal skyline is much as I remember it, scanning the skyline from the broken ruins of the Abbey on Tynemouth hill to the stiletto steeple of St George's church at Cullercoats to the north. But there is one very notable exception. The Plaza was a huge Victorian showcase of a building, perched right on the seafront only a few hundred yards from my viewpoint above The Lido, and it ought to be right in front of me.

The Plaza was built in 1878 and was very grand. It was a massive building right on the beach, rather stern in dark grey brick, and it dominated everything around it. Originally named the Tynemouth Aquarium and Wintergarden, it was re-branded the Tynemouth Palace in 1898, and then given its enduring title Tynemouth Plaza in 1926. Over its time it hosted a ballroom, bars, an ice rink, a billet for first world war troops, restaurants, nightclubs and entertainment of all kinds.

The commercial fortunes of the Plaza were always very much up and down, and by the time I knew it, it was very seedy. Even in my teens there was nothing there to draw me in, and I have memories of it being a lure for those up to no good and in need of a quiet, shady place to congregate and loiter. In 1996 after years of decay it suspiciously caught fire. The great building was destroyed and subsequently bulldozed out of existence. Now, green, sandy dunes roll down to the beach from where it stood. Not a trace remains.

Down a slip road to the beach stands a new café selling fizzy drinks, ice cream and fish and chips. Scattered in the waves just offshore I spot the black, rubber suited figures of surfers. I have never quite understood the desire to throw yourself into the icy waters of the North Sea. The surf here doesn't seem to me to be much to shout about anyway as it's either hardly more than a swell, or rows of pounding breakers. I watch them for a few minutes. The idea seems to be to lie on the surf board, paddle out a hundred yards or so, bob about in the water until the cold becomes unbearable, then leap onto the nearest wave and be carried along on your tummy for the 100 yards back to the shallows, roll off onto the water, get up and do it again. Occasionally, one of them will attempt to stand on the board, but the waves are hopeless and after a sort of wallowing wobble or two the surfer flings himself off with a great flailing of arms and spray. It is obviously very popular though. There is even a specialised surf shop on the beach selling boards, black rubber outfits, and various surf related services. There was no such madness here when I was a youngster, unless you count the horde of strange but charitably generous people who dashed nude into the freezing waves every New Year on the pretext of raising cash for good causes.

***

Just across the wide road which skirts the coast here is the boating lake. If the amusement arcades of Whitley Bay provided the entertainment of my early teenage years, then the boating lake, like The Lido, was a real favourite in younger childhood, only a few hundred yards from home. Oval, about 200 yards long with shallow, sloping stone cobbled banks, it had rowing boats for hire from a small landing stage. My father would shell out a few shillings for my brother and me to struggle in a heavy, wooden rowing boat with oars far too long for us. We had nylon nets on a cane stick with which we would fish for minnows and sticklebacks, which were imprisoned in a jam jar of green pond water, to be returned to the lake later by my father when we had become tired of that and wandered off in search of something else to entertain us.

There was a community of model boat enthusiasts who sailed intricate, radio controlled models of tugs, warships, yachts and all manner of craft genteelly about the lake. Sometimes teenage louts set off hydroplanes from the lakeside, flat hulled contraptions powered by petrol driven fans on the back which reached loud and uncontrolled speeds across the water, colliding with rowing boats, models, ducks and causing immense havoc, much to the glee of the hooligans.

My father was clearly inspired by these models, and as a naval architect he obviously had more than a little idea about building boats. And so he installed himself in the kitchen, covered the Formica topped table with a newspaper and set to work with plans, plywood, glue and all the paraphernalia of the model boat builder. He was a meticulous man, often irritatingly so, and he was there for weeks, bent over bits of this and bits of that while my mother fretted about how to get dinner ready or how to get blobs of glue off the lino floor, or out of her children's hair.

The result though, as we ought to have known it would be, was a boat of fine craftsmanship. He had built a fire tender, which we knew because it had "FIRE" in capital letters painted on the side. It was sleek, about 2 feet long, and had an exciting petrol engine which we imagined, rightly as it turned out, would make it very fast. We were beside ourselves with excitement at the prospect of taking it down to the boating lake where, we confidently expected, even the hooligans would be impressed.

And I expect they would have been, had it not been for one thing. My father was a generous man, and as I have said, meticulous, and so why he built such an impressive boat but failed to install radio control, or indeed any means of controlling it, I have no idea.

The boat was taken to the lake, where it was set up on two wooden cradles, filled with petrol, and a short rope thing deployed around a flywheel. While my brother and I hovered excitedly, father rapidly cranked the flywheel to and fro with the rope, supposedly to fire the engine. It rarely did, and then he made adjustments to various levers, tried again, and again, until our enthusiasm abated and we went back to fishing for minnows.

But occasionally the engine did fire with the sound of a swarm of angry hornets and father rushed to get the propeller into the water before it over-revved. With renewed excitement we crowded him, crouched at the water's edge, the engine snarling and water boiling about the stern as he held it while making adjustments to the rudder.

The idea was that the rudder would be set so that the boat would curve out across the lake in such an arc as to bring it back to the point from which Dad had released it. It was usually pretty soon we realised that was not going to happen. Either it was obvious the arc set was too shallow and the boat was going to crash into the bank on the other side, in which case Dad would sprint ferociously around the shore to try to catch it before it damaged itself, or worse shot up the shallow bank and caught a child or a pensioner on the ankles, or the arc was too steep which was the usual case, and the boat simply roared round in ever decreasing circles until it conked out in the middle of the water. Dad got fed up of rolling his trousers up to wade into the lake, knee deep in slimy green weed, to retrieve it while we squealed with delight from the shore, so being the engineer he was, he invented a recovery device which consisted of a tennis ball on a length of string which was hurled out towards the wallowing boat in the hope of snagging it and pulling it back to shore. Our endeavours with Dad's model boat probably caused more entertainment and amusement for onlookers than anything else on the coast.

Like The Lido, visitors from all over thronged to the lake. It was, again like The Lido, a break from the labour of the shipyards, a place to take the children, watch Dad with the boat, and to get in a pint or two in The Plaza or at The Park just over the road. The Tyneside Riviera, as this coastline north from Tynemouth has been called, provided working class entertainment. I don't think the residents of Percy Gardens were frequent visitors.

Today, as I walk slowly around the lake, there are few other people about. The chill breeze ruffles the surface of the water so that the light sparkles in a brief opening of sunshine. The hut on the landing stage is closed up, and at this time of year the rowing boats have been taken away. A few ducks paddle lazily or sit on the bank with their heads tucked in closely as if asleep for the winter. There are no children running about, no model boats, and no young hooligans.

Behind the boating lake and before the railway line which carries the Metro line around Tyneside are pathways between rose beds, brown, flowerless and pruned for the winter. The bowling green is closely cut and pristine, the little wooden clubhouse painted a fresh white, ready and waiting for a new party of cream-flannelled, elderly competitors. I stop briefly by the wire mesh enclosure of the two gravel tennis courts, nets rolled up until next season, unchanged since I last passed by here over 50 years ago.

I am momentarily startled by the huge lizard which appears before me through the bushes. It glares at me, and its companion rears behind it on great thighs, little forelegs clutching the air and its mouth wide with rows of teeth in a silent roar. Where once I played crazy golf with Little John, the windmills, bridges, bumps and hollows have been replaced by a small Jurassic Park, monstrous figures rendered in fibreglass and plastic.

I walk back to the water's edge and take a seat to gaze around for a while and take in the sights around me which, apart from T Rex and his fellow dinosaurs, don't seem to have changed at all, even though my whole career, from a junior desk to a metaphorical gold watch, has passed by far from here since Dad's boat was last dispatched in noise and spray from that far bank.

***

Walking from the boating lake towards Whitley Bay I pass the Park Hotel where I started out today. Wide dunes and sands border the sea and then over the road more green space. There were horses tethered there, and in these fields I can remember Billy Smart's circus being set up. There was a big top, and as little boys we could not control our excitement when the circus came to town. We expected to see animals, elephants probably, and maybe a lion or two, all persuaded to perform outrageously unnatural acts which you wouldn't see today. But there were also clowns of course, trapeze artists, unicycles and other silly forms of entertainment which thoroughly engaged us.

Just a little further on, tucked into the dunes and below the low cliff at the northern end of the Longsands, is yet another new café. I am struck by the abundance of these new establishments. 50 years ago there was little more than a mobile ice cream van on a nearby car park, and then only in summer. If you wanted lunch when visiting the beach you brought a picnic. I can still taste the gritty cheese and sand sandwiches, eaten in the lee of a billowing nylon windbreak, my father desperately trying to keep track of unrestrained pieces of napkin, food and children.

This new café is a good example of the Tyneside Riviera re-inventing itself to take advantage of the currently increasing popularity of taking holidays in the UK. Staycations, I believe, is the word for it. There is money to be made from tourism, as the North East has known since early Victorians discovered the train, and having lost the plot in the late 20th century there is now investment which, in parts, is beginning to return the area, if not to a former glory, hopefully to a new one. It's a work in progress, but the signs are there, and I am pleased to see it.

The View is rather box and steel looking from the outside, like an oversized shipping container, but once inside it is a full-on restaurant with a proper restaurant menu, furbished in a very nautical, seaside style with solid wood tables, beach debris ornaments, hanging lanterns, ropes, and ships wheels. The View is an appropriate name. The panorama from my chair over a very acceptable espresso is spectacular. The sea surfs onto the curving Longsands down to the cliffs at the Lido, the rugged priory and the long line of the pier outlined on the horizon. Only the bulk of The Plaza is missing from the view from here 50 years ago. I could sit here for a long time.

***

Just a little further on, past the tall, sharp spire of St George's church, the grand parade of Beverley Terrace overlooks the coastline. Not as grand as Percy Gardens, the terrace is nevertheless a splendid Victorian row which at the end of the 19th century would also have housed the more well-to-do. Opposite, a wide grassy space on the top of the cliff looks down onto the piers and the small crescent which is Cullercoats Bay. Steps lead down to the sand, firm under my feet from the outgoing tide.

It seems to be the inevitable case that beaches, and in particular beaches I am walking on, attract dogs, one of which on this occasion, loose of its leash, shows a disturbing interest in my trouser leg and has to be pulled away by its owner, or perhaps it was a concerned passer-by, reluctant and growling by the scruff of its neck.

Cullercoats is a charming little bay, bordered by rocky cliffs. Its two short piers enclose a small crescent of seaweed strewn sand. A great deal has been written about the history of Cullercoats, its position in maritime culture and the Marine Research Facility it hosts, its lifeboat station and its importance to the local fishing industry, but for me as a young lad its principal attraction was its cave. Set into the cliffs below the town the cave was dark with a floor of damp sand. It was a dank, smelly, litter beleaguered space where local romantics might steal a kiss or more from a willing lass, and teenage ruffians would drink from bottles, smoke, set off fireworks or simply urinate.

But the effluence resulting from such activities didn't put us off. The cave was our pirates' headquarters, our hide and seek refuge, or our commandoes bunker when we were in combat with the Japanese. We went home covered in sand, salt and worse, but it was a far better education, a much healthier nurture, than playing out our battles on a bedroom computer or a games console.

Today, the cave is clean, free of litter, and smelling only of the sea. It's smaller than I remember, but then so was I, and the roof seems lower as I have to crouch to reach into the further dark recesses. If I close my eyes I can hear the shouts and squeals of my little pals running from one point of cover to another, clutching machine guns of driftwood with which death was delivered with rat-a-tat-tat noises.

There are small boats pulled up here, highly coloured blue, yellow and red fishing boats filled with ropes, nets and cages, and with names such as "Jingling Geordie", "Silver Coquet", "North Star". An old, rusty tractor waits for someone to try to start it.

Cullercoats is more full of memories than I had expected. Beyond the piers, far out beyond the breakers and coastal swell lie the shapes of ships at anchor, waiting for tide or permission to enter the Tyne. Colliers, tankers, bulk carriers, cargoes from all over the world headed for the Port of Tyne's unloading cranes and a destination that may well be your corner shop. There are half a dozen, at least, as I stand on the sand in the cold sea wind and the piercing cries of seagulls. Stand on any part of this coast, at any time of day or night, in any season, and these are the sights and sounds. Seagulls and ships. It is a very pleasant place to be.

***

Above the bay was The Ship, where as an older teenager I drank Newcastle Brown Ale and listened to folk singers in a small, crowded upstairs room. The privileged space which The Ship occupied, looking out with uninterrupted views across the bay and out to sea, is now taken by a modern apartment block.

From Cullercoats the road winds around a headland crowded with small cottages and small terraced houses where the seafaring folk of the village would have lived, now smart and freshly painted. The street names reflect its position; Cliff Row, Promontory Terrace - names I had forgotten. It also accommodates The Queens Head, which holds the accolade of being the smelliest pub I have ever been in. I had forgotten about that too. I never knew if it was sour ale, a leaking toilet or just the customers. I think I only went in there the once, obviously.

The last cove before I reach the expanse of Whitley Bay is Brown's Bay, and Table Rocks. Slabs of rock under the cliff form natural bathing pools which the Victorians built up with concrete and where people thronged in bathing hats and costumes to lie about on the rock slabs and splash in the pools of weedy salt water. The pools and the concrete are still very much in evidence, but bathers are not. Like the Lido, it is no longer the tourist attraction it used to be, forsaken for bars and restaurants, shops and computer games.

Rocky fingers stretch far out beyond the bathing pools, dipping below the surface of the sea but not deep enough to avoid being a treacherous hazard for shipping. These fingers have claimed many ships over the years, and a heritage board records the fate of The Zephyros in 1942. The great steamship, bringing wartime supplies to the North East, was stranded high on the rocks, her back broken. According to the notice, parts of the wreck can still be seen at low tide, but I can't today and I don't remember ever seeing them.

I then find myself on The Promenade, Whitley Bay's answer to the Las Vegas Strip, where I turned into a teenager.

If Tynemouth provided a mainly refined style of entertainment, Whitley Bay offered the alternative. Tynemouth had the Abbey, The Lido, the Boating Lake and a refined shopping street. Whitley Bay had nightclubs, amusement arcades, cheap fish and chips and The Spanish City. It was litter strewn, noisy, and often intimidating. The sixties were the years of mods and rockers, and the seventies brought the skinheads, thugs whose uniform was a shaven head, trousers rolled up to the calf, and big boots laced to above the ankle. They were a truly evil confederacy whose common purpose was gratuitous violence. The disturbances caused by the confrontations between Mods and Rockers not many years before were mere light fisticuffs compared to what you might expect at the hands of cudgel wielding Skinheads.

The North East was by no means alone in suffering their odious presence, but it certainly had its share and during the fortunately short time that they gathered arrogantly in the streets there was an air of constant malevolence. For young teenagers with no appetite for receiving a complimentary beating for no other reason than existing, I can recall more than one occasion when we ran for our lives from a pursuing gang of them. I would have welcomed Oz's company on those occasions. At least he had a reason for his belligerence, even if it was lager, and his fists would have come in handy. I wonder what became of the shaven hooligans when they grew up. Are they now languishing at Her Majesty's pleasure somewhere, banged up for violence with a walking cane, or did they all turn into used car salesmen and estate agents?

***

The Rex Hotel, at the beginning of The Promenade as I approach the town, used to be a thriving venue for rock and roll, blues and heavy metal in the late sixties when I was in my teens. A fading, scruffy place even then, it made no pretence at any sort of sophistication. It was crowded, loud, and loads of fun. Smoke and the fumes from bottles of Broon Ale mingled with crowds of long haired rockers nodding heads to heavy rock pounding out from stacks of Marshalls and Fenders. I was younger than most of the patrons, and our boarding school haircuts rather singled us out from the hairier majority, but there was rarely trouble at The Rex. We felt grown up, and slightly anarchist.

I had expected to find that the old, worn façade of the Rex had been replaced with tasteful modern brick and stonework, proclaiming itself a care home for the elderly. I thought that because that is what I read about it before I travelled north. I was hoping that, if I went in, I might find some familiar faces. I thought maybe they never left.

But sadly, and yet again, the promises and ambitions have not, at least not yet, come to anything. The Rex still stands in corrosion and decay, a shabby wreck. The windows and ground floor entrance doors where we queued for rock bands and the sounds of the sixties are boarded up. Security warnings are displayed alongside torn event posters. It is such a grand old building and such an outstanding feature of the sea front here that I cannot imagine it would be simply bulldozed, but I fear that if nothing happens soon it will die of its own accord, and that would be a shame.

The terraced housing lining the seafront continues, but becomes noticeably less grand towards Whitley Bay. The terraces are interspersed with uninviting private hotels and cafes. The imposing High Point Hotel, where my parents would go dressed to the nines for business dinners and dances, is now demolished and replaced by another apartment block.

On the roadside railings, next to some car parking bays, is a bold Notice which states "*Please Use Discretion When Undressing*". That there is even the need for such a Notice speaks loudly of something, but I'm not quite sure what.

The terraced housing facing the seafront approaching the town of Whitley Bay gives way to a long row of amusement arcades, fish and chip cafes and 2-star hotels lining The Promenade, much smartened up, with enticing parasols and inviting seating out front, enabling the consumption of lager and chips facing the wind off the sea, and the fearless seagulls. There has been much improvement of the seafront infrastructure here. The pavement promenade has been widened and is now as much as 30 feet of clean paving, new street furniture, seating, lighting and new railings where all I remember is fading, peeling paint and rust-streaked ironwork. Below, the seafront promenade has also been cleaned up in a similar way, but in the centre of the new prom is the kidney shaped blue paddling pool, filthy and green with weed and algae. I am at a loss to understand why, when millions are spent on improvements like the new promenade, the cost of a scrubbing brush and a bottle of bleach seems to have been ignored or forgotten. Another Lido. Another Rex. Another blemish on the Riviera.

***

Whitley Bay. When I was too old for the boating lake or the Cullercoats caves, but still too young for Brown Ale or

The Rex, this where I headed, and where, should I close my eyes and roll back the years, I can conjure vivid memories of the old sea front here, the amusement arcades and the seedy dominance of the Spanish City, the place to be if sporting a Kiss Me Quick hat.

The Spanish City was, and still is, the iconic feature of Whitley Bay. Set in an acre or so right on the sea front, its white dome can be seen from miles away. Opened in 1910, it was a concert hall and a ballroom, a tearoom and a permanent funfair with a helter-skelter and dodgem cars, rifle shooting galleries and coconut shies. I am sure the nuts were nailed to the posts. Around its perimeter were amusement arcades glittering in neon, welcoming punters with promises of prizes from rows of one-armed bandits and push-penny machines. For us, the banks of pinball machines were the lure where, if fortune was with us, we could play for hours on one sixpence. Fish and chips were served in newspaper, cockles and vinegar in paper cones. It was all delightfully vulgar. There was candy floss and ice cream, and at night there were thugs and yobs.

I have read that the Spanish City has undergone a massive regeneration project since then, and is said to have been well scrubbed up and no longer vulgar, tastefully equipped with restaurants, event spaces, a tearoom and, I am taken aback to read, a champagne bar. As I approach along the sea front, negotiating the new road and pedestrian system, I do so with a great deal of apprehension. I've heard this sort of thing before, about The Lido for example, and The Rex. I am quite prepared to encounter peeling paint, crumbling masonry and the smell of decay.

I am, in fact, first confronted with a Beefeater restaurant the likes of which I thought had disappeared into oblivion in the eighties, but it's new and gleaming. Next to it is a rather ugly, but nevertheless actually there, brand new Premier Inn. I don't even recognise the old Spanish City next to the hotel. The amusement arcades in which I spent many a sixpence are now high end shops, an art gallery, a restaurant, a waffle and pancake outlet. I am astonished at the elegance of it all, from the brass and mahogany framed glass doors to the wide paved pedestrian area in front, complete with art installations.

Only the white dome above me bears any resemblance to my memory of it, and even that is gleaming white and gold. At the glass entrance doors are brass-framed menus set on stands offering a sumptuous selection of food. There is a long wine list. I am surprised, not only by the offerings, but at the prices too. I'm not going to get a bag of chips for a shilling here anymore.

Through the doors and underneath the dome is a palm court restaurant, beautifully set with dressed tables, tasteful lighting and a sparkling bar. Above, the dome is white and gilded. A balcony runs around at first floor level. Signs direct me to conference and meeting rooms, another restaurant upstairs and, true to its word, a champagne bar. It sounds kitsch, but it works, wonderfully well.

I have to have a wander around, past doors leading to reception rooms and displays offering wedding venue services. It's all nicely carpeted, a far cry from the cold, damp concrete floors I remember in here.

I've never been one for champagne, but I have to have a look. I didn't really believe it when I read that there was such a thing in the Spanish City, or if there was I expected it to be a poor attempt at one. But from what I have seen, I'm beginning to envisage something special, and I am not at all disappointed. I think the label "*Champagne Bar*" might be pushing it a bit, for although no doubt champagne is available should anyone want it, it's really a very nice café bar with feature windows looking out over the green links to the sea and the white pinnacle of the lighthouse on St Mary's Island in the distance. There are several customers, mainly older people enjoying cake or seafood. I have a commendable espresso and sit to enjoy these rather exceptional surroundings. Indeed, it is so comfortable and I am so staggered by what has taken place here that I have another, to spend more time in this place. This is a transformation indeed. I wonder where the hooligans go now.

The Geordie girl who serves my coffee tells me, when I express my admiration, that it is all part of the rejuvenation of the town. Hen parties and stag weekends were spoiling it and the town was in real danger of falling not only into disrepair, but into serious disrepute. With that came decreasing revenues and the inevitable decline of the town itself. The townspeople are strongly behind what is being done. When I ask her about The Lido, The Rex and the other decaying features I have encountered, she shrugs them off. It will take time, she says, but it will happen. Clearly, it has already started.

This is a place where memories of the past merge with the discoveries of the new. It feels right. I feel a stirring here, an emotion which may be telling me something about how I feel about this place where I was born. I do wonder if the word "*home*" is trying to make its presence felt.

***

The road from the Spanish City and out of Whitley Bay north, runs for about a mile until it reaches the limit of my childhood playground, St Mary's Island. The road is bordered to the seaward side by wide, green links which run down to the sand. Tucked into the dunes there is a Victorian café and shop building where mother used to take us for cake and ice-creams. To the land side the residential properties are good quality, mainly detached and semi-detached post war housing which have, of course, wonderful views out to sea. A singular fifteen storey block of executive flats holds particular memories, as my first proper girlfriend lived there. Past the Briardene pub, much improved from the shabby place it used to be, and before we get to St Mary's there is a quite remarkable set of four art deco houses. White, curved balconies, flat roofs and exactly in the style of The Park Hotel, a bit vulgar perhaps, a reminder that it is still Whitley Bay after all.

At the end of the links before the small road which leads to St Mary's is the pitch and putt course. I am amazed it is still here. My father used to bring us here when we were very small, knocking golf balls about in any and all directions with wooden handled, iron headed clubs hired from a green hut kept by a sour old man with a yellow stained moustache. I can see him now, the miserable old goat. We would beat Dad every time and dance about in excitement when the final putt fell. Or perhaps he let us win, which would have been his way.

St Mary's is a tidal island, and from the small car park where there was usually an ice cream van in summer, it is reached by a concrete causeway at low tide. A couple of hundred yards out along the causeway is the rocky island on which is clustered a small group of cottages and towering above them the white lighthouse. Constructed in 1898 it has not been operational since 1984, but it was alive when I was a lad and I remember the great light sweeping across the bay and out into the darkness of the North Sea. Now, it is fully preserved by North Tyneside Council as a visitor centre, complete with café, gift shop, video displays, and the opportunity to climb the 137 steps to the top. I have never been up, and am relieved to discover that the ascent is closed today. It's 46 metres up, which is a long way above my comfort zone.

The island is surrounded by rock pools, boulders and pebbles, green and slimy with weed, and is just right for a curious young boy to go exploring. We are about 3 miles from where we lived, and it was with great excitement that we would jump on bicycles and pedal furiously through the town to reach this place. Hours could be spent studying the pools and lifting rocks in the hope of disturbing a startled crab, or a starfish.

We had a great deal of freedom as children. My mother and father seemed to think little of letting my brother and I cycle down here on our own, or indeed to the Spanish City or the North Shields Fish Quay come to that. But they were by no means neglectful. We were constantly warned of the dangers of traffic, deep water, slippery rocks and we were always dressed for whatever activity or adventure we set out on. Interestingly, I don't recall them ever cautioning us against that scourge of modern society – the predatory adult. Although the likes of Myra Hindley made the headlines from time to time, society did not much adjust itself in the light of people like her. I don't think it ever occurred to my parents that we might encounter one. So we were given a long leash, and apart from a scraped knee or a wet sock we never came to any harm. I'm in no doubt that it was an education from which we benefitted greatly, and one that is probably less available to, or even less desired by, the children of today, to their significant disadvantage.

It seems to me as I recount this and re-live those years that childhood sounds as if it was one long holiday - fishing, cycling, boating and playing pin ball machines. But it can't have been entirely like that. Both my brother and I did fairly well at school, Little John rather better than me I must admit, but well enough nevertheless. As indeed, my father would have sternly insisted, determined as he was that we should not only receive a good education, but profit from one too. It is my memory which must be selective. There were undoubtedly days at school and evenings reluctantly consumed by spelling homework, but apart from the teacher's chalk and the warm milk I have no recollection of any of that. I cannot bring up an image of a classroom, the face of a teacher, or even the name of one. Perhaps, I would like to think, although my schooling taught me to spell, add up and get through exams, the real education, the valuable lessons which ultimately steered me through life, were learned around the rock pools of St Mary's Island, the Geordie fishing folk on the quayside, and the freedom to explore and discover for ourselves.

***

There is an overwhelming sense of space here at St Mary's island. Out to sea I can see a new windfarm and looking back south the great expansive crescent of Whitley Bay, past the headland at Brown's Bay and beyond to Cullercoats and Tynemouth Longsands from where I have come today. The great pier is outlined on the horizon and I can just make out the rising banks of County Durham far on the other side of the river. It is a marvellous view.

Before returning, I spend a little while at the crematorium just over the road. It's not only at the limit of my childhood playground, but my father's final resting place. The grounds are well kept and peaceful. It is a place to dwell a while, and reflect.

***

On the way back to the hotel at the end of this day, I travel along the Broadway from Whitley Bay, to the house I lived in. It was sold after we moved my mother. It is a semi-detached house, solidly built at the end of the 1940's, on that part of the Broadway which is wide, with verges and service roads. It is at least 100 yards between the houses on each side. It had a good sized, enclosed back garden with an oval lawn on which my brother and I would play cricket, much to the silent irritation of my father who spent hours caring for the grass. I can see that the house has been significantly extended, but there is much that I remember. The same front porch and door, the same windows with their cream, false shutters and the same shallow curved bay window. In my memory I can see the furniture, the carpets, my father's piano and the bedroom I and my brother slept in where we played out battles with miniature plastic soldiers, made lines of Dinky cars, and indulged in the mischief of childhood.

I don't know who lives there now, and I'm not going to knock on the door. This is one memory I would prefer to leave alone.

***

Just two or three hundred yards along the road from our old house is the roundabout which forms the intersection of The Broadway and the road from Newcastle to the coast. Neither the coast road nor the roundabout existed when we moved there in 1959, but the pub which was built there soon afterwards provided entertainment for me for years to come. During its construction, we used to play in the foundations, and because a cellar was being built they were deep. They were often filled with water and we would wade about, make boats out of wooden planks, and just muck about in the mud, much to the irritation of my mother who had to wash not only our clothes, but us too. But she never stopped us.

With astonishing originality the pub was named The Broadway, a flagship of the Scottish and Newcastle Brewery, celebrated for the blue star logo and Newcastle Brown Ale. They furnished and equipped it in the same way as they did with every other pub they owned or controlled. Down went bright, swirly carpets. In went plastic wooden beams, a long dark mahogany bar, ships wheels, brass bells and velour covered stools.

The long bar was festooned with beer pumps. Newcastle Exhibition, Watneys Red Barrel, Vaux Gold Tankard and a host of other gassy, pasteurised keg pop. We drank it because it was all there was and, I suppose, because we knew no better then in the dark ages of beer, the days after real ale had been lost to the tasteless fizz of corporate monopoly and before its resurgence courtesy of CAMRA's long, resilient campaign.

By the time I had reached the permitted drinking age and before the attractions of The Chain Locker had been put before me, The Broadway's carpets had become sticky underfoot, the walls were crowded with fruit machines and sports televisions, and the clientele was less flat cap and more white tee shirt. Lager had become the drink of choice. The pub staggered on in much that way throughout the time I was there, and I can't resist recording, if only because it is an important memory and I don't get to meet famous people as a rule, that I met Alan Hull of the band Lindisfarne in there one day. Lindisfarne were a big name Geordie band at the time, and had performed not only at The Rex but also at Newcastle City Hall, where there is now a memorial plaque to Alan, following his death in 1995. The appropriate response to a young adolescent coming up and saying "You're Alan Hull," ought to have been "I know. Get lost," but being a true northern gentleman he pretended to be pleased to see me, and bought me a pint.

By the late 1980's the pub struggled, failed, and in the way of so many pubs these days, re-invented itself as a local Sainsburys, in an annex of which is Woods Café Bar. I make my apologies to Pete. I don't need to go in.

***

The comfort of a high stool at the Park's bar is welcome now. The night is drawing in and the lights of the coastline shine yellow through the dark windows. A gratifying pint of Hadrian & Border ale sits beside me on the mahogany bar top as I idly swipe through the photographs I have collected today on my phone.

The big picture, the coast and the skylines, the wide horizon out to sea and the solid Victorian terraces are all profoundly familiar and resonate harmoniously with the memories I have from my childhood. There is much that has not changed. The image I took at St Mary's Island could have been taken on my junior Instamatic 50 years ago. Only my father smiling in his cap for the photo, and my mother gripping his arm at his side are missing. The Longsands still sweep from Cullercoats to Tynemouth in the same, shallow crescent, and the pier at the mouth of the Tyne still reaches out solidly into the North Sea. The waves still crash onto the rocks in King Edward's Bay.

Yet in the detail, in the close-ups, there are many changes. Some of these, like The Lido and The Rex crumbling into an uncertain future, invoke in me a poignancy that the source of such prominent memories may be irrecoverably lost, like The Plaza, and looking back to yesterday The Chain Locker, the dockyards and the way of things five decades ago.

But it is inescapable that others, strikingly The Spanish City but others too like the reborn promenade and the clean, sea-fresh ambience, are exciting developments which I am glad indeed to witness. There is new life here, and if my friendly Geordie girl in The Spanish City is to be believed, even The Lido and The Rex may get a chance, given time. As I felt sitting in the café in The Spanish City looking out over the green links, I am drawn to this. I like the rebirth I have seen. It sits most comfortably with my memories of long ago.

As my pen hovers above my notebook Geordie Ben the barman, without any prompting, provides me with another pint of Hadrian & Border, and tells me that the essential Tyneside, its soul, has not changed. It is alive and well here, which is a pleasing thing to feel a part of.

Across the bar I show Ben a picture of The Spanish City I took this afternoon, and I ask him if he has ever been inside. Certainly, he tells me in his Geordie lilt. He often goes there with his girlfriend for coffee, a drink or dinner, and when I describe to him the disreputable place it used to be, the dull cracked white plaster and damp concrete, the dodgy funfair and the menace when the sun went down, he can only say that he has heard about that. Ben is several decades younger than me, but I have got to know him a bit over the last couple of days. He is a confident young man, a new Northerner proud of his native land, a cosmopolitan. He doesn't have the memories that I do, but I think he holds the heart of Tyneside.

I think I might have another freshener, just to make sure I'm getting this right, before I settle down in advance of tomorrow's journey to the City of Newcastle.

FIVE

Newcastle

The original rail infrastructure, of which Tynemouth railway station is a part, was built in the mid-19th century, and the station itself opened in 1882. It's a typically Victorian structure of arched iron beams and pillars. With remarkable early foresight the line which linked the coast to Newcastle and south of the river was electrified from as early as 1904, but by the time I stood on the platform in the 1960s British Rail had got hold of it and diesels had replaced the quieter, cleaner electrics.

Today the old Victorian station has been preserved, but integrated into a bright, modern transport system now known as the Tyneside Metro, which I am going to take up to Newcastle to see how things have moved on, and to see if Oz is still there.

The ticketing system is a challenge. I have arrived at the station this morning from The Park without giving it much thought, and I am a bit baffled by the array of ticket options which are presented to me by the stoic machine at the entrance. Back in 1969 there was a ticket office with a window, behind which sat a man who sold two types of ticket – single or return. He did not offer day returns, day hoppers, weekend specials or off-peak discounts. He did not provide reductions to students or pensioners, and he would have nothing to do with an Oyster Card or a Tyneside

Tourist Pass. Nothing less than cash would persuade him to issue a ticket.

Eventually I manage to acquire a Short Day Excursion Saver (certain services excluded – see terms and conditions) or some such thing, which gives me entrance to the platform, and I am able to take stock of how things have changed.

For a start, there are no louts making a nuisance of themselves, but then it is before lunchtime and Newcastle United are not playing at home today, so far as I am aware. But it is an encouraging sign.

The station concourse is much, much wider and more spacious than I remember it. Victorian pillars and iron work support the multiple ridged, glass roof, and artisan shops have appeared where the ticket office and waiting rooms once were. Modern signage and electronic displays have replaced the uniformed man with a whistle. It is clean, free of litter, remarkably uncluttered, and fag ends are no longer strewn across the concrete platform. But there are no toilets, no staff, and the only way to seek assistance is by way of a button and a speaker on a device hung on a wall.

The Metro system runs a circular route to and from Newcastle and the coast. The southern side of the circle runs from the coastal stations of Tynemouth, Cullercoats and Whitley Bay westwards following the river and largely the route of Hadrian's Wall to the city stations of Manors, Monument and Haymarket. Then the circle returns by the northern route through Jesmond, Gosforth, Benton and Shiremoor. There are spurs which run across the river to Gateshead and on to South Shields and Sunderland in the east, and to the airport in the west, but my journey will retrace the route I took to Newcastle to see the bands at the City Hall, and to visit the music shops where we could spend hours for free in an audio booth listening to Deep Purple, Black Sabbath and bands like them through tinny headphones while eyed suspiciously by sales assistants who knew we had no intention of actually buying anything.

The Metro Light Transit System that exists today was conceived in the mid-1970s and opened in 1980 by HM

Queen herself. The tunnels and underground stations serving the centre of the city did not exist back in the 1960s, but the lines to and from the city follow the same routes as they did back then, and I am looking forward to encountering the views as we pass through places with familiar names.

The electric train which collects me from Tynemouth is modern, clean, bright, unexpectedly quiet, on time and offers free Wi Fi. There are brief stops at the stations of North Shields, Meadow Well, Percy Main and Howden. I am impressed by the modern, clean infrastructure, marred only by the inevitable trackside graffiti.

At Hadrian Road station the train jolts to a stop rather suddenly. Almost immediately there is an announcement from, I assume, the driver who apologises in broad Geordie for something to do with the brakes sticking. At least, that's what I think he said. No one seems to take any notice, but his engagement with the passengers is a nice touch.

As we approach Wallsend, I notice an unfamiliar tall structure like an airport control tower emerging from the landscape between the track and the river, a few hundred yards away. And beyond the tower a great cleared area at the riverside surrounded by the infrastructure of an industry slipping into extinction. Although I have no idea what the tower is, I realise that beyond it is the remains of the great Swan Hunter shipyard, one of the grandees of Tyne shipbuilding, and a place my father often visited in the course of his work. Urgently, I grab my things and get off at this station to explore.

At first I thought perhaps the tower thing might be some sort of control or observation platform for the Port of Tyne Authority to monitor the passage of ships, for it looks to be about 35 metres high with a raked glass cabin at the top. Approaching it on foot not at all far from the station, much to my surprise it turns out to be part of the museum at Segedunum, the most eastern Roman fort of Hadrian's Wall. Wallsend. Of course.

What I can't understand is why I didn't know this was here. I knew the docks of Swan Hunter just behind it because occasionally my father would take me there when he had business and I would potter about the shipyard, or at least those parts of it where I wouldn't encounter death by crane or riveting hammer. But I have no recollection of this at all.

The answer, as it turns out, is that it wasn't here then. Or rather, being nearly 2,000 years old, it was here but lying hidden under the foundations of the terraced housing built in the 19th century for the dock workers. It wasn't until the mid-1970s when the derelict terraces, as redundant as the men who worked at Swan Hunters, were demolished and the underlying archaeology exposed. The University of Newcastle was called in, and armed with their trowels and geophysics discovered a site of such historical importance that the plans to build flats and suchlike were abandoned, and the museum as it is now was founded. The tower was built as a viewing platform to look down on the site from above, the better to appreciate its construction and layout. All this, since I left.

Entering the museum from its car park, past a rather startling, larger than life, Roman Centurion, I am greeted by a very nice, and knowledgeable, Geordie man who is overjoyed to hear that I am on a voyage of remembrance to the North East, and that my father had connections with Swan Hunter. He tells me that he worked at the yard himself and is old enough to remember all this before the demolition and the redundancies. He is now a tour guide for the museum.

He shows me some photographs of the area taken during the demolitions. Rows of terraces at the mercy of bulldozers and diggers, rubble and open gable ends exposing torn, fluttering wallpaper. In one photograph, a digger with its hydraulic arm raised in a position of imminent destruction stands next to The Ship Inn, below which was found the Bath House of the Roman legions who inhabited this place 2,000 years ago.

My guide encourages me that the place to start is the viewing tower, a prospect which does not appeal strongly to my aversion to heights as it is, as I estimated, 35 metres.

But I want the view at least, and with resignation I head for the lift. Press button 9, my guide tells me, which sounds an awfully long way up.

The lift glides silently upwards, and when the doors open I find a viewing cabin fitted with several rows of tiered, theatre style seats, several video information screens and a 360 degree panorama over the river Tyne from the piers at Tynemouth to far upriver towards Newcastle. After an initial wobble at the distance between me and the ground, I am mesmerised at what lies spread before me.

The tower is principally designed to provide a bird's eye view of the layout of the Roman site, which is actually rather flat and uninteresting to look at. It is no doubt of immense historical importance, but it is the prospect before me, out over the river, which captivates me. I have looked out at the Tyne from some decent vantage points, but this is beyond anything I have seen before.

More or less below me are the old offices of the shipyard. I can see one of them still displays the sign "*SWANS*". A jumble of buildings, some brick some steel, a surprisingly new looking 4 storey office block although it's probably 1960s, appear deserted. They give way to the vast cleared area down to the riverside and which I had seen from the train, the concrete bases of the yard's industry. Here were the slipways, the great sheds and cranes amongst which I pottered while my father did whatever business he had come for. I don't know what development is proposed for here, but the trend seems to be apartments, restaurants, and leisure.

I do linger a while here, as memories of places long forgotten arise from the vast landscape, and then take the lift back down for a look around the rest of the museum. As one might expect, there are a lot of Roman helmets and pottery artefacts displayed in glass cases, but the museum has also dedicated a couple of rooms to the history of shipbuilding which, if not very Roman, is fitting given its location next to the site of one of the great docks of the Tyne. There is some marvellous artwork depicting the ships and yards, and a couple of incredibly detailed models of great ships, complete down to the last rivet. But what unexpectedly arrests me is a big screen video playing in a dimly lit room.

There is no one else at the exhibition, and I sit down alone to watch an absorbing archive film of the launch of the gigantic Esso Northumbrian from the slipway of Swan Hunter in 1969. Made by Turner Films and preserved by the North East Film Archive, it documents the launch by a young Princess Anne of the 250,000 ton vessel, the largest ever built in the UK at the time. It is astonishing to think that what is being shown on the screen, a little grainy and very much of its time, happened not more than a couple of hundred yards from where I sit.

The camera takes shots from street level, down a cobbled street closely built with terraced houses which would have been pretty much right on this site. At the end of the street rises the great bow of the ship, far above roof level, towering above crowds of onlookers in coats and scarves, caps and boots. It is so close, almost in the street itself. Children lean out of windows. Flags and bunting are tied across the street and at upstairs windows. It is an outstanding sight.

When HRH pulls a lever which operates a device which swings a bottle at the bows, agonisingly slowly, inch by inch the ship begins to slide towards the river, gathering pace slowly, the great hull gliding past the rooftops to be guided by the tugs which await her on the river Tyne. The crowd raises cheers. It is clearly a momentous occasion as another great ship leaves its birthplace on the banks of Wallsend.

And for me, it is also personal. In 1969, it is likely that my father had a hand in that ship somewhere. Something of my history rode down that slipway.

After that, when the 20 minute film is over and the credits have run, and after a moment to reflect, it's time to re-join the Metro system and continue to the city.

***

One stop past Manors where I frequently alighted for the City Hall is Monument Station, so called because it is built beneath the 130 feet monument to the 2nd Earl Grey, constructed in 1838 and widely regarded as the centre of the City of Newcastle. It's all new to me as the station wasn't opened until long after I had left. It is strongly reminiscent of the City of London as the train trundles through dark tunnels and emerges into the bright underground station platform, signed and designed just like its London counterpart. Hot draughts of air, a slightly oily smell, escalators and automatic ticket barriers complete the illusion. Happily, my super saver discount ticket is accepted by the automation, and I emerge from below slightly dazzled into the bright but rather damp Newcastle air.

Familiarity breeds contempt, and although I thought I wouldn't even need a map here, I am a little bewildered and find it difficult to get my bearings. The huge pinnacle of the monument towers above, and the streets are bustling with people.

Newcastle is a big, heavy city, built of great Northern resolve and determination. The powerful stones of Grey Street and Grainger Street spread like spokes from the hub of Monument Square, south towards the river. Everything seems much higher, taller than I remember it, but I do remember the drizzle in the air and the cold draught which clutches at my coat.

Newcastle is not just a place of big architecture and industry, it is also a city of culture, featuring among its many attractions the Laing Art Gallery, which happens to be pretty much right behind me as I stand in the monument square. The Laing is world renowned and houses much of great value, as is immediately evidenced by the peculiar anatomy of the Henry Moore which confronts me as I enter. Turner and Edward Lear are among those represented, and although there is much to see I am particularly interested to see the art depicting the lives and industry of the Tyne, both in painting and photography.

It is a splendid exhibition. Several connected rooms in the gallery are dedicated to portraits and landscapes from an earlier age of shipbuilding. Figures, coarsely clad, are captured on monochrome film. An old man with a leathery, wrinkled face gazes into a camera lens with a world weary expression. Rough and grimy shipyards are painted in exquisite detail. In almost all, the hardship endured by those whose lives depended on the shipyards is a prevailing feature; men hauling heavy chains, sitting soberly on a bollard smoking, wielding hammers, manhandling crates and machinery; women in grubby shawls and headscarves, lines of washing hanging across back lanes between closely built terraces. Any one of them could be an ancestor of mine.

Backgrounds of great hulls, ships in the course of construction, tall cranes, slipways, oily pools on concrete, men with faces streaked black with grease and ingrained dirt. The river crowded with vessels from lighters to tankers, vying for space on the congested water. Steam, smoke and steel, grease, cloth caps and grimy overalls. Noise and more oil. These are the images I take away.

Beneath the subject matter there is a beauty in the art. In many of the portraits, below the surface of deprivation and poverty in the faces of the subjects, there is a discernible stoicism, a hint of a smile even. And in terms of actually getting a ship built to the point you could fill it with cargo, or bombs, and sail it off to do its business in some other part of the world, these people were as important to the process as the designers, financiers, and dock owners. That they did so, without any prospect of betterment, in the conditions which are depicted in art here before me, is humbling indeed.

***

I am anxious to move on to those places which feature strongly in my memory. I'm keen to see the place known as Bigg Market which had a fearsome reputation for unruly, loutish behaviour, and which has probably given rise to, or at least significantly contributed to, this overwhelming recollection I have that Newcastle is a city of belligerence. I also want to visit the quayside under the feet of the great Tyne Bridge where as a child I watched the ships and the opening and closing of the Swing Bridge which let them through to the upper docks and further reaches of the Tyne.

As I leave The Laing and head for Grey Street which will take me down to those places, I see the entrance to Eldon Square Shopping Centre, which was the largest indoor shopping centre in the country when it was opened in 1976, again by HM Queen. To make way for the development, a large part of historically important Georgian Newcastle was lost, and what was put in its place was architecturally controversial. The writer Christopher Booker who co-founded Private Eye and wrote in the Telegraph described it as *"the greatest single example of architectural vandalism in Britain since the war"*. Harsh words, and with a different agenda I might have a closer look, but I am not in need of new shoes or a fashionable shirt and I don't remember it anyway, so I press on.

I am also surprised to notice, across the road from The Laing and amidst the modernity of new shop fronts, a crumbling concrete abomination which appears to be, or to have been, a multi-story car park of some sort. It is a truly awful sight, and just visible, stencilled in the grey front, faded and hardly legible are the words "Dex Garage". Dex, of course, the memory instantly surfacing - the car park of choice for my parents when we travelled up to town to shop in Binns and Bainbridges department stores, The John Lewises of the time. We would seek new shoes for Dad, a dress for Mother, school uniforms for us. I can hear my father's words "We'll park in Dex", every time. But memories apart, it's an unpleasant wart on the fabric of Newcastle, and I am at a loss to understand why it still stands there, festering and mouldy.

In some stark contrast, just past the extremely weird Stack market complex, which seems to be constructed from shipping containers, is the grand façade of Northern Goldsmiths with its ornate corner pinnacle, rather brash, illuminated Rolex crown and extravagant gold clock suspended above the street. The clock is a Newcastle icon I remember from all those years ago. The container market is not.

The northern weather, which had been merely damp when I emerged from Monument station a short while ago, has taken a turn for the worse and as I make my way back past Grey's towering pillar towards Grey Street, the heavens open into a full deluge. It is sudden and fierce, and I dive into the nearest refuge available, which happens to be a Pret a Manger, not my preferred option, with my apologies to those who prefer the coffee in a paper cup experience.

And so, the rain blattering down and pedestrians scattering under straining umbrellas and hoodies, I find myself at a window stool with a paper beaker of espresso and the opportunity to sit awhile and watch the world of Monument Square go by.

It's hard to see much at all while the rain comes down in stair-rods, but it soon eases off and the street seems to slow down. Office suits and overcoats, tracksuits and hoodies, high heels and trainers all mingle in the swarm of people criss-crossing the square, all headed for somewhere, all with a destination. Plastic shopping bags, briefcases, rucksacks and designer handbags conceal their business of the day. It would be fascinating to know their purposes.

I can see no young Geordie men in white tee shirts, oblivious to the cold wind. Perhaps that is just a myth, or maybe they will come out later when it's a bit chillier.

Eventually, the last of the rain moves off elsewhere, and leaving the dregs of my instant espresso, I head out for Grey Street and the road down to the river.

***

I'm still a little unsure of my bearings, although when heading for the river a downhill path is usually a safe bet. I accost a gentleman walking towards me. He is about my age, wearing a smart suit and tie, and carrying a professional looking briefcase. I ask him if I am headed the right way for the quayside. He speaks with the slightly refined Geordie my father did. Yes he tells me helpfully, and asks if I am looking for anything in particular. "*Memories*" I tell him. This raises an enigmatic smile. "*Aren't we all?*"

As I watch him walk away from me he has the same shape, the same bearing as my father. I linger over that accent, the almost lyrical, dignified version of dockyard Geordie. Softer than the Geordie of the shipyards, devoid of the more gratuitous oaths common on the streets and in the pubs of Tyneside, it identified him, as it did my father, as a man who had achieved a measure of success and status. Yet it was still, unmistakably, Geordie. It is an accent which not only distinguishes the people of Tyneside, but cements them together. Whether spoken with the direct rudeness of the dockside or the restraint of the drawing office he is regarded as a Northerner by other Northerners and as such part of their community, a compatriot in the face of the misalignment of class.

Bill Bryson, in his travelogue "*Notes from a Small Island*", in which he wandered about the country in a reminder of things which give rise to essential Englishness, noted with some surprise, he claims, the extent to which the North feels like another country. He put this down, in part at least, to the manner of speech. He tells us that it is "*to do with the accents, the different words, the refreshing if sometimes startling frankness of speech*".

I loved the manner of my father's speech. He spoke softly, and his sentences rose slightly in tone, as is the Geordie way. Like any child would, I copied his use of Northern words and phrases, his vernacular, and I copied his smile too. He didn't show his teeth when he smiled. He "*smiled with his lips*", according to my mother's affectionate description. He had a slim face, like the rest of him, and he had a Roman nose. His eyes narrowed when his smile widened, giving a mischievous look to his face.

But my father was a practical man, and he knew the value of a well spoken word. Today a Geordie accent, or at least one that sounds like one, has helped propel the likes of Jimmy Nail, Cheryl and Alan Shearer to the status of celebrity. It wasn't always like that. When I was a boy in the

1950s it was associated with an uncouth rudeness and a disadvantage to social improvement. Simon Evans put it succinctly, and courageously, to a Newcastle audience, when he told them "*30 years ago if you had a Geordie accent you were virtually entitled to a disability pension, so detrimental was it to your prospects in life.*"

And so my father discouraged it in me and in my brother. He often attempted to speak in a neutral voice in our presence, although the Geordie accent is impossible to conceal and the result was hilarious. My brother and I sniggered behind a handkerchief, much to his bewilderment. But the job my father attempted was completed by a few years at a boarding school and now I have little of it left except for a persistent hard "a", so I'm told.

***

I've often wondered if I missed out.

When I was at school its incumbents were an eclectic mix from all parts of the country, and indeed the globe. There was a smattering of ex-pats, local day boys from around the border of Durham and Yorkshire, southerners whose parents felt an expensive Home Counties education was probably not worth the investment, and others for whatever reason pushed off up North. And there was a significant contingent from Tyneside, north Durham and Northumberland who contributed a hefty dose of Geordie to the mosaic of accents.

Just as a combination of the colours of the rainbow distil into white, the school's natural accent was similarly colourless. The individuality of dialect which every first former brought to school was bleached over time and melded into a flat, neutral English which left little trace of its origins except, in my case, that flat "a".

But the Geordie accent is persistent and resistant to all but the stoutest redaction. I must have succumbed to my father's well-meaning persuasion and the natural influence of the school, but there were a few who didn't submit, and for those whose Geordie did not leave them it has sometimes served them well, which is what has caused me to wonder, frequently over the years, if the course of my life might have been any different if the Geordie of my early childhood had been allowed to persist.

In about the fifth form, aged about 15 and by then well on the way to Universal Dialect, I was approached by the Drama Master who suggested that I audition for the lead part in that year's play, performed at the end of term by whatever motley assortment could be mustered. I had no idea why he chose me, for I had no pedigree on the stage, but I remember feeling rather flattered by the invitation, although with a hint of suspicion lingering somewhere in the back of my mind. A justified suspicion, as it happened, when my audition turned out to be a mere formality to lend credibility to the casting of the fellow student who had already been pre-selected and allocated Top Billing.

It was an Irish play. I can't remember which one but probably James Joyce or Bernard Shaw or something like that. I was given a page of lines and sent up onto the stage to recite them before an audience of one Drama Master and the other, already preferred, auditioner.

I recited my lines. I gave emphasis in all the right places. I even waved my arms about I think, and I raised an eyebrow when the text demanded a moment of reflection. It came out, of course, in School Speak.

My opponent then took to the stage, and delivered his audition in a rich Irish brogue that would have done credit to Bob Geldof. I was thanked and dismissed, as had been the plan all along. My opponent got the job and delivered an admirable performance when the play was produced a few weeks later. His name was Kevin Whately, known today as Inspector Morse's sidekick, Lewis.

I'm sure that Kevin is quite unaware that he is responsible for the consignment of my putative acting career to the receptacle of things that are Not Going To Happen. He was a year above me, so he couldn't be a mate, even if he'd wanted to be which I'm sure he didn't. But I knew him well enough and we had a mutual interest in rock music. He gave me a few guitar lessons in fact, although I wasn't much good at that either. Kevin was a natural on the stage, as has become clear over the years, and even back then when he was but a sixth former with an eye on accountancy he could turn out a capital Irish accent should he need to. But in the natural world he was always a Northerner.

Whether Kevin hung on to his accent by design or otherwise I don't know, but I suspect he was simply one of those who was naturally resistant. And this, as I am sure even he would agree, has served him well. From the hapless Geordie Neville in Auf Weidersehen Pet, to John Thaw's Detective Sergeant in Morse, Peak Practice, the eponymous Lewis and many more besides, Kevin's easily articulated northern voice has been one of his most enduring, and appealing, features.

But that's acting for you. If Kevin hadn't turned to drama and had pushed on with accountancy, he would probably have done well to stay in the north east where the accent is socially irrelevant. I'd go further. Whether on the shop floor where Oz would be found or in my father's boardroom, anything other than a northern accent is the distinguishing stripe of someone who is not one of us, and treated with suspicion and probably distrust. At least, it was back then in the 1970s.

I'm not sure where the demarcation line is, probably somewhere a bit south of Durham, where the opposite is true. Certainly, when I came to East Anglia in 1974 to embark on a career in law, the only people who spoke with a local dialect were the people who drove buses or grew potatoes. If I had brought a Geordie accent with me I might as well have had leprosy. My accent, as Simon Evans noted, would have been detrimental to my prospects.

So I have not, on the whole, regretted that my manner of speech renders my northern origins indistinguishable to all but the keenest ear. But sometimes, when I observe the Geordie accent regarded with the modern favour that it is in the likes of Ant and Dec, Sting or Robson Green, I do wonder whether I might have got more girls, or become an actor like Kevin.

But the resilience of the Geordie accent is strong, even in me and in spite of my well-meaning father and the thorough washing it got at school. As I wander the north east, and in fact whenever I find myself among friends from the North, I find myself lapsing. My sentences engage the music of the dialect, rising towards the end. I say "Aye" with a knowledgeable inflection, and the use of words like "clarts" mysteriously arises from time to time without me thinking about it. I feel quite proud when this happens. I am glad it comes back so easily. It genuinely gives me a sense of cordial fellowship, a feeling of belonging. Something, somewhere, doesn't really want to let go.

***

Passing between the brown block stonework of Grey Street and the modern high street shops, a short detour takes me to Bigg Market. It is not a market at all, although in years gone by I dare say it might have been, but in my memory it was a collaboration of drinking places which attracted those whose standard evening entertainment was to drink until all social reasoning was lost, and to fight.

I know that I ventured down here when I was a teenager because I can remember the anxiety of simply being in the place, but why I ever did so I cannot recall at all. It is not as if it is on the way to anywhere specifically, or at least not on a route that cannot be avoided. Perhaps one of my friends was braver than me, and I just tagged along. But for whatever reason, I do remember Bigg Market.

Men in black tie suits stood guard outside dim doorways. Neon advertised the best place to buy your fill of lager. There was always shouting, aggressive belligerent shouting. And then one group of shouting people would fight with another. They fought with fists, and with bottles. The big men in black ties stayed in the doorways. They can fight on the street as much as they like, but not inside. It was not a good place, and I am sure that Newcastle was not proud of it.

It doesn't seem much like that today as I stroll down the road which is now descending towards the river. There are fewer bars and dingy doorways than I remember. It's fairly litter free and there is no vomit in the gutter, no smashed glass on the pavement. But as Bigg Market turns into Cloth Market, the buildings become seedier and I begin to see boarded windows, barred doorways, and a more desolate perspective than I had expected.

On the corner with the narrow street known as High Bridge is a pub, The Beehive Hotel, although I can't imagine why anyone would want to stay here. It has a dark green tiled façade, arched grimy windows, and a dingy unwelcoming feel. I have no intention of going in, but I can see through the window it is a long narrow bar at which sit perhaps a dozen men, many of them in flat caps, huddled over beer. It's hardly mid-morning. I can see a crudely written sign behind the bar, "*Cash Only*". This is an uncomfortable place.

Cloth Market disgorges me onto Neville Street and immediately in front of the Cathedral Church of St Nicholas, before which a dark statue of Queen Victoria squats very sternly, as if casting her disapproval at the goings on in Bigg Market just a couple of hundred yards away. From there I take Dean Street, steeply descending to the river and the quayside. I had forgotten how steep Dean Street is and how high the city is built above the river. I don't look forward to the walk back up, but under the towering arches of the bridge which carries the main line into Newcastle Central Station I find myself, at last, on the flat open pavement with the Tyne quayside before me.

Before exploring the quayside, I need a break from the Bigg Market and Cloth Market experience, and my feet are weary from the walk down to here. I have come out right underneath the majestic arches and stone supports of the Tyne Bridge, squeezed between buildings which were there long before the bridge was built. There wasn't much here as I remember it, just under the towering bridge, but now I find wide, clean pavements, pedestrian walkways and many smart looking cocktail bars and restaurants. I can only pick one at random, find myself a coffee in a window overlooking the quay, and settle down to write up my notes so far.

Gazing absently out of the window watching the world go by, my eye is caught by a passing white van. Not by the van itself which is unremarkable, but by what is written on its side. It says in professional lettering, and I promise I am not making this up (and I didn't make up the bit about the dog being fed lemons either, in case you thought I had), "*Manufacturers of the Famous Craster Kippers*" I have a fleeting image of some massive machine into which, at one end, are fed ingredients of some sort and from the other emerge perfect kippers, flopping down a chute to be stamped "*Made in Craster*". Personally, I like kippers, but I'm going to take a closer look at the labelling from now on.

***

As I walk out from the bar onto the wide quayside, I have my first view of the broad river from down here at water level. I am immediately struck by three things. Firstly, the great white ship which was permanently moored on the Gateshead side underneath the Tyne Bridge has gone. Secondly, the horizon is blighted by the enormous silver slug of The Sage building. And thirdly, the millennium bridge, which actually looks very pleasing. All of these things are quite new to me.

***

The great, white ship was the Tuxedo Princess - or the Tuxedo Royale which was a temporary replacement for a few years but was much the same thing - a vast floating nightclub which was parked under the bridge for 25 years between 1983 and 2008. It was the brainchild of a local businessman who was also a club owner in the city, and saw the opportunity to profit from the expanding leisure and entertainment industries. He wanted something big, brash and eye-catching. He certainly got it.

It was originally intended to moor the ship on the Newcastle side of the river, but the authorities in the city didn't want such a thing on their doorstep and gave it a firm thumbs down The folks over at Gateshead were more amenable to whatever incentives were on offer, and allowed it a berth on their side, right under the great arch of the bridge.

The ship was built as a car ferry, and so had masses of internal space. It was given a dozen bars and restaurants, a revolving dancefloor created from the turntable used for manoeuvring vehicles, and bedecked with light from bow to stern. It was hugely successful and became a Tyneside icon, one of the most recognisable landmarks of the region. Celebrities adored it, and its roll of guests included Frank Bruno, Kevin Costner, Noel Edmonds, Ian Botham, Paul Gascoigne (inevitably), Les Dawson, Freddie Starr and many others. It even featured in the television series "*Our Friends in the North*".

Actually, I never went in it. If it had been moored on the Newcastle side I probably would have done at some point, but I didn't venture over the river. Nevertheless, its sight was iconic and I am surprised to see its berth empty, replaced on the quayside by a pile of brown shipping containers known as the Gateshead Container Village where can be found a micro-brewery, street food and artisan offerings. I do wonder what it is about the North East and old shipping containers.

Anyway, the ship is gone, and I wonder why and what happened to it.

***

The silver carbuncle blotting the skyline above the southern banks of the river is Sage Gateshead. Opened in 2004 primarily as a concert venue, it was designed by the otherwise talented Norman Foster, and has hosted numerous internationally renowned artists, from rock bands to classical orchestras from around the world. It is the home of the Northern Sinfonia.

I think that I must be missing something because its architecture has been widely praised. Although Gavin Stamp of Private Eye described it as "a shiny condom" and in 2004 it was awarded the medal for the worst building of the year, it does seem to be highly regarded by those who know better than I. Still, as I observe it from the Newcastle quayside it looms like a great shimmering slug, and I cannot, for the life of me, see any merit in it.

Perhaps I am just mourning the Tyne as it was, and not celebrating its new clothes. I find myself lamenting the absence of something many regarded as a symbol of unwanted decadence, yet similarly lamenting the appearance of something many applaud. Well, I have seen many new developments which no doubt enhance, renew and excite here on Tyneside, but I cannot bring myself to place Sage Gateshead in any of those categories.

***

The millennium bridge, however, is altogether more appealing, only a short distance from me down the quay. Two slim arches elegantly span the river, one acting as the footway and cycleway and the other as a counterbalance. Rotating the bridge allows river traffic to pass beneath, a process which takes only minutes to complete.

The bridge was opened by HRH Queen in 2002. It strikes me that Her Majesty has been up and down to Tyneside on many occasions, opening things like this.

The quayside here is broad and open, bordered by bars and restaurants set into the ground floors of grand buildings where there were once shipping offices and the trading houses of the river, and where it nears the bridge is free of traffic. A wide pedestrian area hosts a glazed café/bar complex. I am not disappointed to find that the bridge has been opened to allow a ship to pass, as it allows me the opportunity to see the mechanism in action. After a short while the whole bridge starts to rotate, silently and smoothly until the pedestrian arc is flush with the quayside and the waiting citizens can cross to Gateshead and The Sage, if they really want to.

***

I notice that there are two marked police cars parked next to the pedestrian area. They don't seem to be on any sort of a call or emergency, as one of the officers is leaning on the door of one of the cars in a nonchalant manner. I've always been wary about approaching policemen, in case I have been doing something inadvertently unlawful such as walking on the cracks in the pavement or breaching a local bylaw by wearing a hat, and I have equally regarded the expression "*if in doubt ask a policeman*" with some caution for the same reasons. But it occurs to me that he may be able to tell me about the white ship, and what has happened to it.

As an introduction which is intended to indicate both that I am not up to no good, and that I am perfectly aware he has better things to do than bother with me, I tell him that I am, honestly, a law abiding tourist seeking the memories of my childhood and that I thought there ought to be a big white ship where now there is only a pile of old containers, and does he know how this happened?

I ought not to have been so anxious, of course, as the officer is most approachable and quite happy to chat. I think he might even be relieved to have something to do. Perhaps crime in Newcastle is at a low point at this time of day.

He tells me, in a fine Geordie accent, that the ship was a great attraction for the North East, as I knew already. But although originally the ship had a dress code and a code of behaviour, this was eroded over time and then the celebrity patrons stayed away and hen and stag parties took over. The venue became a binge drinking den, unruly behaviour became the norm, and eventually the authorities got fed up with the nuisance and started to clamp down on its activities. When Newcastle and Gateshead were preparing for the 2008 Capital of Culture bid, the ship and its rowdy customers were considered unsuitable features for the city's CV, and it was closed down, eventually to be towed away to Turkey, where it was scrapped.

As we chat, and his colleague in the police car eats a sausage roll, I mention my recollection of Bigg Market and the fighting I witnessed there back in the 1960s and 1970s. It seems to me, I tell him, that the area has been cleaned up and I wonder if this is the case and that Newcastle is now a safer, more sober place on a Friday night.

It hasn't and it isn't he says. If anything it is worse. Drugs have joined alcohol, and the combination fuels confrontations and hostility. I think he fears I may be planning to see for myself later, and sternly warns me against it. Bigg Market is to be avoided. Even the police will only attend in force.

There is a trend, he tells me, for young people to get fuelled with cocaine before they even start the evening, and then alcohol completes the lethal cocktail. The result is loss of control, inhibition and common sense. There is no easy solution he says rather tiredly, so just stay away.

***

I feel rather despondent at that as I walk back down the quay. I had hoped for different news of the city's night time perils, and it is a sadness to hear this. I don't think that even Oz would have approved. On top of that it has started to rain again, and so I take shelter in a bar called Charts, which is no doubt intended to give it a nautical feel, fitting for the quayside.

It is a nice bar, and I'm able to take a high stool against a counter in the window overlooking the river with a fine view up though the arch of Tyne bridge, the swing bridge, the High Level rail bridge and beyond. Sitting in contemplation of all I have seen today, the rain turns heavier, I stay longer than I had intended, and my coffee turns to beer.

SIX

Reflection

Tomorrow I will leave The Park Hotel, the Northern Riviera of Tynemouth and Whitley Bay, the old docklands and the City of Newcastle, for the land of my ancestors over the river in County Durham, and sitting in the bar of The Park on my last night, trying to put together what these past few days have meant to me is actually not something that comes easily. Pete was a great believer in Guinness as a lubricant for this sort of thing, and it seemed to work for him so I have a pen in one hand and a glass in the other. I have instructed Ben the barman to stay close at hand.

I have enjoyed my time here, more than I thought I would, wandering the coast and the quaysides. I have seen the old and the new, the decayed and the restored. I have felt excitement at things discovered, and disappointment at things that have gone. Many of my discoveries have been things I actually knew about, but had quite forgotten until I came upon on them, locked away in some filing cabinet of my mind only now to be brought out and examined. The smelly pub for example, the turbulence of King Edwards Bay, the fine architecture of the city and many of the things I have written about so far. Much of this I knew, but it had been in the dusty storeroom at the back of my memory.

Finding the new and the renewed, such as The Spanish City, the museum at Segedunum and its stunning film, the reincarnation of quaysides and dockyards, has been a stimulating experience. Even The Sage, in its way, contributed to this.

I know I haven't been to the city on a Friday night, and from what my friendly copper told me that's just as well, but I have been gently reminded that Tyneside is not a warzone. It is not ubiquitously belligerent. Everyone I have met here, Geordie barmen, people in the street, waitresses and shopkeepers, policemen even, have all been outstandingly welcoming. I have understood nearly everything that has been said to me, and no one has said "*are you looking at me?*" I thought Geordies were lairy by nature and that belligerence went with the territory, but it behoves me to concede that I was wrong.

What I have found very marked is the stark difference between my early memories and those which emerge from my teenage years when I made the transition from childhood towards an adult world, too old for one yet too young for the other. A place of games and caves, Dad's boat and ice cream on the beach gave way to the land of Oz, of Bigg Market, The Chain Locker and trying to grow up in a world I was not quite prepared for. The recollections of my teenage years, typified by that memory of Newcastle that I recalled at the beginning of this story, seem to have overshadowed those of a carefree childhood. I had remembered the former too much, the latter too little.

Although I have not sought them out because they are not part of this journey, Newcastle now has fine restaurants, cocktail bars, a highly regarded University, a culture of art, inclusive toilets and gay bars. I wonder what Oz would have thought about that. I remember Oz because I met him. I didn't meet his antithesis.

I came here genuinely thinking that I may never again return. The passing of my father and the departure of my mother had left me no reason to come back, and it is very largely the influence of Pete's writing that has inspired me to do so. Now that I have done, I think that I have discovered a connection with the North East that I did not expect. Whether it amounts to a sense of belonging is, for now, something I have yet to work out. "*Belonging*" is a deep, social connection. If that's how you feel about a place you should go and live there and be done with it. But life, over time, levies baggage – friends, a family, a wife, a house, the pub on the corner. I wonder if I were free of all that, where I would stick the pin in the map. Would it be here?

I will return to this place. I want to know what becomes of The Lido, The Rex, the North Shields quayside, and the yet barren docks of Smiths and Swan Hunter awaiting their regeneration. I want to see how this work in progress evolves.

My journey will now take me to County Durham on the far side of the Tyne. I will leave behind this place and my own childhood to find the lost coalfields and the heritage of my parents, and their parents before them. I will look for the deeper memories that can arise only through my ancestors, through the line of my family who came before me. This is a past which concerns others, yet perhaps I am still connected. A genetic memory, if one is to be found.

I will leave this place reluctantly, sadly even. I am sorry not to have seen the round, bespectacled figure of Brendan again, full of optimism and anecdote. I shall miss his hand clutching a glass of Merlot. I think of him and the landscape of Tyneside as I am drawn to the lights of the bay through the darkened windows of the bar. Or is that just the drink talking?

PART TWO

THE COALFIELDS OF COUNTY DURHAM

Chester-le-Street, Grange Villa, Beamish, Tanfield, Esh
Winning, Cornsay Colliery, Lumley

"Is it possible to have some kind of genetic memory of a
place where you have never lived, but your ancestors have?
Or am I just a sentimental fool, my judgment fuddled by
nostalgia, Guinness and…romance…?"

Pete McCarthy

SEVEN

Over the River

The road to County Durham will take me over the river, not under it by the Tyne Tunnel, but up to Newcastle and across the great arching bridge which I stood beneath only yesterday, although for some reason it seems an age ago now.

I take my leave of the staff at The Park who have been wonderful hosts. They beam widely at me as I shake their hands. I don't know if they have enjoyed my company too, or if they are just glad to see the back of me.

From the hotel it's 8 miles or so to Newcastle passing by the fork to the tunnel road, and past the old Formica works and the former Wills cigarette factory, a huge 1940s art deco building bordering the road which has become something of an icon and is now, perhaps unsurprisingly, luxury residential apartments. At least the front part which housed offices is. The factory at the rear had to be demolished because it was so contaminated with nicotine that it could not be restored, which is a sobering thought for those who indulged in its products, or even just worked there I suppose. The remaining building is listed as historically important, and its dramatic façade is one of the images that always comes to my mind when thinking of our family trips to and from the city in the 1960s.

The road takes me past Jesmond Dene, a narrow steep sided valley through which runs the small river Ouseburn, a tributary of the Tyne. There was a good restaurant here in the dene, The Fisherman's Lodge, which was a favourite of my father and to which he would take us as boys, smartly dressed in shirts and ties, mother in a posh frock, for a treat. I am told it closed in 2013 and was then damaged by fire in 2016. Its future apparently remains uncertain. It's reminiscent of The Plaza, and I hope it doesn't follow quite the same fate.

I remember crossing the dene by the tall, iron bridge constructed by Lord Armstrong who created a public park here. We'll meet that great industrialist again when we get far up the east coast to Bamburgh. The bridge is now closed to vehicular traffic, and the road sweeps past on a new by pass. I would probably sweep past too if it wasn't for the traffic, nose to tail approaching the city.

Past the familiar Cradlewell pub on Jesmond road where many a pint of Exhibition was taken, the road joins the motorway which now runs south of the city centre and takes me towards the Tyne Bridge. Passing under the green ironwork of the arch, if I could take my eyes of the road and the traffic, I would see, to my right, upriver to the High Level rail bridge and beyond, and to my left the millennium bridge and the silver carbuncle on the southern bank.

And so into Gateshead and County Durham, land of The Prince Bishops.

***

The traffic eases on the continuous urban sprawl south of Gateshead, through Low Fell on Durham Road and the crease of Team Valley on my right, when into view rises the reason I have taken this route today, the outspread wings of The Angel of the North. There's a car park here, for those who want to explore it. I have never stopped before, but now I do, pulling the car off the road right below the wings of the massive structure. The Angel was erected in 1998, long after my time in the North East, but nevertheless it is important to me, and to this story, for a number of reasons.

The Angel is aligned to look south, addressing those arriving in the north on the Great North Road and on the main East Coast line which runs close by. It is expressionless in its features, yet projects a welcome to those arriving in its domain. It has a noble bearing, the keeper of the kingdom, the regal gatekeeper of its realm.

Anthony Gormley, who designed The Angel at the invitation of Gateshead Council, said that one of its significances was that beneath its feet coal miners had worked for two centuries.

"When you think of the mining that was done underneath the site, there is a poetic resonance. Men worked beneath the surface in the dark.... It is important to me that the Angel is rooted in the ground—the complete antithesis of what an angel is, floating about in the ether. It has an air of mystery."

This is no generalisation. The statue sits on the site of the baths of the Betty Ann pit, part of the former Team Valley Colliery. The baths would have been hot with steam to purge the miners' bodies of grime and coal dust, and noisy with laughing, complaining, swearing and banter. I doubt there was much modesty among them.

My mother's father, Harry, worked at this pit for many years between 1930 and 1960, first as a locomotive fireman, a driver, and then as an engine winding-man operating the great spoked wheel which towered above the pit shaft, raising and lowering the miners' cage to and from hundreds of feet below ground. My grandfather may not have worked down there in the dark perils, but he had in his hands the lives of those who did.

There were many fatalities here in the 250 years of its operation between 1726 and 1973, as there were in all of the pits and drifts in the area. They were most often caused by the explosion of firedamp, a gas comprised mostly of methane which accumulated in pockets and could be easily ignited, but falls of stone, collapses and flooding were also common.

There is a serenity to this place as I walk around the statue, set on a green mound with tracks and walks through the neighbouring grass and shrubs. The surface infrastructure of the industry has gone, the towers, rail-tracks, engine sheds and winding wheels replaced by fields, woodland, new housing and the tarmac of new roads, but below ground the shafts and tunnels remain, sealed, entombed, their truths eternally preserved in silence and in darkness.

The view from here is immense, and if I could climb up to the height of The Angel's eyes 66 feet above me it would no doubt be more so, but you're not allowed to do that and with my phobia of heights I wouldn't anyway. Even so, from here I can see over the industrial steel roofs in Team Valley far into the rising land of Durham, and south to Chester-le-Street, Stanley, Beamish, the core of the Durham coalfield, and my heritage.

Leaving The Angel the road takes me further down Durham Road to Birtley and past the Red Lion, where we held the wake for my father's brother, Uncle Albert, who died of Woodbines in 1986.

***

The Lambton Worm is both a legend and a pub. The legend is a stirring tale of young Lord Lambton who, while fishing in the river Wear, discarded an unwanted worm down a well, where it grew to a monstrous size and terrorised the local people by eating babies and sheep. Lord Lambton, grown up and returned from victorious foreign wars, dispatched the worm and attained the status of true hero. As with all folklore, various forms of the tale have evolved over time, but it is usually said that in spite of Lambton's gallant endeavours, it did not end well due to some misunderstanding over a witch's instructions and the line of the Lambtons was forever cursed not to die peacefully. At least some of this seems to have come true, as it is a matter of record that a number of Lambtons have perished by the sword, by falling off a horse, or by a surfeit of one thing or another.

The story is usually told by way of a rhyming poem recited in a strong local dialect, which I shall resist narrating in full, tempting as it is. My father would frequently recite it to my brother and me when we were very young, scaring the living daylights out of us with the gruesome parts involving children and livestock. I know it off by heart.

The pub, on the other hand, while named after the famous tale, is not scary at all, and appears welcoming on the Durham Road just before I reach Chester-le-Street. It is here I shall stay a while and perhaps learn more about the worm before exploring the town and the place of my mother's birth, and her romance with my father, tomorrow.

EIGHT

Ancestral Lines

My mother was born in a garage, and my journey has brought me here to the Lambton Worm at Chester-le-Street to explore how this unlikely event came to be, just a few minutes' walk down the road from the pub towards the town centre.

The bar has a low, ambient yellow glow, and I like the sturdy pine tables, wood floor and stools set before a bar lined with beer pumps labelled with the curious and inviting names of local breweries. I see that there is a full recital of the famous poem on the wall in that curly longhand script favoured by trendy bars, but I can see no further reference to The Worm itself, or indeed the hapless Lambton.

Once I've slung my paraphernalia into my quite adequate room upstairs, dined well enough and refreshed my glass, I push my knife and fork aside and sit back to give some thought to the history which has led me to this agreeable bar and my mother's birthplace in the garage down the road. It might be worth having a finger in the family tree page as the lines of my ancestry unravel.

***

My mother's grandmother Mary Hannah Pearl was born in 1878 in Perkinsville, a tiny mining village close to the former Urpeth and Ouston collieries, just outside Chester-le-Street. Her father Thomas had come here from Suffolk, and her mother Susan from York, no doubt drawn by the work available in the mines of the mid-19th century.

Perkinsville is one of a cluster of places closely strung out to the west of Chester-le-Street and south of Gateshead, all falling under the watchful gaze of the Angel of the North. They include names which feature persistently in my family tree – Pelton, Ouston, Grange Villa, Beamish and Stanley to name but a few. The village was built by, and named after, Charles Perkins in the very early 19th century. Perkins was a successful mine owner and industrialist, and he built simple housing for his pit workers. With no other purpose than to accommodate his workforce it was set out as a small grid square of back to back terraces. Perkins didn't even bother to name the streets, which were designated A to F. The Pearl family lived in D Street.

Nevertheless, Perkinsville had a pub, a Wesleyan Methodist Chapel and a working men's club, as you would expect in a mining community. Now, save for a solitary line of terrace houses facing the main road it is all gone. Behind the terrace where the grid of rough streets were is now a small estate of 1980s bungalows. Where washing lines hung between the backs of terraces and scruffy children played football in the back alleys there are now green verges and Fords parked on driveways.

A website which offers suggestions for things to do in the area has a page for Perkinsville. It is blank.

Mary Pearl, or Gran Elliott as we came to call her, was a tiny woman with a long face and wispy hair. She looked like Piglet out of Winnie the Pooh. She lived in and around Perkinsville and, in 1907, she married George Elliott, a miner who worked in the deep, underground shafts and seams. They had two children, my grandmother Irene in 1908, and John in 1910.

Sometime after John's birth they moved across what is now the A1 to the east of Chester-le-Street where George worked in the Lumley pit. He was a strong Geordie man with steel eyes and a big, bushy moustache. Together, he and the diminutive Gran Elliott must have made a curious couple.

George was injured by a fall of stone in the Lumley pit, and died of those injuries on 20 February 1915 aged 44. He is the only one of my ancestors who died as a result of a mining accident, so far as I am aware. He was one of thousands who did, of course.

Their daughter Irene, my grandmother, was only 7 when her father died, and John was only 5. How the family managed after George was killed is hard to imagine. With no longer any family member employed by the colliery Mary Elliott lost her entitlement to the company house near the pit which went with George's job. Alone, aged only 37, with no wage earner, no state benefits to fall back on and with two young children in tow, she moved the short distance to Chester-le-Street where the need to provide for the family took her to work in shops and as a greengrocer's assistant, as did Irene after she left school. Eventually, sometime before 1928, Gran Elliott became employed by Jack Aunger.

Jack had a garage business just outside Chester-le-Street town centre on Newcastle Bank, the road leading out of the town north towards the Durham Road to Gateshead. He sold petrol, car repair and motor services, and new Morris and Wolseley cars.

The people at the Chester-le-Street Heritage Group have been able to show me some photographs of Aunger's Garage from their archive. It is difficult to date the photographs precisely, but a black and white print looks to have been taken in the 1920s judging by the old car shown in it. The garage looks a dirty, oily little place, a curved front gable over a shabby concrete front and four slim petrol pumps with big, round heads displaying the names Shell, Cleveland and ROP Oils. The roadway in front looks to be cobbles and mixed, loose stone. It appears just like the dark, grubby businesses carried on beneath the arches of London's rail bridges.

In 1923, before Mary Elliott turned up, Aunger's had suffered a devastating fire the garage had been rebuilt, shown in a later photograph with the front gable arch replaced by steel cladding, glass showroom windows, and a small two-storey house built on the side. This was Allotment Cottage, later known as Morris House after the prestigious dealership Jack Aunger commanded, and was the accommodation which went with Mary's job as clerk to the business, and where she and the family went to live.

In 1928 young Irene, now grown up, married the Harry Ritchie who took his baths under the Angel of North. Harry moved in to live with them at Aunger's Garage where in 1929 my mother was born, and her sister Mary, my aunt, three years later.

***

My mother and her sister grew up in the little house next to the garage with their parents Harry and Irene, overseen by Irene's mother Mary, who came to be known by us all as Gran Elliott. By the late 1940s the war had come and gone. The miners were in a reserved occupation and avoided the fields of conflict. They stayed at home to dig the fuel of the war and face their own perils below ground. Some women lost their husbands on the battlefields of Europe and beyond. Others lost theirs below their very feet.

Harry continued winding his charges up and down the shaft of the Betty Ann pit, and Gran Elliott kept Jack Aunger's books in order. Irene, now in her thirties and with my mother and her sister Mary at school, managed Roger Watson's grocery shop on Chester-le-Street High Street. Unknown to her, she was about to benefit from the death of Uncle Arthur, Harry's mother's brother.

Arthur William Hinkley was born in 1859 in Ellingham, far up in the north of Northumberland, which is why he is important to this story as well as for remembering my grandmother in his will. He was the grandson of John Hinkley, the coastguard who lived in the little white cottage in the remote, seashore outpost of Low Newton where I shall be spending a few days in the next week or so. He is a link between the far north and the coalfields of Durham, and I will be exploring the footprints he left in the fabric of my heritage later in this story.

Uncle Arthur became a school teacher. For some years in his twenties he taught at a church school in the curiously named village of Tockholes near Bolton in Lancashire. There he married Isabella who had been born in Durham, although what had taken her to Tockholes is unknown, as it is also unknown whether it was her connection with Durham which brought her and Uncle Arthur back there to Tanfield, not far from Chester-le-Street, at about the turn of the century. There Arthur furthered his teaching career, remaining in Tanfield and rising to Head Teacher until he and Isabella died within months of each other, childless, in 1937.

I have no idea how much Uncle Arthur left to Irene, or perhaps more likely to Harry, but I doubt it was much. Nevertheless, according to my own mother, whatever it was enabled Irene to buy the grocery business off Roger Watson. I expect that she only took over the lease of the premises and paid a bit for the stock and something for goodwill, for there was certainly no fortune or even the hint of one, and they still lived on in Aunger's little house.

Uncle Arthur and Isabella are buried together in the churchyard of St Margaret of Antioch in Tanfield. We'll be meeting them later in this journey.

***

My mother's teenage years seem to have been a mix of church, the local cinema and hanging around on the streets with her school-friends. Next door to where Gran Elliott's house and the garage stood is the Chester-le-Street Community Centre. It's a well-cared for, church-like building and was once the Miners' Welfare Hall, where there was dancing and music, and during the war it attracted soldiers billeted nearby, much to the disapproval of Gran Elliott. Despite her meagre stature, she seems to have been a stern matriarch with a Victorian morality. I imagine that she must have felt heavily burdened by the fact that my grandmother was two months pregnant with my mother when she married Harry. I envisage a silent but discernible disapproval.

Licensed premises were off limits to her, so my mother tells me. She and her friends would congregate on the street to chat, or visit the cinema, The Palace or The Savoy, where they would watch cowboy films. They would also go to church, The Wesleyan Chapel, as decreed by Gran Elliott. It sounds riveting.

My father came into my mother's life at this time. He had gone from school to Technical College in Sunderland where he had learned to draw ships and had found himself in the drawing office of one of the Tyneside shipbuilders. He lived with his family in Grange Villa, a small mining village only a stone's throw to the west of Chester-le-Street, and he courted my mother, so she told me, by taking her on long walks. Dad became a regular visitor to the little house next to Aunger's garage, and made friends with Jack's son, Ben. They would all, the Grandmas, Harry, my mother and her sister, Dad, Ben Aunger and whoever was Ben's girlfriend of the moment, pile into one of Aunger's cars for a trip down to the coast at Tynemouth and Whitley Bay. I expect they were frequent visitors to The Lido and The Boating Lake, but probably not the Spanish City.

The long walks and trips to the seaside must have done the trick, for in 1950 my father married my mother and took her to Whitley Bay where he had moved to a job with MacGregor's. The young firm of naval architects founded by brothers Joseph and Robert MacGregor soon became a globally recognised force in the design and manufacture of ship hatch covers. My father seems to have been highly regarded by the brothers, for Joseph became my Godfather, and Dad was made a Director. The job came with a new Mark 2 Jaguar, and a new-found status in the world.

***

Looking about the bar from my comfortable chair, there aren't many people of an age to have any memory of the period my family occupied Aunger's garage, and certainly none who could recall the two grandmothers and Harry. But two gentlemen occupying a couple of stools at one end of the bar attract my attention. They are both men in their late sixties, comfortable in what I imagine to be their regular space, and they are receiving privileged attention from the barman.

I feel awkward going up to people I don't know and attempting to engage them in any sort of personal conversation. They might have an aversion to southern speaking outsiders, and it wouldn't be the first time I have encountered that, but needs must and encouraged by my beer I smile and affect my best Geordie.

In fact, Brian embraces my approach most genially. He is stout, with grey swept-back hair and a fleshy face, perched on his stool, arm resting on the bar in the effortless composure of a man at one with his ale. At the mention of Aunger's garage he throws his arms wide and tells me he has lived just a few doors away all his life. He embraces the opportunity to dispense his knowledge about it, and I find myself, whether by way of invitation or not I cannot recall, on a stool between the two of them. I ask Brian if he remembers Jack Aunger.

"No, not Jack," he says, "he was before my time, but I remember his son Ben. He was older than me, but yes I remember Ben Aunger."

"Ben, yes, my Mum and Dad both talked about him," I say. "When would that have been?"

Brian thought for a moment. "Well, it would have been in the late fifties, sixties I should think." Brian has a Durham accent, not Geordie but close to it, a little softer.

"That's well after my mother left the garage," I tell him. "She married in 1950, so it would have been before then that she knew Ben. I think he used to knock around with my Mum and Dad. I've seen a few photos of him with them."

Brian tells me about Ben Aunger. At least he tells me his personal view, which may or may not be the view of others, and as I didn't know him I cannot tell. It's far from complimentary which is surprising as my parents not only spent a great deal of time with him but spoke well of him too, especially my father who was not inclined to take fools lightly. But Brian is acerbic. Ben Aunger drank too much, and he tells me a story about him giving short measures in oil cans. Brian's face scowls as he recalls his memories.

"Well, my mother never said anything about that," I tell him.

Brian's friend, Simon, who has said little up to now, leans towards me. He speaks quietly but not quietly enough that Brian doesn't hear. "Take no notice of him, he's always talking rubbish."

"Aunger was tight and I'll tell you what, if he was in here tonight he'd not put a hand in his pocket. I'd call him worse than that, if there weren't ladies present," he says oddly, as there aren't.

I am wondering what my mother would have to say about this assassination of her friend Ben Aunger. "I expect he's dead by now," I venture.

"Aye, he will be by now. But not of generosity, I can tell you."

And so it goes on, and it turns into a long evening. Eventually, they both declare it's time to go, and with the slow deliberation of men on the wrong side of sobriety, shuffle off their stools into overcoats and out the door into the damp streetlights of the night.

I'm left alone on a bar stool. I smile to myself at Brian's brusque acerbity and Simon's quiet, contrary interjection. Ben Aunger was not my family, and although he may have touched it just a bit, he is no catalyst for any sort of genetic memory. I'm still waiting for that.

***

Back in Whitley Bay, in 1953 I was born, Irene became Grandma Ritchie, and Mary Hannah became Gran Elliott. They stayed on at the little house on Newcastle Bank with Harry, and I remember as small boys my brother and I being taken to visit on Sundays, for tea.

Morris House was a cheeky label for a two-up two-down, and I can't remember much of it, except that it had a small front parlour where Little John and I would sit in our Sunday best - a white shirt and tie, short trousers, short white socks and Clarks sandals. We sat quietly, maintaining a respectful silence while the adults talked in the kitchen. There were crudely laced antimacassars on the backs of cloth upholstered chairs, and our little legs dangled not quite reaching the floor. There was cheap Indian Tree china only ever used on special occasions, Battenberg cake and iced fancies for tea, and the steady tick of the wooden mantle clock.

It does sound a tedious experience for a small boy full of energy, but I didn't hate it by any means. I enjoyed seeing my grandparents, Grandma Ritchie especially. She smiled a lot and made a fuss over us with cake and fizzy pop. But it was a bit of a duty for a little boy to sit, on show for the family elders, until the cake had been eaten, the tea drunk, and it was time to pile back into the car for home. The goodbye kisses smelled of soap and something else I only ever associated with my grandparents. It was probably moth balls.

Irene, Grandma Ritchie, died of chronic bronchitis in 1967 at the age of only 59. The determined and diminutive Gran Elliott came to live with us in Tynemouth after that until she followed in 1969 at the good old age of 91, 54 years a widow. Harry went in 1971 having spent years under the grim burden of a form of multiple sclerosis. Even Aunger's garage succumbed, taken over and re-named Johnsons before demolition in 2009.

And so with the passing of time my mother's family disappeared into the past.

***

It must have been a jolt for my mother, hauled out of work in a shop and a life squeezed into a two-up two-down with her mother, colliery worker father and her grandmother. Naïve, I'm sure, unworldly certainly, in the blink of an eye she was thrust into life as the wife of a Director, a man who went to work in a suit. She had to learn how to meet my father's business colleagues, how to behave, wear a posh frock and how to shop. They were able to own their own house, take dinner in restaurants, and my mother was expected to accompany my father at business functions. MacGregor's bought holiday property in Majorca, and there were company meetings in Italy on the shores of Lake Garda, which is probably where my mother developed a taste for the wide-brimmed hats and dark sunglasses she wore on Tynemouth beach. Not rich by any means, but a far cry from the pithead.

And to be fair to him, it must have been a rollercoaster for my father too. By a combination of talent, study, good fortune and sheer persistence he progressed from the mining village of Grange Villa to the bosom of MacGregor's and a world of business and technical innovation. Before MacGregor's in the 1940s ship hatch covers consisted of wooden planks laid over a hole in the deck. In weather these were easily washed off, or in wartime they were blown off. A lot of water got in and the ship sank, usually very quickly. MacGregor's developed steel covers which concertinaed over the hole in one single unit and sealed it. Later they were hydraulically operated. They saved time in port, money, and many lives.

My father was the technical man. He designed the covers, the pulley systems and the hydraulics, and he travelled Europe, particularly France, Germany and Scandinavia, troubleshooting the newly developing technology. Ask any man who worked in the dockyards of London, Bergen, Liverpool, Cherbourg or any of the great ports of the world, mention the name MacGregor's, and he will tell you they were the best thing to happen to the shipping industry since the invention of the lifeboat.

And so the company flourished, withstanding the decline of the shipbuilding industry in the 1970s and 1980s. It is now part of the international marine logistics Cargotec Group. I think my father would be very proud that he had a hand in guiding the business in its early, formative years.

As a small boy a great deal of this passed me by. I remember my father in a dinner jacket and black tie, my mother in a long, pretty dress, ready for a dinner-dance somewhere. I remember other dressed-up couples passing through our house, my father's business colleagues and their wives, whisky and orange, adult talk and laughter I did not understand. There must have been babysitters I suppose, but I have no memory of them. I do remember my father coming home with small toys from business trips abroad, often a small Dinky car to add to my treasured collection. He always brought us a gift.

What I remember most is the time we spent together - my father sitting playing the piano for us, gathered around the dining room table playing Ludo or some board game at which Little John and I would shriek with delight, pottering with Dad in the garden on a sunny day, or setting off for an afternoon at the beach or The Lido, or with the boat down to the lake. I remember my mother making cake icing in the kitchen, which we were allowed to lick from the spoon, Pinky and Perky records on our new, state of the art stereogram, and walking with Dad on the pier. And the wonderful, quiet excitement when Dad came home after work on a Friday evening, our bags and cases packed and ready to pile into the car for the long drive over the Pennines, dark and mysterious in the night, to the Lake District for the weekend.

Those are special, treasured memories, almost a whole lifetime ago.

***

Breakfast is included at the Lambton Worm. There was a time, when I was office bound and my living depended on actually doing some work, that breakfast consisted of little more than a quick black coffee. These days, released from that commitment, I still take little more than toast and orange juice. So I often wonder why it is, and I am convinced this is not just me, that when "*breakfast included*" appears on the hotel menu, you just have to have the Full English. And this is even though I am labouring slightly from the effects of Old Scroat or whatever it was that Brian and Simon insisted we kept drinking last night.

And so, even though I've been up less than an hour, I have to have another lie down to let it all settle, before I can even begin to organise myself for the walk into Chester-le-Street this morning.

***

I am comforted by the fact that Aunger's is only about a mile down the road, although I know that the garage itself is now long gone. The Durham Road which leads into Chester-le-Street is a wide avenue of middle class housing and it's a pleasant walk, before passing the newly built Durham Police Headquarters, and then the allotments from which the house built by Jack Aunger took its early name. Opposite, only a hundred yards from the beginning of the town's main street, is the small block of five modern townhouses which occupy the site on which the garage and Gran's house once stood.

I haven't forgotten why I am here, but it is difficult, standing in the road looking at a block of modern town houses and full of breakfast, to draw much of a sense of heritage. I can imagine the garage standing there, the house built on the end, and the allotments over the road, but I can't help feeling that is probably because I have seen the photographs.

Nevertheless, and even though there are no ghosts, no apparitions or wafts of diaphanous history, this is irrefutably a place where threads of my heritage were spun. And they didn't just pass through here on a whim, they lingered for more than 40 years. Here my mother was born. Here my father appeared and joined two bloodlines together. I can't help thinking that if there is a place where a genetic memory would be sticking its hand up and demanding attention, it would be here. I feel there ought to be something, but try as I might I can't produce anything except for the nostalgic equivalent of a bit of wind.

Perhaps I am expecting this to happen all too soon. After all, I do have my own memories of this place, even if they are limited to Gran Elliott's front parlour and her iced fancies. I remember the people who lived here when they were alive, so maybe it doesn't work like that, and I have to wait until there is no trace of living memory before the names on my family tree, the places on the birth certificates and on the old census returns take on an unexpected shape and familiarity.

The trouble is I have no idea what to expect when, and if, I should come across a genetic memory. How will I know if I get one? I don't know if some ancient long departed ancestor might suddenly manifest before me and moan about having to live in a dump like Perkinsville, or if the essential yet intangible soul of some place will present itself to me, appearing spectre-like from the Asda or Tesco which actually lies before my contemporary eyes. In fact, and in spite of Pete's premise for his journey, how can I be sure there even is such a thing?

I had the presence of mind to read up on this before I set off on this journey. I got through everything from Darwinism and Lamarckism to the copious wafflings of the online community. I read what psychologists and evolutionary geneticists had to say about it, and became befuddled with countless definitions and postulations, epigenetics and biogenetics. And that's before you even start on the physiology of it, the cellular biology which explains how something as intangible as memory is translated into actual stuff.

Respected neuroscientist Rodolfo Llinas said it is "*a memory present at birth that exists in the absence of sensory experience.*" Carl Jung said "*we're born with the experiences of our parents and ancestors imprinted on our DNA,*" and Freud too said similar things as, in fact, do most people. Although Max Robinson, a molecular biologist and evolutionary geneticist answered the question "*Is there really such a thing as Genetic Memory?*" with a simple "*No, there isn't,*" he seems to be in a minority of one and I'm left with the conclusion that it probably is a Real Thing.

And I have no doubt that a sense of belonging is a Real Thing too, but not the Same Thing. If I find a sense of belonging in Tynemouth and Whitley Bay it will have arisen from my own memories. Only I and my parents lived there, and that's not a genetic memory, it's a real one. I was actually there and I don't need an evolutionary geneticist to tell me what I remember and whether I liked it.

Yet if a sense of belonging turns up in a place I have never lived but my ancestors have, that must arise from the genetic memory that Pete went off to Ireland to look for. All very well, but I don't imagine that a genetic memory would necessarily give rise to a sense of belonging. I would be surprised indeed if I developed a yearning to pop down a pit shaft just because some ancestor of mine shows up and tells me what a lot of fun it was.

So you can have a sense of belonging without a genetic memory, and you can have a genetic memory without a sense of belonging. They are not mutually exclusive.

And more, I have to be careful not to confuse a sense of belonging with an attraction to the aesthetics of a place. It might be nice to sip a Pina Colada in the sunset on a beach in Puerto Rico, or stand in awe of the silence and panorama of a Lake District fell, and there is many a bar I have felt extremely at home in, but these are, for most people, but interludes in real life. An intimate alignment with a place, such as might arise from a sense of belonging, is not a mere amiable pause to take in a different view. So I shall tread with caution, as I have done through the, mostly, pleasant vistas of Tyneside, the colossal seascapes and wild beauty which is yet to come in the north of Northumberland, and even here in the rolling country of Durham, which I know will deceive in its soft greenness the blanket of industry which used to cover it.

Anyway, whatever a genetic memory turns out to be, I don't think I've had one yet.

"*I'll know it if I see it,*" I muse, as I turn and walk away from the site of old Aunger's garage and the little house, down the hill to Chester-le-Street town centre. If there are any spectral faces peering at me from the windows of the town houses as I leave then they will have to shout a little louder.

***

The folks at the Chester-le-Street Heritage Group know a thing or two about Chester-le-Street, as you might expect. It was they who sent me the photographs of Aunger's garage from their archive, and one of their members, Catherine Button, was brought up only doors from there and would have been a child when I visited with my parents and took tea in the parlour of the little house.

The Heritage Group meets every Tuesday throughout the year, and I'm keen to discover what they can tell me. Apart from the garage I also want to hear about the Wesleyan Methodist Church where not only did three generations of my mother's family seek their salvation, but is also where Harry and Irene were married in 1928, and Gran Elliott and George before them in 1907.

***

I don't know Chester-le-Street at all. Once Grandma Ritchie had passed away and Gran Elliott came to live with us in Tynemouth for a few short years, there was no one left there. I went off to college in Leicester to further my drinking education and then on to Norwich to be confronted with Real Life and the need to earn a living. I returned to visit Mum and Dad in Tynemouth of course, from time to time slogging up the A1 in a battered Ford or, as my career advanced, a slightly less battered Ford, but there was never any time in all those years that I set foot in Chester-le-Street. It is not that I don't remember it, I just have never been there, like most of the places I shall be visiting on this stage of my journey. If I remember anything of them, it will be, well, unnerving to say the least.

Just a couple of hundred yards down the bank from where Aunger's stood is a modern intersection, where the old street configuration has been cleared to make way for the road which bypasses the town centre. Over there, the High Street sets off up a small incline and the old street closes in.

The street is clean and largely pedestrianised now, encumbered with a mix of modern shop fronts accommodating building societies, charity shops, food outlets and shops for mobile phones, for betting, and for nothing particularly exciting. I have no idea on which street corner my mother used to hang around, but today I'm struggling to feel anything particularly stimulating about the place, and I don't wonder that cowboy films in the old Savoy cinema were a popular attraction.

The Savoy was located on the High Street itself, but it is long gone as a cinema and I don't know where it was exactly. The Palace, the other one my mother told me she used to visit, was on a small lane off the High Street called Low Chare, which is where I am headed now to meet The Chester-le-Street Heritage Group in the brand new Salvation Army meeting hall.

Most of the original buildings on Low Chare have been demolished, but the United Reform Church still stands in its plain, grey, disapproving morality, and I know from old photographs that the cinema was directly opposite on what is now a used-car sales lot. A website which is dedicated to the record of old cinemas describes The Palace as "*a flea pit*" where one might truly be bitten by fleas. The Savoy, the website also tells us, had a ramp up by the side of the screen which led to the toilets. The crowd would chant "*we know where you're going*" when an audience member, usually female, had the need to pay a visit, and "*we know where you've been*" when they returned to their itchy seat. As Lord Blackadder remarked to his uninspiring gaol staff Baldrick and the hilariously unrelated Mr and Mrs Ploppy, "*The long winter evenings must just fly by.*"

***

The Salvation Army headquarters is a low, modern building, and entering cautiously because I don't want to be converted or recruited, I find myself directed by handwritten arrows on walls and doors pointing to a small room with chairs around the sides and a display set up in the middle with old photographs and newspaper cuttings pinned to a board. There are at least a dozen people, some seated and some standing, and some computer terminals at which people of at least my generation, or older, seem surprisingly at home.

A small, grey-haired lady immediately pounces on me and offers an enthusiastic welcome and a cup of tea, which arrives almost instantaneously in a light blue institutional cup and saucer. I need to find Alex, who sent me the photographs and I think is the Hon. Sec. of the Heritage Group.

Alex is a tall, slim, kindly looking gentleman who immediately identifies me as a newcomer and as the one with interest in Aunger's, as we have exchanged a fair bit of email correspondence about it. He produces some more photographs of the old garage, and some of Chester-le-Street High Street and the very shop in which Grandma Ritchie worked. He is fascinating to talk to with tales of the garage and the town itself, but of course he doesn't remember my family. At only 70 years old he can't be expected to. However with regard to Aunger's garage, he tells me that the person I need to speak to is Malcolm Smith, and he waves his arm at a man sitting at a desk in front of a screen.

Malcolm is ex Met. Police. He now lives near Lumley Thicks, the tiny outpost near the Lumley pit that George was killed in. He tells me that his father, James Smith, worked as a foreman to Jack Aunger in his garage in the years before the war. He would have worked closely with Gran Elliott who kept the books. She probably even handed over his pay to him.

This is a startling connection. I was hoping for something more than memories of the physical garage, and I had wondered about the possibility of there being a people connection. But of course, his father's time at the garage was long before my mother was old enough to have any recollections, and his own memories belong in the more recent past, as do mine.

I spend some time chatting with Malcolm about those who lived before us in these places, places of which we have no personal memory. Photographs of them are displayed around us on the bulletin boards and pin boards in the little room. Photographs of Chester-le-Street 100 years ago, brown prints of streets lined with the shopfronts and awnings of a bygone era, old buses with thin tyres and a spiral staircase up the back, horses and carts. The sepia of the photographs promotes nostalgia for an age in which we have not yet been born, a place we have never lived, but our ancestors have.

When the time comes to leave, I have learned a great deal about the life lived in this place so many years ago, and that comfortably translates into the lives of my own ancestors. I can see them a little more easily, more vividly in my mind. All that I have heard from my mother, learned from old photographs and from long, laboured research, have been given a little more colour, a little more life.

Our parting handshakes are firm, genuine and accompanied by smiles and promises to remain in touch. Email addresses are exchanged. I feel I have made some friends here, and I take away a welcome feeling that my personal memories have been greatly enriched.

***

Just a short way up the High Street at the junction with Station Road is the Wesleyan Methodist Chapel in which the marriages took place of Harry and Irene in 1928, and Mary Hannah and George in 1907. It's a very solid, well presented building with none of the patriarchal severity I had expected. Arched windows, leaded panes with part stained glass are set into three storeys of light, clean stone under a shallow pitched roof. At the top of the façade the stonework is boldly inscribed "Wesleyan", and "AD 1880".

Above the kitchen and schoolroom on the ground floor the dark brown, heavily panelled and lacquered front door is set at first-floor level, approached by a broad flight of stone steps with black iron gates and balustrades. Two Grecian busts mounted on the wall flank the doorway. The wall in front bordering the pavement is of heavy stone, topped with rounded coping and black iron railings. A heritage plaque on the front wall facing the road confirms the building is now a private residence.

So I can't go in. I would have liked to, perhaps to stand at the place where grandparents and great grandparents also stood to receive God's blessing, exchange rings and engage in whatever Wesleyan formalities their faith prescribed. The unions of those two couples, cemented as they were in this place, ensured the continuation of the line which has resulted in me, and I give thanks to whatever Higher Authority had a hand to play in the matter.

The rounded copings on the wall provide a moderately comfortable place to sit. I half hope that someone will come out or go in, or in some way be identified as a person I can go up to and announce that two generations in the line of those who conceived me had their alliances approved in their lovely house and would it be alright for me to go in and have a look around? And by the same token, I half hope they won't.

There will, of course, be nothing left anyway. The altar, pews, all the ecclesiastical trappings will be long gone. In fact, since the Wesleyans moved out it was occupied for a time by the Jehovah's Witnesses so I've since come to understand, and that would have put paid to most of it.

I do have a hint of those who attended these weddings, in addition to the brides and grooms. From their marriage certificates I know that George and Mary Hannah's marriage was witnessed by Fred Burn, whose name is not familiar and may have been hauled in from off the street for all I know, and Frances Pearl who was Mary Hannah's sister, 5 years younger. They all signed their names too, which means they were all literate, not a flippant observation for 1907.

Harry and Irene, my grandparents, had their union witnessed by Susan Pearl who was Irene's Aunt, Fred Ritchie who was Harry's brother (and who went off to deepest Africa and grew thousands of acres of Kenyan coffee before President Kenyatta pinched his land and fortune in the early 1970s and packed him off back to England where he settled, and finally expired, in Brighton – which is another story), and John Elliott, Irene's brother. So all in all quite a family affair, as it should be.

I would like a memory to form here, to be honest, as I sit on the wall. I would like to see the bride and groom arriving in their finest, their little congregation of family and friends stepping up to those doors. I would like to be able to see, rather than just imagine, the great moustache of George Elliott presiding over the diminutive, probably prim, figure of Mary Hannah Pearl, soon to be an Elliott as well. I wonder what she looked like at the age of 29. Was she pretty? What did she wear? Or, in the case of Irene, did her bump show?

I ease myself off the wall and push gently through the small crowd of wedding guests gathered at the foot of the steps, dressed finely in wing collars, tail coats with buttonholes and hats. A minister stands among them, smiling in religious geniality. Ladies chatter quietly, but there is excitement in their voices. I smile and nod slightly at a tall man with a moustache on whose arm a small woman in a white dress holds a posy of flowers, but my great-grandfather doesn't see me.

Like a figure viewed through frosted glass his shadow ebbs and wanes, then fades and is gone, as a candle's flame is snuffed, leaving nothing but a wisp of something and a lingering memory.

***

Contrary to the affectionate relationship with my mother's parents, my father's side of the family were much more remote. His mother, Grandma Wood, was a stern woman, a widow by the time I knew her properly. I don't recall her playing games with us, or laughing at some silliness. She wasn't frightening or particularly formidable, but I think she had a real problem with open displays of affection. Like all small children would, we responded to that by treating her with a well-behaved, respectful caution, which was fine but it didn't involve the cuddles and giggles that Grandma Ritchie bestowed upon us.

I didn't know my grandfather, Albert. Grandad Wood died when I was just 9 months old. He was only 56. My father talked about him, and I have seen some photographs. He had a striking physical resemblance to my father, and I can imagine he may well have had a similar temperament. Like my father, Albert had made the effort to haul himself and his family, if not out of the mining community, at least up from the underground seams and a relentless life of coal-dust. He established a small grocery and general dealer business which he ran from the back of his house in the small mining village of Grange Villa where he had been brought up. By all accounts he made a decent fist of it, made a bit of money, acquired a bit of local status, and gave my father the opportunity of education and in turn another step up the ancestral ladder of self-improvement. My paternal line advanced from the dark depths of the coal-pit to international commerce in just two generations. That's an impressive evolution, and Albert Wood was the man who enabled it. I do, truly, wish I'd met him.

NINE

A Glimpse of the Past

Albert stood on the pavement outside his terraced house in Queen Street, Grange Villa, and surveyed the road. He was a slim man, not given to overweight, of medium height and a shock of white hair. He wore a long, navy and white striped grocer's apron which came down to his knees, tied round the back at the neck and the waist. He had on nailed boots over brown cloth trousers. It was 1953 and he was 56 years old.

Albert took a long draw on his Woodbine cigarette, and regarded the horse and cart over the street. The flatbed cart was stacked with bags of coal, the dirt and black coal dust spilling over the cart and onto the road. The side of the cart was stencilled *"Joicey Collieries Ltd, Ouston"*. The horse, a big, sturdy animal with enormous hooves and a brown and white coat, stood motionless, its head slightly bowed. The street was quiet, the time before the miners returned from the pit to their wives, their supper, and their identical terraced houses.

Albert dropped his Woodbine to the ground and squashed it out with his boot. He had done quite well here, he reflected absently. His little grocery and general dealership which he ran from the back of the house had saved him from the pit, and even enabled him to buy the house next door and two over the road, in one of which he had installed his mother and father and in the other his sister. There was a Co-op shop only 3 or 4 miles away in Chester-le-Street where they sold most of what you would want, and cheaply too, but you couldn't haul a bag of potatoes all that way, even with the bus. And he gave credit where it was deserved, so he had plenty of local trade.

"Afternoon, Morris," Albert called to the man approaching up the street. "Not had your bath at the pit, then?" Morris was black in the face, black on his hands, black on his clothes. It was unusual for a miner not to scrub the coal off him in the pit baths before coming home.

"Had to get back quick, like," Morris answered as he drew near, "One of the bairns is sick and I need to see to him. Peggy's run off her feet with the others."

"Aye, I heard," said Albert with a nod of his head. "Will he be alright?" He waved an arm round the side of the alley which led to the back of his house where he kept his stock of provisions and necessaries. "Do you need anything?"

"You're alright, Albert." Morris paused a moment. "We've got the doctor coming."

Albert pulled a Woodbine from his apron pocket, and took a moment to light it. "How much does he want, the doctor?"

"Two and six. Just for the visit, you know. Medicine's extra, I should think."

A moment passed, slightly uncomfortably, then Albert straightened. "Hang on, Morris. Just a minute," and he turned and went down the alley at the side of his house to the back.

The back room of the house was stacked with the business of the general dealer. Tins and cans, piles of cloth, towels, soap, boxes of vegetables, a couple of sacks of potatoes, bottles of paraffin and lemonade. Further through was a small wooden desk where Albert kept his books, meticulously, every penny accounted for in proper, blue ink. Albert looked about him, up and down at the shelves of this and that, and then selected a small loaf of white bread. It was 3 days old and hard, but they could soak it in lard and it would make a tea for the bairns.

Morris was still standing in the street, on the corner of the alley and Albert's house. Albert held out the loaf. "Go on, Morris, take it."

Morris hesitated, but took it in his coal grimy hand. "I'll pay you back, Albert," he said, defensively.

"Aye, I know you will." Albert watched Morris's back as he walked off up the street, and he knew that he would, and that when Morris did offer him payment for the bread he would have to take it, even though he wouldn't want to.

The horse and cart had gone. Albert could hear the hooves clopping and the iron rims of the cart wheels clattering on the road around the corner. He pulled a silver pocket watch from his apron and looked at the time. Not long till tea time he observed to himself. Meggie would be in the kitchen, which was actually in the next door house, getting something ready. A hot pot, maybe. Albert liked hot pot.

"Albert!" Another neighbour approached with an amiable greeting. Not filthy with coal dust though, this one. Percy didn't work in the pit, or anywhere if he could help it. "All right?"

"Aye, Percy, all right."

"That Morris just then? Isn't one of his bairns poorly?"

"Proper poorly. They're having the doctor."

Percy sucked his teeth, and shook his head. "Will he get something from the Welfare? For the cost?"

"I expect he might, if he asks. You know what Morris is like."

"Aye, proper proud is Morris." The men dwelt on that observation for a moment, then "How's your boy then, Albert? Over the river isn't he?"

Albert brightened. "Aye, Tynemouth. He's doing very well thank you Percy, what with the shipyards and all that. He's got a bairn now. A little lad." Albert rummaged in his apron pocket and pulled out a small, dog eared, black and white photograph. He held it up for Percy to see. Albert in an open necked shirt, sleeves rolled up, the bush of his white hair looking dishevelled, is standing next to a much

119

younger man holding a very small child wrapped in cloth or blankets, its eyes tightly closed under a white woollen hat. Both men are smiling at the camera. "Just 2 months," said Albert proudly, lighting another Woodbine.

"He's a bonny bairn," said Percy. "What's his name?"

"Stephen."

"Aye," said Percy sagely, as if it required his approval. "That'll suit."

The two men peered at the photo for a minute or so, then Percy announced, "I think I'll pop down the Miners Welfare, see if there's any dominoes on tonight. Might even have a pint."

Albert waved him off as he walked away down the street, between the terraced houses of Queen Street towards Front Street and the Miners Welfare. He will probably stay all night and get home late in a cloud of beery unsteadiness, and then there will be an almighty row with his suffering wife which the whole street will hear. Again.

Albert stood on the street a while longer. It was good to be a grandfather, and he thought about the day when the little lad would be old enough to play with, kick a football about, or take him down to that boating lake in Tynemouth and feed the ducks. Aye, that is something to look forward to.

Albert coughed into his hand, twice, a rasping, expectorant cough. He wiped a gobbet of brown mucus on his apron and looked at the Woodbine held between his thumb and brown stained forefinger. "I should give these up," he muttered to himself.

He should. But it is already too late.

TEN

Chester-le Street, Grange Villa, The Alma Pit

So I did meet my grandfather, apparently, if only at a couple of months old and from under a woolly hat, before he died of Woodbines six months later, as did his other son, my father's younger brother Uncle Albert in 1986. I wonder if they called him Little Albert, in accordance with what seems to be a trait in the Wood family to name younger sons after their father without providing any other means of distinguishing them, to which my brother, Little John, will testify. It is fortunate that there was no father named Willy, otherwise his second son would have endured a mortifying adolescence.

I do remember my father talking about Grandfather Albert, or Grandad Wood as I expect he would have been called should he have survived. He kept chickens, Dad told me, and from the sale of the eggs he bought houses. I took that with a large pinch of salt, as it occurred to me that he must have sold an awful lot of eggs, or bought very small houses, if the egg to house price ratio was anything like it is today. But although I don't know about any chickens, he certainly did well enough with his backyard dealership to have acquired four houses in Queen Street, Grange Villa – the two next door to each other which he occupied and from which he ran the business, and the two over the road in which family members were installed.

Mind you, house prices in Queen Street are even today at the dog-kennel end of the market with a two bedroom terrace costing little more than a family car, so perhaps that explains on the one hand how he came to acquire them, and on the other why no generous inheritance seems to have filtered down in my direction, or indeed in any direction.

***

I have left the Wesleyan Chapel in Chester-le-Street to come to Grange Villa to see for myself what has become of it, and to reflect on what it may have been like in the days of Albert, and his father Joseph.

It's about 3 miles, which my father used to walk in their courting days, or so my mother tells me. In fact, she told me that she sometimes walked it herself which makes Dad sound less than chivalrous. From the town centre it's out along the Pelton Fell Road, Bluehouse Bank then turn right onto Newbridge Banks, over the Twizell Burn, then into the small village of early 20th century terraces.

The road from Chester-le-Street is remarkably rural and leafy, and to the south the rolling green fields and woodland of County Durham stretch to the horizon. From old maps I can see that it was so even back in my father's day, and before him. There were indeed great expanses of the county unencumbered by the detritus of the coal industry, in spite of what The Times had to say about it being "*one huge colliery*".

So for my father it would have been a long country walk. Even now there are few footpaths at the side of the road. A few short lines of terraces pop up here and there where they would have served some local works, now long gone. Passing through Pelton Fell there is much in the way of new housing development and to the north of the road were massive sidings and railway marshalling yards. Waggonways criss crossed the landscape, the rail lines that carried the heavy clanking coal trains to and from the collieries of the area. But here along the road it is largely hedgerows, fields and woodland. It must be said, it seems like a long 3 miles and my father's tenacity in slogging to and from Chester-le-Street in his boots to see her must have been at least one of the virtues my mother so clearly saw in him. For my part, I'm glad of the car.

If the pleasant countryside to the west of Chester-le-Street is one thing, the approach to Grange Villa up the short Newbridge Banks is another. Or at least it used to be. Just outside of the village, and which is of course why the place was built in the first place, is the site of the West Pelton Alma Pit, with its chimneys, shafts, headgear, railway and sidings. I pull the car over here, because I want to take a closer look. It is where Albert's father worked before his son identified grocery as a cleaner, more amenable career.

There is an unmade earth track, hardly the width of a car, running off the road just before the village. It runs for as far as I can see between a low bank and a high, brown, woody hedge on the right and a post and wire fence on the left which gives on to acres of grass fields running down to woodland. The track runs to a slight rise on the horizon, several hundred yards away. There is no gate to the lane. At its entrance there is a "*Public Footpath*" pointer, and a couple of bench seats are placed underneath a semi-circular, metal "*Welcome to Grange Villa*" sign heavily embossed with an image of a filled wheelbarrow, chickens and ducks. In the fields cows stand lazily chewing. It is a scene of quiet, timeless farmland.

In my father's day, and in the days of generations before him, it was not like this at all. It is a story which is repeated all over County Durham, and doubtless throughout the coalfields of Lancashire, Yorkshire and elsewhere too wherever the black gold of coal was there to be mined. Here, at Grange Villa, is a striking example of how the hand of man has altered the aspect of the land, not once but continuously over the centuries, and although I know that I will come across this time and time again wherever I go on this stage of the journey, this is a place in which the connection of my great grandfather, who toiled here and walked this very track, draws me to discover, imagine, and perhaps even feel, the history of the industry which took this pristine land, contaminated it with filth and ugliness, then put it all back again.

Albert's father was Joseph Wood. He was born in Pelton in 1873, a stone's throw from here and in the midst of all the works and infrastructure of the mines. He never moved more than a couple of miles throughout his life. He is described in 1901 as a *"coal miner hewer"*, which confirms his work deep underground. Joseph's father John Wood, in turn, was born in Bolton, Lancashire in 1843 and he came to Pelton sometime before 1861. What brought him and the line of my family here to Durham is unknown, but work in the mines is likely as he was a miner too, as was his father before him. Coal was in the blood of the Wood family, literally so in all probability. It was brought here to County Durham by great, great-grandfather John Wood in the mid-19th century.

I sit on the bench under the Grange Villa sign and regard the fields, the hedgerows and the cows. I have a small sheaf of maps on my lap.

The earliest Ordnance Survey map I have of this place is dated 1859. This track is marked but un-named. To my left only some 50 yards away from where I sit is the West Pelton Waggonway which crossed what is now the field of cows to the Pelton West Colliery about 200 yards into the field. The map shows a few buildings, a water engine and 3 round structures described as *"gins"*. These were the usually circular structures which housed horse driven gear engines. The village of Grange Villa does not exist at this date.

The 1896 map shows that there has by then been massive development. The waggonway is now several lines with sidings and engine sheds. The colliery is described as the *"Alma Pit"*, and several large buildings are marked along with a gasometer, 3 chimneys, a brick works and 2 rows of terrace housing set amidst it all. This is all in the field before me, to the left of the fence. Just 100 yards further up the road where I stopped the car is a long, single line of terrace houses, the beginnings of Grange Villa.

In the 1920 map more buildings have appeared, a sewage works to accommodate the needs of hundreds of workers, and Grange Villa has been built up with the square of terrace streets which exist today. Queen Street can be seen right in the middle.

Then, by 1960 although the rail tracks and the buildings of the colliery are shown, the brickworks have gone and in the middle of the field before me is the legend "*Disused Mine*". By 1981 all the buildings are gone as are the rail tracks, taken up, dismantled and the land repaired. Even the disused mine annotation is absent. The map shows only the contours of the land, symbols for trees and fields, and the line of the pretty, gurgling Twizell Burn which runs through it.

***

I ease myself up from the bench, gather the maps, and set off down the country track. As I walk I discover that exposed in the earth and mud, which is all that can be seen in contemporary photographs, is the broken and uneven red brick of the original pit road.

In 1920 I would have been jostling with mine workers, blackened faces and grimy work clothes. Were they silent under the burden of their labour, or chattering, laughing, bantering in their comradeship? Over the fence to my left would have been a coal train groaning and puffing hard under the strain of a line of waggons loaded high with coal. Beyond that a line of blackened, sooty terrace houses and then the hefty stone buildings and belching chimneys of the brick works.

After a couple of hundred yards before me is the pithead. The track opens into concrete yards and bases. A 40 metre brick chimney spewing black and grey smoke, a spoked winding wheel spinning in its tower of iron above the shaft, engine sheds and rail sidings. Brick buildings blackened with soot house offices and engine gear. Stables and carts, horses and waggons. Black nailed boots and cloth caps. All around me is noise, activity and the acrid stench of the mine.

I stop on the track, exactly where all this would have been almost 100 years ago. I give some thought to how the dismantling of this industry in the years that followed caused such unrest, such discontent, such deep feelings of resentment. The miners fought hard against it then, the Great War in 1985 between the Prime Minister Margaret Thatcher and the President of the National Union of Mineworkers, Arthur Scargill. It was a bitter contest. Strikes and unrest crippled the country and, for some, when Thatcher prevailed, irreparably consigned industrial relations to the trash can and sealed the divide between the them and us of industry, and to a large extent between the North and the South.

But the reality is that whatever the outcome had been in 1985, the coal industry was already fated to succumb to the pressures of environmental concern. It's a new world, in which coal has an uncomfortable place now, and a limited future, if any. I feel no sadness at the loss of this place.

But I am feeling a connection with the men who laboured here. If my great-grandfather Joseph walked past me now on this track, coal-blackened face, another day spent doubled up in the dark narrow coal seam deep underground, hewing at rocks with a pick and living day to day on a meagre wage, I would stop him and tell him that things will change, that the time will come when no one will have to do this anymore. But I expect he would look at me in bewilderment. My history is his future, and while I can look back and offer encouraging hindsight, he can't see the future any more than the miners of 1985 could do. This is Joseph's world. It is not mine. With that thought the connection is broken and I am left alone on the track amidst birdsong and the smell of grass. In the field the cows regard me with curiosity.

The images of the Alma Pit wash away into the green field, the woodland, the standing trees and hedgerows. Not a trace of it remains. Not a brick, not a bent piece of iron. Nothing. There must have been a great determination in those who did this, to sweep away every piece, every scrap of evidence, to put it all back as it was. I think, as I look out over the countryside, it was very much the right thing to do.

***

But it's not all gone, actually. The green fields and quietly grazing livestock are deceptive of what lies below. Not everything was brought back to the surface when pits closed, and what was not remains undisturbed down there in the dark depths.

The main vertical shafts which could descend hundreds of feet were capped off at the surface or in modern times filled with concrete leaving exhaust openings to vent gasses. But the horizontal workings which spread out under the surrounding countryside, sometimes for miles like the threads of a fungus, were largely just left.

The tunnels will be mostly flooded, but down there from the 19th century and early 20th are the wooden props and piles, broken picks, rail tracks, pulleys, ropes and gear. Perhaps discarded lamps, shovels, bottles and coal carts. In more modern mines huge, state of the art machines were abandoned in the seams. The last deep pit mine in the UK, at Kellingley, Yorkshire, closed in 2015. There were 2 main shafts there descending to 2,600 feet, almost a kilometre below the surface. Advanced mining machinery used to produce 900 tons of coal an hour, a staggering statistic, but the equipment employed to achieve it was not worth the cost of recovery and there was no market for the salvage, so it was abandoned to the still, airless darkness.

Even in the advanced mine at Kellingley there were fatalities, and we know that over the last 200 years many thousands of miners died underground. In cases of explosion, flooding and rock fall not all bodies could be recovered. There remains down there, under the grass and cows, the motorways and housing estates, more than just machines and old pit props.

***

As I walk up Queen Street from the High Street where I have left the car I see front doors and windows replaced with UPVC and there are Fords parked at the kerbsides. The air is clean. No coal dust or smoke from the colliery pollutes it. Yet the atmosphere is heavy with a depressing, soulless languor. There is no one on the street, no voices, no birdsong. The silence is overwhelming. A bored dog languidly ambles across the road. The sky is a miserable grey and there is a misty dampness in the air.

Front doors open directly onto the pavement of uneven flags. There are no front gardens here, not a bush, not a tree, not even a green leaf to break the bleak, unrelenting plainness of the houses. Such improvements as have been attempted - new doors, windows, guttering and fascia boards - seem to have been carried out with a bland, uninspired design.

There would have been a community here, bound by the common purpose of the mine. The street would have been filled with activity, chatter, clothes lines and children playing. Women talking on doorsteps, carts and barrows would have clattered on the road. There is none of that today. No sense of belonging could possibly arise in this dreary, drab place.

***

I am standing on the pavement on the corner of Queen Street and the alley next to No. 34. This is where Albert stood and smoked his Woodbines, where he chatted with the likes of Morris and Percy, and where he stood in anticipation of his Hot Pot supper. It is where he probably gave thanks for not having to spend his days down the mine, and where he looked forward to feeding the ducks and playing football with his grandson.

I'm glad he did that. It gave my own father the opportunities which led him to MacGregor's, and which in turn gave me mine, the chances to grow up in the way that I did, to gain the memories I have so far described, and ultimately to be standing here.

Stepping down the alley that runs to the side of the house I am at the back of the little terrace where Albert kept his stock. I can see him there with his shock of white hair, rummaging about among the boxes and bottles, perhaps sitting at his wooden desk, bent over a ledger of neat, blue handwriting. He might look up. "Be with you in a minute", he might say, going back to his books for a moment before standing and edging towards me through the sacks and crates in his striped apron and nailed boots.

"Albert?"

"Aye, what can I do for you?"

"I was just passing," I say, and hold out my hand to him. He takes it cautiously, a slim, slightly bony grip. It is a brief handshake, then an awkward moment of silence between us. "It's a fine little business you have here."

Albert's eyes narrow, just very slightly. "Do I know you?"

"No. Not really. Not yet." A slight pause. "I just stopped by to tell you that...well...everything will be all right. It will all work out fine."

Albert regards me. He has a kindly face, and I see my father in his features. He studies me for a while, holding my eyes, then nods slowly. "Aye, it will." He smiles without showing his teeth, a smile with his lips.

I walk back out of the alley onto 21st century Queen Street and down the road to my car. My throat tightens slightly as I walk. I wish I had known Albert Wood, grocer, dealer, candlestick maker.

ELEVEN

Tanfield, Lumley

From Grange Villa it is about five miles to Tanfield and the church of St Margaret of Antioch where Arthur William Hinkley, my schoolmaster Great Grand Uncle and my grandmother's benefactor, is buried together with his wife Isabella. Although the day has turned grey and the wipers flick occasionally in the damp air, it's a pleasant drive with much in the way of leafy, green undulating countryside, although we know that not so long ago it would have been heavily scarred by pits, chimneys and the effluence of coal. It is really quite hard to get used to all this fine outlook in a place with such a legend of industry.

The road takes me by the curiously named village of No Place, which had the residents spluttering with indignation when the local authority offered to rename it for them, and past the highly renowned Beamish Museum to which I hope to return tomorrow. Skirting East Stanley on a new bypass which I know from old maps traversed what used to be a great railway marshalling yard and row upon row of tightly packed terrace houses, the road descends to the no doubt sleepy village of Kip Hill then on westwards to Tanfield.

But first I take a short detour to Flint Hill to see where Great Grand Uncle Arthur taught, and as Head Teacher presided over his young scholars.

Many of the old mining villages I have passed through on my journey around Durham have not worn well, and Flint

Hill is no exception. The road brings me to a small, mini roundabout at the top of the hill down which the drab village descends away from me. Like Grange Villa it has a soulless disposition. It feels grey, unkempt, dilapidated.

Stopping at the side of the road, on the far side of the roundabout is the Prince of Wales pub. It's a low, dull cream, scarred building with carelessly whitewashed windows, flaking paint and torn sport events posters stuck haphazardly about its façade. Straggly weeds grow from its footings next to a muddy footpath. It's about as welcoming as a gas bill.

I guess there must be little incentive to improve things. The industry for which the villages were created has abandoned them. The houses themselves were built with tiny rooms, no aspect either at front or rear, and they must be difficult candidates for modernisation.

The schoolhouse in which Uncle Arthur ruled with a clipped beard, trim moustache, and I would like to think a moderate hand, occupied a substantial corner plot just over the road from the pub. The Victorian schoolhouse is now long gone, and in its place there is a surprisingly pretty new cottage, attractively constructed with solid, light coloured stone and clean matching paintwork to the leaded pane windows and French doors to the front garden. It has a sizable ground floor area suggesting generous interior space, and smart gates open onto a wide smooth black driveway and a double garage, all set amid close cut lawn and beds.

So the question I ask myself is this: as the cottage clearly would have cost a fair bit to build and whoever designed it had at least some modicum of taste, who on earth would spend the effort, time and money to live here, on the edge of a grubby roundabout, fifty yards from the wretched Prince of Wales?

I have stopped the car on the road opposite the cottage, just before the roundabout, and as I am leaning on the stone wall next to the new, steel gates to the driveway thinking about this, a new Mercedes drives in. Parked in front of the double garage a young man gets out. He is smartly dressed and confident. He's close enough that I don't have to shout too much, and I ask him if he lives here. I try to sound less weird by explaining about Uncle Arthur and ask if this is where the old schoolhouse used to be. He tells me that it is. He seems friendly enough but doesn't approach me before turning towards the front door. There is so much I would like to ask him. Who is he? What does he do? Why on earth does he live here, of all places? Has he taken leave of his senses?

But I can't ask a total stranger such personal stuff, so I don't and in any case he has disappeared inside. But I would love to know. He is obviously not blind, so perhaps there is some hidden attraction, some benefit to living in Flint Hill known only to those who live here, a secret never to be divulged. The sort of thing that, if ever made public knowledge, would sell millions of tabloid newspapers. Or perhaps he was just born here and can't bear to move away. I suppose I will never know.

***

Just a few steps back up the road is a straggly row of houses before the fields and hedgerows begin. Next to the old schoolhouse plot, set well back and slightly higher than the road, the first of these is the austere form of South View, the house in which Arthur lived with his wife Isabella from about 1895 until their deaths in 1936 and 1937.

It went with the job, of course, and as would befit a Head Teacher the house is larger than an average terrace by a good margin. It is very square, architecturally functional. It has a generous front garden, and a front aspect over the surrounding countryside which no doubt gives it its name, although that view may well have been more industrial back then than it is today. But in spite of that it is a brown, bleak looking place.

There is no one about, and I have time to linger at the front gate without arousing suspicion. I can see Arthur stepping out from the front door of an early morning, misty perhaps with the smell of coal smoke in the air from the numerous village chimneys, fires set to warm the workforce before they set out for the labour of the day. He would take the few steps down the road to the schoolhouse where he would unlock the doors and walk over the wooden flooring to his study. He would have a desk, an inkwell, ledgers of handwritten timetables, notes, and lesson plans. It might be cold and he would set a fire in the black iron grate, the smell of coal smoke soon wafting through the air.

Shortly, the sound of footsteps attracts his attention. A teacher pushes the door ajar and offers a cheery greeting. "Good morning, Headmaster." She is dressed in a long skirt, a shawl and her grey hair is tied back in a bun. "Good morning, Emily," Arthur smiles at her and she pulls the door closed behind her as she walks to her classroom, footsteps echoing in the corridor and Arthur returns to the business on his desk.

After a short while he hears the sound of many little footsteps and the chattering of children, the occasional squeal and Emily's soft admonishment. Arthur smiles to himself as he pores over his desk, imagining the little rosy scrubbed faces and the delight in their eyes at some pleasure found in the company of their friends. And then, when the chattering has subsided, he pushes his chair back and walks slowly to the classroom where the children are seated quietly and attentively at their little desks.

Arthur will preside over an assembly. They will say the Lord's Prayer in unison, perhaps a short hymn, and Arthur will read out the names to receive a child's response, "Yes Mr Hinkley". It is ordered, yet friendly. The children are respectful yet not fearful. There is learning here, but there is also play.

I remind myself that Arthur has no children of his own, and I wonder if that gives him an affectionate, paternal approach to his little charges. I have a photograph of him, a studio portrait, sepia in a grey cardboard frame. He looks to be about 55 years old and so it would have been taken in about 1920. He is a professional looking gentleman with neat cut, grey hair, trimmed beard and a bushy moustache. He is wearing round rimmed spectacles, a white wing collar shirt with a spotted bow tie, and a heavy looking woollen jacket with waistcoat. A white handkerchief pokes from his breast pocket. He has a genial, kindly face.

There is no coal in Arthur's blood. He was born in the far north of Northumberland to James William Hinkley and a family in the coastguard service. His grandfather was John Hinkley, the coastguard from the far north east coast whose remote cottage I shall be visiting in a few days. James William brought the family south to Durham where he worked as a gardener. He also brought with him the Church of England, the religion to which his Northumbrian family was aligned, and the reason Uncle Arthur was buried in the Anglican Church of St Mary of Antioch, just 2 miles down the road at Tanfield.

***

Nearly every mining village in the coalfield area, however small, had a Wesleyan Methodist Chapel. Frequently a Chapel served only a few houses, like Perkinsville for example. Communities engaged with what was simply referred to as "Chapel". The expression meant not just the physical building. Chapel was a conformity, a lifestyle.

Local Wesleyan Chapels were built to a utilitarian standard, without the spires, domes, towers and complex architecture of a church as we think of it. Transepts, internal columns, the display of art and icons were rarely employed in village chapels. This was not out of ideology, but of need, cost and practicality. They were plain, functional places, but still they provided an important adhesion for the communities they served.

There was a Wesleyan chapel in Tanfield Lea, but that is a different village about a mile away, and to the best of my knowledge there was never one in Tanfield itself. The purveyance of religion there was the domain of the Church of England. It is to here that Uncle Arthur would have come to pay his respects, and why he and his wife were buried here. I have arranged to meet the churchwarden, Margaret Goodchild.

***

My first impression is that Tanfield is a village apart from the usual closely built, terraced places I have been accustomed to seeing around here. It is clean, leafy and the buildings are of solid stone. It would not look out of place in the Cotswolds. The pub, disappointingly closed on my visit, looks attractive. Tanfield is a small place, with only a little modern development, and very much dominated by the church which sits in the large grassed area of its cemetery. There is more cemetery over the road and there are acres of gravestones and memorials. I am glad of Margaret's unexpected and generous offer to seek out Arthur's grave in advance, saving me the trouble of ferreting about for hours, especially as there is a drizzle in the air, punctuated only by periods of heavier rain.

I am met by Margaret, as arranged, at the heavy doors of the church. She is a small lady with grey hair, about my age I would guess, and has a charming smile which is echoed in the welcome she gives me. She is clearly proud of her church, and is anxious to show me around.

The church is rich in stained glass and the icons of Christianity. Several rows of dark wood pews, divided by a stripe of red carpet, lead to the draped altar with the usual adornments – silver goblets, a crucifix and a gold sash. There is a splendid pipe organ to one side with polished wood, upholstered seat and lots of interesting stops and pedals. A slightly musty smell hangs in the still air reminding me of damp plaster. The rough surfaces of the old iron radiators spaced sparsely around the walls are cold to the touch. The building feels switched off for now, idle, waiting for the time when the heavy oak doors open again and a few well wrapped people bring movement and a little

135

warmth. And then they will leave again, the doors will close behind them, the temperature and silence will fall and the church will sleep again.

Margaret shows me behind the altar, woodwork engraved in gold lettering with remembrance and reverence to those with names such as Joicey, one of the main names of the coal industry, which surprises me in a religious context. I expect he was a generous benefactor.

Although I don't ask her, I'm sure I am safe in assuming that Margaret holds her allegiance to the Church of England, but to what extent and in what tradition I don't know. Certainly I can see her pleasure in showing me around, offering explanations of this and that, and pointing out some memorials on the white walls. She tells me something of the history of the church, how the original monks who settled here many centuries ago to escape the Viking ravages from the north even dug a small mine beneath the site on which the church stands.

For me, although I have no religion save for an alignment with the social principles associated with Christianity, I am glad to stand in silence, which Margaret allows me to do. She clearly understands my need to engage with this place, gazing around me in its tranquil solemnity, its history. I wonder, as I always do when I stand in a place like this, at the quiet gravity it induces in me.

For one who takes the cautious view that religion has, in its many forms, drawn out the worst in mankind more than it has the better, and has been the instrument of division more than it has of unity, I always wonder that nowhere provokes in me such moments of personal tranquillity and reflection than does a place of religion like this church, and equally a great cathedral to Catholicism, a mosque to the sanctity of Allah, a ruined Abbey or a hermit's silent cave. There seems to be a power at work which I cannot begin to understand. I sometimes wonder if I have more religion than I think I do, a thought that seems easier to reject than to accept.

We stand for a few minutes while I allow myself to embrace the potency of these surroundings. All the events which have taken place here over the long years and centuries are distilled into one feeling of calm serenity.

And of course, and as Margaret agrees, this is where Uncle Arthur and Isabella would have come to sit in these very pews. I try to imagine him sitting there, dressed as he is in my photograph amid a congregation united in a service, singing their hymns and offering their prayers. A priest in white, a small choir perhaps. Sunday best suits, long dresses, ladies in fancy hats and men in polished boots. And after the service they will leave slowly and quietly, perhaps gathering outside the doors in small groups to talk and smile together, the vicar offering his contribution as he wanders from one small gathering to the other.

The imagery, quite frankly, comes easily. A community at peace, not only with their God but with themselves.

***

Eventually Margaret leads me from the church, across the road and through a gate into that part of the cemetery where she has located the grave. Through the wet grass and surrounded by hundreds of gravestones and memorials she shows me a low-set, dark, granite headstone. Spots of green lichen grow on the top surface but otherwise it is clean and looks well cared for. We stand before it quietly and I read the clear inscription.

In Loving Memory of
ISABELLA
BELOVED WIFE OF ARTHUR WILLIAM HINKLEY
DIED DEC. 21st 1936, AGED 82 YEARS
Also the above ARTHUR WILLIAM HINKLEY
DIED SEPT 6th 1937, AGED 79 YEARS

So, below me the two coffins and the remains of two relatives, childless, who lived an extraordinary life from the coastguard community of the north east, to the beginnings of a teaching career and marriage in Lancashire, and then to Durham and a life of education and worship in this local community. A life I gain pleasure in imagining. I think it would have been an ordered life, of simple pleasures and companionship. I find myself hoping that they had great love for each other.

***

Before we leave, Margaret says she wants to show me something. Just a few yards from Arthur's grave is the headstone of Thomas Armstrong, the Miners' Poet. Born in 1848, Tommy was a short man with bow legs from childhood rickets, and he worked in the mines and pits around Tanfield and Stanley from the age of 9. He became a songwriter, a concert hall performer and something of a celebrity. His songs and poetry, although often humorous, reflected the harsh lives and working conditions of the mining community. He lived in and around this area all his life except, I am surprised to discover, for a period in Whitley Bay. He had 14 children, which seems to me quite a feat in itself, what with his theatre, poetry and his bow legs. He died in 1920.

***

In the early years of the 20th century, let's say prior to 1909, while Arthur stood before his children in the schoolhouse on Flint Hill dispensing the three Rs and Christian scripture, my great grandfather George Elliott, who we met getting married to Gran Elliott in the Wesleyan Chapel in Chester-le-Street this morning, was getting dirty down the coal mine at Lumley, only a few miles down the road.

George is Arthur's sister's son's wife's father, or put another way his nephew's father-in-law, a relationship for which there is no genealogical term, as although I am related to them both, they are not related by blood to each other.

I take the country roads east from Tanfield, back past Beamish, Grange Villa and Pelton Fell, passing Chester-le-Street to the south to Lumley New Road where almost immediately before the road passes over the A1 motorway, I make the turn onto a track which will lead me in a couple of hundred yards to the extraordinary hamlet of Lumley Thicks, where George and Gran Elliott lived for about 10 years after arriving here from Perkinsville.

The hamlet is a disorderly jumble of a dozen or so buildings set in the middle of a huge field. The rutted track from the road shortly splits to left and right forming a central area where sit the buildings, rather like a large farmstead. There are several "*Private*" and "*Residents Only*" signs, which I cautiously ignore and drive into the small enclave of dwellings. There seems to be no one about, although I imagine several pairs of eyes and curtains twitching in the windows.

There was, as always, a Wesleyan Chapel here too, serving just these few houses, and although I thought I would easily identify where it is or was I cannot. Perhaps it has not survived, for the old buildings are not only restored but brought right into the 21st century. There are expansive plate glass windows, French doors to patios, and Range Rovers and Mercedes are parked on the forecourts.

There were several pits in and around Lumley, but I am sure that the one George worked in was the nearest to here, only about 400 yards across the fields. A track led from Lumley Thicks to the pit which no doubt would have been a familiar walk for him, day in and day out, fair weather and foul. I have a decent photograph of Lumley 6th Pit, and although I can't be sure that is the one to which George toiled across the fields from here, it probably was and is typical of the pithead gear and the structures and rail tracks of the time. I can see now across the fields to where this would have been. I can't get out of the car for fear of being mistaken for a burglar, or an estate agent, but holding the photograph up to the window I can compare the views. It's a typical story, and one I have seen before, at Grange Villa for example, but this one gives an idea of the sheer size of a pit like this. In the foreground there are a dozen coal waggons on rail tracks, behind them engine sheds and a row of hopper bays from which the coal would be loaded into the waggons, and beyond high, brick buildings housing engines, machinery, offices, baths, boiler-rooms, steam and dust. And above the pitched roofs and chimneys of the sheds arises the great spoked wheel, lowering the men down into the depths and hauling back up the tubs of black coal.

One day, deep below where I stand, or certainly somewhere not far from me, a tunnel collapsed onto George and he was badly injured. He died of those injuries on 20 February 1915. And as we know, the house at Lumley Thicks in which the family lived, and whichever one of these it was I cannot tell, was a company house and Gran Elliott had to leave, taking her small children and whatever belongings she might have had to find work in Chester-le-Street.

I wonder at her leaving, and the manner of it. Did she walk down the lane with a few bags leading her children by the hand, perhaps to find a bus? Or did she ride on a horse drawn cart, her belongings piled beside her? It must surely have been a lonely, frightening time, leaving her home and life with her husband behind. George is buried in the Ropery Lane cemetery in the town.

***

On the way back to Chester-le-Street, I take a short detour by the village of Great Lumley. There I find, on a wide green verge between the road and an estate of modern bungalows, a memorial erected to commemorate the miners who lost their lives in the Lumley pits. Although it has come on to rain again, I park the car and walk over the wet grass to stand before it. Set in a red brick plinth, the memorial plaque is black, about 3 feet wide and 4 deep, with gold lettering.

This memorial is dedicated to
THE MEN & BOYS OF GREAT LUMLEY
Who worked in the numerous mines in the parishes of
Great & Little Lumley for almost 700 years
In particular we pay tribute to those who made the
ultimate sacrifice,
Giving their lives to winning coal for the security of their
families,
While contributing to the progress and prosperity of
Great Britain

The inscription continues to record that the youngest known to have died was John Cusby, just 9 years old, who died along with his father in 1799. And it concludes:

Lest we forget those lost and those that suffered the cost

a reference not just to those who died, but to those widows, children and families left behind.

I note with interest that alongside the commemoration to those who lost their lives, there is also a note of patriotism in the acknowledgment that duty to King and Country was being done. At least, if I were to put on a cynical hat, there was patriotism in those who wrote the inscription.

***

By the time I get to Ropery Lane cemetery the rain has eased off leaving a damp stillness in the air which I find quite pleasing, and I am glad to leave the car and stroll in through a pointed archway flanked by ornate pinnacles. The cemetery is a beautifully created and maintained space. It's green, leafy, and the headstones and memorials are well ordered. The Chester-le-Street Heritage Group have mapped much of the cemetery and I easily find George's grave, where he lies together with his wife, Grandma Elliott.

For the second time today I find myself standing before a grave where husband and wife lie together. Arthur and Isabella died within months of each other, while George and Mary passed away more than 50 years apart. They were both of my blood, but standing in the wet grass before that low memorial stone I think about what different lives they led. Arthur with his suit and wing collar in his classroom, George with his coal-streaked face and calloused hands down a pit.

And for the second time today I stand in admiration of their lives, their courage, their beliefs and their strength in what today we would see as adversity. And it occurs to me, do I admire them simply because they survived without washing machines, or pizza, or free Wi Fi? Is my respect for them borne of an arrogant assumption that the modern world with all its technology and material advancement is better?

Of course, it would be fruitless to deny the benefits of modern medical science, and working conditions are not only better today but enshrined in law. We have information technology, the internet, the ability to travel wherever we want, mobile phones, and we can operate our central heating systems from the other side of the globe, should we wish to do so. Human rights, inclusivity, freedom of speech and expression are words and phrases we hear day to day. In most parts of the world, although I concede not all, the 21st century has afforded us a safe, comfortable and affordable existence.

But then, might not a descendent of mine 200 years in the future regard me with the same sad compassion that I might now feel for Arthur and George? Might my life, absent of the technological, medical and social advances of 200 years hence, be considered deprived, primitive, difficult?

Harold Macmillan, the then Prime Minister in 1957, told a party conference "*Most of our people have never had it so good*", and that was more than 60 years ago when they didn't have smart televisions and the M1 had not even been built. A lot of people disagreed with Macmillan, of course, but compared to the lives of George and Arthur, he was right.

These thoughts come to me as I look down on George's headstone. He was man who worked hard, in conditions which today would not even be allowed. He lived in a house without electricity, or any of the comforts we take as essential today. He lost his life too early, and left a widow too young. He was a man for whom I am feeling, frankly, sorry. But again I wonder, if he was listening to my thoughts might he not arise before me and express some indignation? Might he not stab a finger in my chest and ask me how the hell I think I can be the judge?

George would be right to remind me of a few things. He did not have global warming and climate change. He did not have nuclear armament or international terrorism. His world was not encumbered by the insidious contamination of global pandemic, disease spread by overpopulation, our insatiable appetite for travel, and an arrogant disregard for the health of our planet. His job was secure and his children were not obscenely fat. His house was free, and so was his coal.

George might suggest I consider the contentment of sitting before a blazing coal fire with his wife and children, of the camaraderie of the mine, of the pleasures of a meal hard won, or the exquisite pleasure of no one's company but his own. Who knows what he enjoyed, or in what he found his delights?

He would be right, would he not? The quality of life of a generation cannot be assessed with reference to the quality of another.

***

My feet crunch on the gravel path that leads back to the cemetery gates and my car. I walk slowly, thinking about what George has said to me. I do still feel a sadness that he led a life of hardship, by my standards at least, that he died so tragically and so young, and that he didn't survive to see his children grow or hold my baby mother in his strong arms.

But if George tells me that actually it was alright, then who am I to argue? Perhaps that is just the way it was, as it is now, for me.

TWELVE

Beamish Museum

Not many years ago if you took the road from the north to the south of the river Tyne by way of the Tyne Tunnel, you emerged out of the yellow dimness into the brightness of County Durham at Jarrow, where you were presented with a colourful roadside billboard which proclaimed "*Catherine Cookson Country*", celebrating the author who wrote nearly 100 novels, most of which were set in this landscape where she was born.

In what South Tyneside Council described as a rebranding exercise, the signs were removed in 2012. It replaced them with those brown ones which indicate heritage sites, local attractions and that sort of thing. This was, it said, to "*raise its regional, national and international profile in relation to tourism and economic regeneration*". I suppose this sounds fair enough, but I would have thought that the signage could have been additional rather than a complete substitution because Cookson was, whether you read her or not, a hugely important social observer, in a Downton Abbey sort of way.

Although Cookson became a millionaire, was made a Dame in 1993, and had films and television series made of her stories, she had a pretty rough start being born in Jarrow, and you might think that reason enough to abandon any hope of future prospect. But on top of that she also had an alcoholic single mother who, for much of her early childhood, she believed was actually her sister. Her father was a gambling addicted absentee and she suffered from various illnesses throughout her life, including depression. All in all, it's a pretty impressive career progression.

Cookson's novels were often tales of personal anguish of one sort or another. She told of social and class divides, domestic service, love conquering all sorts of obstacles, or not conquering them as the case may be, and she frequently dwelt on the living conditions of the poor. Her book covers were often designed with a *"young girl with wind-blown hair gazing resignedly into the distance"* style of illustration, which made it fairly clear what sort of story you were in for.

The reason I mention this is because Cookson was a meticulous researcher. She felt it necessary to experience the things she wrote about, and famously when she drew a character who was a mine worker she actually went down a mine to suffer the working conditions for herself. An extreme but nevertheless admirable approach to ensure the authenticity of her work, I would have thought.

It might be appropriate then, as this section of my story is closely connected with the mining industry, for me to follow suit, and get a bit dirty for the sake of my art. Happily, and I can honestly confess with some relief, I can't do that because there are no deep mines anymore. But there is the museum at Beamish, a recreation of the everyday lives of the mining communities in detailed reconstruction. There is a whole street, cottages, a colliery pithead with winding gear, a railway station, a farm and even a drift mine, much of it built with reclaimed or relocated original material. It's world renowned, just down the road from Chester-le-Street and hardly a mile from Grange Villa.

It's not a cheap visit, although I have no doubt there is much value to be had in the nearly 20 quid standard entrance fee. But I do notice in the promotional stuff I have read that there is a generous reduction for the more mature visitor. So I have checked my wallet for my bus pass which should be adequate proof of my entitlement to a pensioner's discount.

I have never been to Beamish museum before. When I was a child in the 1950s it had not yet been built. A museum to the mining community back then would have been like creating a replica Marks & Spencer or a dummy Wetherspoons today. It actually opened in 1972. So I am looking forward to seeing whether this exceptionally authentic replication of the lives of my ancestors might provoke anything in the deeper recesses of my mind. A genetic memory, perhaps, if the odd soul or spirit from the past were included with the metal, bricks and timberwork they have brought and installed here.

***

I survived the previous evening by joining up with Brian and Simon on their regular stools, and half listened to Brian's further pronouncements on the failures of modern society and his encounters with Ben Aunger, but there was nothing new to write in my notes about it. I ate a nice meal and treated myself to a brandy before bed, which I assumed would ensure me a good night's sleep but in fact gave me wind.

This morning my Lambton Worm Full English has settled. I have packed my bags, paid the bill and loaded the car. Tonight I am booked into The Black Horse at Beamish, which has more stars than the Lambton Worm but where breakfast is Not Included. Nor, I expect, are Brian and Simon. But first, the famous Museum.

***

Once I have passed under the great, red entrance arch which seems to have once been a big, heavy piece of industrial engineering, the first things I notice are the size of the car park which is massive, and the car park attendant who is dressed like a 19th century policeman, giving me the first taste of the museum's quest for authenticity.

Having parked the car and changed my footwear for some sturdy boots because I am, honestly, expecting to go down a mine, I enter the doors of the wide, sweeping entrance building, past the inevitable gift shop and a large room which appears to be a café staffed by scruffy labourers and milking maids, to a long hallway which offers me a choice of no less than five lanes of tills. This is a place which in 2017 attracted over 700,000 visitors. That's an awful lot, and accounts for the massive car park and all the tills, which are staffed by women in pinafores and bonnets.

But today is well out of season. The car park is almost empty, and in the till hall there are but a few stragglers and a small party of children. I notice a prominent sign which advises that dogs are welcome but must be kept controlled on a lead, which at least suggests there will be no sniffing slobberers bounding about on the loose. And the weather is much improved from yesterday. The sun shines from a blue, almost cloudless sky.

I'm a bit irritated that I don't have to produce my bus pass because the actress at the till doesn't dispute my entitlement to an age-related discount. I put this down to the peaked, grey tartan, cloth cap I have selected for today. It used to be my father's and I think it gives me a sort of gravitas. My wife says it makes me look like Victor Meldrew, which is not a compliment.

Following the signs directing me into the museum, I pass through the rear of the building onto a wide, stone veranda. Steps lead down a steep bank to a road, and across the road there is a wide vista as far as the eye can see, a bowl in the land over a mile across, mainly trees and woodland from up here. The site is so vast that I can see nothing of the town, the pithead, the farm or any of the other features I know exist out there.

I take the steps down to the road. There are tramlines in the tarmac, and a bus stop in original 1913 design and livery sits beside a signpost which offers disturbingly long distances to the various attractions a visitor may wish to see. The small group of schoolchildren are being herded at the bus stop, and so I decide to follow them, for want of other inspiration.

***

While waiting at the bus stop, I take a look at the abridged guidebook I have downloaded to my phone.

It tells me that Beamish Museum was the vision of Dr. Frank Atkinson in the mid-1950s. Born a Yorkshireman he spent his professional life in the North. With an interest in science and history he was led into a career in museum curation. In 1958 he was appointed curator of the Bowes Museum in Barnard Castle, highly renowned in its own right and next door to my old school, as it happens. That position gave him the influence, the authority and access to finance which enabled him to realise his dream, and he put forward ambitious proposals for a museum which would be about "*the everyday, recent past*".

The site selected at Beamish is a whopping 300 acres, and from modest beginnings in the early 1970s and an introductory exhibition in 1971 the collections grew. Not only artefacts but whole buildings were acquired. In 1975 the Royal Family again braved the long slog north to visit, HM Queen Mother on this occasion, and in 1987 Beamish was named European Museum of the year. Gradually the street took shape, the mine opened, and Atkinson's vision became an ever advancing reality. Even today it's still growing. As recently as 2014 the 1940s farm was completed, and pit ponies were introduced to the stables.

Frank Atkinson died in 2014.

***

In season this place would be thronging with hordes of visitors, children and groups of foreign tourists. I'm grateful that today is out of season and quiet, which more than makes up for the autumnal chill in the air. The empty bus which eventually approaches is painted in yellow and brown livery, has large, thin spoked wheels and an open spiral staircase at the back. The driver, seated in an open cab in front of an enormous, flat steering wheel, is dressed in a black woollen uniform and a peaked cap. I notice the engine is remarkably quiet, which suggests something modern under the bonnet, but no matter because to all intents and purposes it is just the bus that would have plied the streets and byways of County Durham in the early 20th century.

The little gaggle of children and their guardians clamber into the lower deck, and so I haul myself up the spiral staircase to the open top and find myself alone on a bench seat at the front with a marvellous view and a pleasant, relaxed anticipation of the ride in the bright yet still chilly sunshine.

The bus moves off smoothly and we travel slowly along the gently curving road between stone walls and trees, and occasionally some low rather modern looking sheds which I expect are something to do with site maintenance. I am thoroughly enjoying the ride when I become gently aware that I am not alone. It's more of a feeling, a sense of presence, but I am quite convinced that there is someone behind me. Someone who was not there before.

I find it very difficult to be surreptitious. I have little talent when it comes to looking inconspicuous, and I would be hopeless if ever required to go undercover. But with an awkward shuffle while pretending to look around at the scenery and which cricks my neck and probably makes me look furtive, I spot a gentleman sitting quietly about three seats behind me.

I have no idea how he got there without me noticing. I have a fleeting concern that he might himself be undercover, employed by the museum authorities to keep an eye on people like me. But he smiles at me and offers a genial "*Hello*".

Graham, who is actually not undercover, has come over from Kendal in the Lake District for the day, having some time on his hands and never having been to Beamish before, like me. He is a slim man, a bit younger than me but not by too much, smartly yet casually dressed, and has an easy conversation. It seems natural that when the bus comes to a halt in the cobbled, tramlined street of the 1913 town, we should alight and amble off to explore together.

***

Walking a little way down the street from where the bus has stopped, I stand and gaze around me at what has been created here. I am truly astonished. I had expected to find a sort of film set, authentic on the surface, superficially correct, but with nothing much behind the facade. But not so. Not so at all. From the cobbled street, the tramlines and the period lamp posts and gas lamps, to the shops which are not just fronts but whole working enterprises, it has a depth of realism I did not anticipate. The street curves in from one end where there is a bank, solid and sturdy in heavy stone, the tram station with its waiting rooms and conveniences. A hardware store displays its wares in a wide glass window, a bakery, a newspaper office, a full Co-op store, a chemist and a pub, and a short row of Edwardian terraces, brought here brick by brick from Gateshead and reassembled, in which are to be found a dentist, a music teacher, and a solicitor.

I remind myself that I need to look behind the bricks and mortar, the cobbles and the museum, and remember that this was the world of George, Albert and Arthur. I wonder if perhaps I might see them in their boots and caps among the anoraks and trainers that walk the street today.

For no other reason than it is across the road from where the bus dropped us off, Graham and I saunter over to the garage. It's really a big shop front with a couple of vintage cars displayed behind a glass showroom window, and to one side there is a car width entrance. Inside, underneath a high pitched roof there is a wooden counter behind which are banks of little drawers for screws and small accessories all labelled in handwritten ink on sepia labels. On the concrete floor are oil cans, tyres, half a gearbox, racks of spanners and tools and a couple of old cars in the course of repair or maintenance. It's all just slightly oily. Behind the counter stands the proprietor, a stout man in his fifties with a bushy moustache which may or may not be detachable. He is wearing a brown apron, a wing collar shirt and bow tie. He tells us that he also doubles as the dentist, whose premises are just over the road.

Standing stiffly behind the counter, hands spread on the top in front of him, the proprietor slips briefly out of role to offer some visitor information, and tells us that the garage, like most of the buildings here, was brought and reconstructed from a real site elsewhere. When I mention Aunger's in Chester-le-Street, I'm quite taken aback to learn that not only does he know about it, he bought several cars from there. I daren't ask if he knew Ben Aunger in case he did, but I do reflect on how well known that little garage seems to have been, and I wonder whether perhaps Gran Elliott may have stood in a place like this, dispensing a wage packet, questioning a receipt, or checking an inventory.

***

Graham and I have a wander around the street, nosing into the bank, the Co-op store, the bakery and several others. In each place we encounter the museum's actors, wing collars and bonnets, waistcoats and crinoline dresses. They are all very good, rarely stepping out of character.

It's time to stop for a coffee. Graham and I have walked a little past the end of the street, and spot a shack with outside benches. Inside there is a stainless steel counter, plastic beakers and it's staffed by two young girls in jeans. I wonder if we have somehow walked off-piste, and glance back outside to make sure. But no, and it crosses my mind that we might get a decent, 21st century espresso. But sadly not, and we retire to a bench outside with our plastic cups of steaming, thin, filter coffee. Nevertheless, it's a pleasant stop in the sunshine, and I get to ask Graham what he does.

He used to be a teacher he tells me, but now he "*does funerals*". He says this with a straight face, but doesn't elaborate much until I cautiously press him and with a little timidity he reveals that he is, in fact, an ordained minister, a full Reverend. And to me, in that modest disclosure, Graham makes perfect sense. I had noticed his gentle, kindly face and his engaging smile. He listens with a quiet encouragement, a benign pastoral interest. I have that same feeling I get when I stand in the quiet solemnity of a church, as I did in Tanfield. It can't be religion, can it? I've always taken the Richard Dawkins position on that. But I so often find that people who do have religion, and places come to that, invoke an agreeable sense of something I find hard to describe. It's calm, engaging, sentient. Whatever it is, I am comfortable indeed in Graham's company, and the fact that he turns out to be a fully-fledged Reverend is an unexpected and welcome discovery. I'm looking forward to the rest of the day with him, if he'll have me along.

Our conversation turns to his home in Cumbria, and Graham tells me how he loves to sail on the lakes among the high mountains and valleys of the Lake District. His enthusiasm is captivating, and as he describes his love of the Lakes, his engagement with the pure nature of the fells, he takes me back nearly 60 years to the shores of Lake Ullswater, and when my father tried to teach me, and Little John, to sail.

By the late 1950s, early 1960s when I was about 9 and Little John about 6 years old, we had been spending more and more time in the Lake District in the holidays when Dad could take time away from work, or at weekends. In the early days when we were very little we used to go to a small, country hotel at the head of Lake Bassenthwaite. It is now a smart, sprawling conference resort, but then it was just a few rooms in a farmhouse.

Later, Dad acquired a caravan. It was only modest but had sleeping for four provided two of the occupants were small and not too fussy. It had a cooker, gas mantle lighting, and an Elsan toilet which consisted of a bin in a cupboard with an inch or two of chemical solution in the bottom. Use of the Elsan was highly restricted.

The site Dad selected for the caravan was secluded with ash trees between the generously spaced vans, on a hillside overlooking Lake Ullswater about halfway down the western shore. It was a beautiful location, a small fell of woodland, bare rocky outcrops and an unbroken view of the whole lake, surrounded by high mountains and Helvellyn towering over it all in the south. The celebrated Lake District artist William Heaton-Cooper sat near here when he painted "*Ullswater from Gowbarrow Fell*". My brother and I were allowed to roam the hillside at will, building hideouts under the massive tangle of a huge rhododendron, shooting bemused but steadfast sheep with machine sticks, and flying around with the energy only children of that age can muster. It was a wide landscape for games and adventure.

We also spent lazy days at the lakeside, paddling in the icy mountain water, skimming stones and picnicking. But Dad hatched a plan, influenced I'm sure, if not seduced, by the triangular white shapes of sails which tacked and ran before the wind up and down the lake. He didn't warn us, or talk about it first, he just turned up one day at home in Tynemouth with a boat hitched to the towbar on the back of the Jag.

It was a day of great excitement as my brother and I too had seen the white sails on the lake. We had regarded them from the shore with curiosity and wondered what it would be like to sail about on the water, catching the wind and racing, but it never occurred to us that we might ever have a boat of our own. We suddenly felt just a little more grown up. We might even join the people over the lake where they had a clubhouse and a gun which they fired to start races.

Soon the boat was towed over the Pennine Hills to our caravan on the hillside, and the very next day down to a shingly cove on the lakeside where Dad backed the trailer up to the lapping water and gradually eased it slowly over the pebbles until the boat floated free and the trailer could be drawn from under it as Little John and I held onto ropes to stop it drifting away.

Until then, my brother and I had not seen the boat with its mast erected and sails hauled up. I have no idea if Dad had tested it all out at home and given it a dry run, so to speak, before we put it in the water. I imagine he would have done as it came with a whole array of sheets and ropes, a rudder, a centreboard and all manner of things. But it was at that point in my memory that the little sailing dinghy was for the first time put together and made ready for sea.

It was also at that point, and gradually over the next half hour, as Dad unpacked things and attached bits here and installed things there, that it dawned on me that the boat, which we had christened "*Seagull*", was not entirely what I was expecting. And for the second time in this story, I have to recall that although my father was undoubtedly talented in marine design and all things ships, when it came to acquiring Seagull, the only expression that came to my mind was the childhood equivalent of "*What on earth was he thinking?*"

The dinghy was not very large, about 10 feet in length. It was made entirely of plastic and fibreglass down to the moulded bench seats and tiller housing, and it had a blunt, rounded bow. There were some silver metal accessories for securing ropes and whatnot, which Dad screwed into pre-drilled holes on the sides, all the while referring to some assembly instructions he had spread out on the shore and held down with four pebbles. These things, in themselves, were not of any particular concern, but as he progressed, bending over the instructions for a moment then back to the boat to do something then back to the instructions again, Little John and I stood by watching with gradually rising doubt.

The mast consisted of a single aluminium pole which slotted into a hole in the fibreglass hull. The sail, note the singular, was a roughly triangular piece of nylon with a stitched sleeve down the longest side and into which the mast was inserted, like pulling on a sock. There was a metal fitting at the thin end of the sail for threading a rope, and that was it, apart from a tiller and a centreboard which dropped into pre-moulded fitting points. I remember thinking that there must be more to it. Are there some bits missing? Have we left some of it at home?

I stood on the lakeshore with my brother and my father as we dolefully regarded Seagull gently wallowing in the light swell, its single sail hanging limp except for an occasional languid ruffle when a waft of breeze caught it.

Dad was the first to summon his enthusiasm. "Right," he declared, "lifejackets on." They were bright orange, heavily padded things and much bulkier than the jackets of today. My brother and I stumbled about in them, our arms held out at the sides unnaturally, like miniature Michelin Men. And so we clambered aboard, my brother and I one on each side and my father in the stern, one hand on the tiller and the other clutching the single rope attached to the sail. My mother stood on the shore, arms folded across her chest with a look that might have been concern, or disbelief, or both.

Dad jiggled the rope a lot so as to catch some wind in the sail, but Seagull refused to budge and sat wallowing next to the shore, occasionally scraping her hull on the pebbles. Eventually Dad took his shoes and socks off and got out. He pushed the boat out as far as he could, the icy water now above his knees and soaking his trousers, then he scrambled back in, grabbed the rope and waggled it again furiously. Eventually Seagull's sail caught a small gust of wind which blew us into a tree overhanging the shore.

There was a lot of bad language that day and Dad used words that I hadn't heard him use before, and from her black looks I'm not sure Mother had heard them either. Little John and I tried to help in whatever way we felt we could, but we had as little idea of what we were doing as Dad. After several attempts to launch the boat there was a heavy atmosphere of disappointment and frustration among the small party of sailors on the lakeshore.

But, with perseverance and probably a fortuitous turn in the wind, eventually Seagull missed the tree and crabbed out sideways into the lake. This was much more like it, the water all around us, the waves lapping at the hull and the sail occasionally catching the wind and pulling the boat one way or another while Dad, with a face of stern concentration, did more jiggling with the rope in attempts to steer us one way or the other.

Across the water, the sails of Enterprises, Mirror dinghies and the futuristic Flying Fifteens whose crew had to lean dangerously and excitingly out over the water, scudded about the lake tacking into the wind or running before it. On this side of the lake Seagull crabbed and wallowed. The sail flapped ineffectively and Dad struggled with his rope and the tiller. It was soon apparent, both to Little John and me, and to Dad as well, that Seagull sailed no better than a bath tub. Eventually, unable to persuade the boat in any specific direction Dad beached it a few hundred yards up the shore and drove the car round with its trailer to collect it.

To be fair, over time and with a few inventive adjustments by Dad, we did get Seagull to sail. At least, we gained sufficient control of it to avoid trees and mostly we could return it to the point of departure. But Seagull was ultimately consigned to the role of rowing boat from which we dangled fishing lines and pottered about close to shore. It was fun, but it was never going to get us entry to the sailing club across the lake, and my putative future as a racing sailor was dispatched, along with the acting, to that repository of activities which were Not Going to Happen.

***

I'm brought out of my little daydream and dragged away from the shores of Lake Ullswater by Graham suggesting we continue our tour and take the tram up to the pit head where we will find the winding gear, the pit yard and the original miners' cottages which are said to recreate the daily living conditions of the miners in the year 1913.

We catch one of the old buses up to the wide sprawling yard, black rutted and stony on the ground, surrounded by corrugated iron and brick buildings for gear, boiler-houses and offices. Across the yard is the pit head where the spoked winding wheel sits over the machinery, the cage, and the shaft down to the depths below. I'm particularly interested in the pit head and the winding gear because my grandfather Harry operated gear like this, electrified by his time I imagine, but similar in most other respects.

We have to clamber up and around a few gangways and corridors, but eventually we find ourselves in a high-up cabin where a large wooden throne sits next to a huge lever. Before it is a mass of cogwheels, gears, ropes and chains which descend through a hole in the floor to the depths below. The lever, I assume, is for the windingman to operate the cage, up or down. Harry, in his oily overall, would have sat in that seat, his hand on the lever. He truly did have the lives of men literally in his hands.

Harry, or Grandad Ritchie as we called him, operated his lever in the Betty Ann pit underneath the Angel of the North which I visited only a few days ago. Harry was a very laid back man. Nothing ever seemed to worry him or draw him to discontent. But as I try to imagine him in his wooden throne with a firm hand on the lever, all I can see is his toothless smile, gaunt and shaking in a hospital bed, the last time I saw him before the burden of multiple sclerosis prevailed.

I was actually 17 when he died, but in my memory I was standing at that bedside as a small child, confused and unable to understand what was happening to him. Death, and in Harry's case the slow but unrelenting decline towards it, may be an inescapable part of life, but the truth, the whole truth, and nothing but the truth are difficult things to absorb for a small boy with no experience of mortality. I did find that hard.

But then, the visits we made with mother to the Hunters Moor Hospital in Newcastle were for my grandfather, not for me. A cream iron bed, Harry in striped pyjamas holding out a bony, trembling hand from below white sheets, a smile appearing on his thin lips as we approached down the ward of 20 men, my mother, Little John and I. If that was a comfort to him, then I'm glad that I was there.

***

Graham and I stroll across the colliery yard to where a short row of miners' cottages has been reconstructed. They don't seem anything like the back to back terraced housing I have seen elsewhere, in Grange Villa, Flint Hill, and the many places like them. All but one of the cottages is only a single storey with small dormer windows in the roofs, looking altogether more rural than I had expected, and surprisingly picturesque. They have long front gardens planted with vegetables, even some wood frame greenhouses and the brickwork is clean, sand coloured stone. Consulting my brochure I am told they were moved here from Hetton-le-Hole about 15 miles east of here past Chester-le-Street, Lumley and well over the A1M. They had been built originally in the 1860s by the Hetton Coal Company which operated a truly massive colliery and brickworks complex next to the village. Three of the little row have been set up now to accommodate a Methodist family, an Irish family, and a miner's widow. An eclectic mix, if nothing else.

Entry to the cottages is round the back, where the little stone yards accommodate, in each case, a coal shed and an outside toilet. Graham and I peer cautiously round the loosely fitting door of one of them where there is a wooden box with a toilet seat on top. The box, apparently, is emptied at infrequent intervals by a man whose job description is likely to be quite self-explanatory.

There are slates hung on the back doors of the yards on which have been chalked times – 5.30 a.m., 6.30 a.m. and so on. These are the times the knocker-upper would arouse the occupants for work, a man whose employment was unlikely to elicit a warm, friendly morning greeting.

We move slowly from one cottage to the next. In each there is a blazing fire in the grate. Each has a cooking range, but the Methodists' is better. In each there are two ladies who do not come out of role. At least, I hope they don't for there is much disparaging banter about those next door. The Methodists don't like the Irish, and the Irish can't stand the Methodists. They both resent the widow who has only retained her right to the house because she has a young son down the pit. As Graham and I stand gazing about the rooms, they get on with the work of cleaning the range, sewing and bickering, as if we weren't there at all. I wonder what they do when there are no visitors, between one Act and the next.

In all of the cottages the downstairs room is larger than I expected. It is warmer than I expected too, with a strong smell of coal smoke. There are beds everywhere, in the front room, in the back room, and some pieces of furniture convert, like a modern sofa bed, into more sleeping places. In the Methodists' house which is the only one with an upstairs, a large room has no less than four beds in it, necessary for a compliment of nine children. In the Irish house there is no upstairs, but a ladder leads to a loft where we are told there is straw for sleeping on. The work of mining goes on all hours so there are always members of the family out at the pit. Even with all the sleeping places there would not be enough beds for everyone at the same time. It's all operated as a rota, one in one out, like the tin bath tub apparently.

I'm still looking out for Albert, or any old relative come to that, as we wander about this place, keeping an eye out in case one should be standing quietly observing us. But if they are here they are keeping out of sight, not yet ready to take the stage.

***

Leaving the cottages and their players, Graham and I wander over to a small cluster of buildings where the mine is located. It is actually a real mine, by which I mean that it is not a recreation mocked up for the benefit of tourists. The Mahogany Drift Mine was opened up in about 1855 and produced coal here for decades until the mid-20th century. The museum has been built around it.

A drift mine, which this is, is a tunnel cut into rising land where the coal seam is fairly near the surface. Unlike a pit, there is no shaft and in theory you just walk into it, which is what we are now proposing to do.

There are two adults and a half a dozen children gathered around the dark archway which is the grimy brick entrance to the mine. They are all wearing hard hats and listening to an older man, our guide who turns out to be called Eric. Graham and I grab a hat from a huge bin of them, as a Notice tells us we must, and join this little group.

I can't tell if Eric is dressed up in authentic miner's costume or not, especially as he seems to be wearing a cloth cap and not a hard hat. He is one of the very few staff who are not in role, presumably because he has an important safety function here, and also because he is dishing out all manner of facts and information for the benefit of me, Graham, and the little group of children who are listening with commendable silent interest. And he does so with admirable enthusiasm, as if he hasn't given the same speech a hundred times a week. It's very refreshing, actually.

And it's very informative as Eric offers some interesting facts. For one thing, he tells us that the miners were actually very well paid, about twice the wage of an agricultural worker. They also had free housing and free coal. This surprises me, as like many people I'm sure, I had thought the miners rather exploited and poorly paid for their disagreeable labour, but this, so he tells us, was not at all the case.

Secondly, and again I am surprised by this, but only because I hadn't given it any thought, the mining companies preferred to employ Wesleyan Methodists. They didn't drink, and could be relied upon to turn up on a Monday morning. All the Chapels serving even the smallest hamlet now make sense.

We set off down the tunnel at a shuffle rather than a walk, ducking down through the entrance arch, hunched over as it's impossible to stand up straight, apart from the children who have an obvious advantage. I'm reminded that children would have been common down here in the 19th century. The tunnel descends at a slight incline. I'm careful not to catch a foot in the rails. It's very dim in spite of the lights strung out at intervals along the wall. I notice an electric cable. Once or twice my helmet catches the roof with a sharp knock, and I'm grateful it's not my head.

I'm sure it's all very safe. There are parties of children down here after all. I tell myself I have to trust this implicitly, that they couldn't possibly allow this to be even remotely dangerous. If there is anywhere that Health and Safety would be top of the list of things to get right, it has to be here. But quite honestly, I am distinctly unnerved, crouched over, shuffling along. I wonder if the miners felt the same apprehension that I do, or did they get used to it? Did they make nervous jokes about it, or was the danger just too real, too present? I imagine an acceptance, a common submission, unspoken but silently acknowledged between them.

I try to keep all this to myself in the presence of the six years olds who seem perfectly at ease.

We stop for a few minutes at an elbow in the tunnel where a small coal wagon has been set, and Eric explains how difficult it was for the miners to crouch here while shovelling coal into the wagon. I can understand it as it's quite uncomfortable just standing there, half doubled, and I find myself wishing he would get on with it, just so that I could move. I feel the slight draught of ventilation.

We edge another fifty yards or so down the tunnel, past wooden props and supports. I look for the signs of some modern steel but I don't see any. There is water dripping from the roof, and a gravelly stream tinkles at our feet. I don't think this is a special effect. The light here is even dimmer, the smell of coal stronger.

At the end, the tunnel widens horizontally at the coal face, although the roof doesn't get any higher and we are still stooping. Eric has a little seat set up, for him but no one else, and he sits down, back against a pit prop, to give us some information about what went on here.

He demonstrates how a miner would have to lie down on his side and hack away at the coal face with a pick loosening off lumps of coal and stone. Still half lying he then had to shovel it into a small wagon sitting on the rails only a yard away. Sometimes, the seam may be only 18 inches deep and he offers a piece of wood to the ground to demonstrate how low that is.

When the tub had been filled, the coal hewer would place a marker on it, identifying it as his own, and it would then be hauled to the surface where it would be checked and sorted. He would earn six pence a tub Eric tells us, with fines for any stones. He would expect to fill 20 tubs in a shift.

"And what do you do if you need the toilet?" Eric addresses the children, which feels as if he might be trying to introduce some levity to this uncomfortable place, but he's quite serious. "You do it on your shovel, and put it in the coal tub," he tells them. The sorters above ground were on the constant lookout for unpleasant surprises in the tubs, which produces some nervous giggles from the children.

"And they didn't have electricity down here in those days," says Eric again principally addressing the children, and by a switch on the wall turns off the electric lights. The tunnel is immediately plunged into an even dimmer, yellow glow, and there are one or two little gasps from the children. It's hard to see. I can't begin to imagine trying to work down here. Claustrophobia, unable to stand up straight, the sense of being trapped is intense and very uncomfortable. The thought of the immense weight of earth and stone pressing down on the tunnel is frightening.

Imagining the rumble and clatter of tons of falling rock and stone, plunged into complete darkness, the shouts and screams of injured men, the utter helplessness is terrifying. I actually feel slightly breathless, and however much I remind myself that I am just on a tour, in a museum, the feeling of vulnerability will not go away.

We've been in the mine maybe 20 minutes, and I'm glad to stand straight. I ask Eric why he is not wearing a hard hat. He taps the top of his cloth cap with a knuckle and produces the sharp tap of bone on the plastic protection concealed beneath the material. It also occurs to me, in passing, that in all the time we have been underground, the little gaggle of children has uttered not one single word. Were they scared? I don't think so. I think they regarded it with the wonderment they would a rearing Tyrannosaurus Rex in the science museum. Fascinated, captivated perhaps, but not scared. I had their innocence once, now I'm just old and cynical and get frightened in museums.

I've received a hearty dose of truth and reality down this mine. I haven't read how Catherine Cookson translated her experiences of the pit into words, but writing these experiences is a serious challenge. All that I have read, all the evocative realism I've seen conjured into text, even candid photography and film did not prepare me for the reality of what I found down there in the tunnel. I find it's impossible to put into words what I actually felt, what was endured by the hundreds, the thousands, of men and boys every day of their lives.

***

By now the day is quite advanced, and we have seen a great deal of this place. But it crosses my mind that the Beamish authorities might be applying 1913 licensing laws, and I'm anxious that we don't miss the lunchtime permitted hours, should they be adopted here in some misguided approach to authenticity.

I have no idea to what extent Graham's life is orientated towards beer, or indeed if his calling imposes any restriction or influence in the matter, so as we stand outside the entrance to the mine straightening our backs and flexing our knees, I tentatively enquire whether he is a man who enjoys a beer from time to time. Graham's cautious response, "*I have been known to*", is code among beer drinkers, and means "*Yes, I could murder a pint*".

"Pub?" I suggest.

"Pub," he responds, and thus we clamber onto the bus, conveniently waiting across the road, and head off to The Sun on the main street.

***

Like the mine, The Sun Inn is also real, moved here from Bishop Auckland, brick by numbered brick, together with its original fixtures and fittings. It's very wooden, from the rough plank floor to the bar and the pew-like seating. The windows are part frosted and engraved with lettering announcing billiards, sitting room, family room, buffet and other such enticements, which I do find peculiar as the whole pub consists of just one room. It's daytime, but gas lamps flicker on the walls.

I have an ambitious expectation that the price of our pints may also reflect the museum's unrelenting pursuit of authenticity, but I know in my heart of hearts this is unlikely to be the case. I am proved right when I'm relieved of the very modern cost of a couple of beers. But still, it's a very amiable place to be, and actually not so different to some existing pubs I've been in on my travels.

I accept that if you look closely you will notice there is no electric light, there are no Fosters or Birra Moretti pumps on the bar, and the barman is dressed a bit like a butcher. But those details apart, it's hard to tell that this is a pub from more than 100 years ago. The Sun would not really be out of place in the ruder parts of any old town. Except, that is, in one very important and surprising regard.

As I said, the day is quite advanced and as I collect our pints of Miner's Finger or whatever it is, I ask the bar person, as you do, if he could point me in the direction of the facilities. I detect just the slightest elevation of one of his eyebrows. "Customers," he says in a Geordie that I suspect is genuine, "usually just go out the back."

"Out the back?" I respond, just to be clear.

"Yes, Sir. Out the back." There is a moment while we stand and simply regard each other, the barman with a totally blank face. If he's acting, as I imagine he is, he's bloody good at it. With near imperceptible resignation he continues, "Or for those requiring a more," he pauses with perfect stage timing, "discreet experience, the tram station down the street offers public conveniences."

Which it does, in a welcome 21st century, stainless steel, flushing way, even if they are nearly 200 yards away. On my return I tell Graham that he holds a unique position in my bank of lifetime experiences, in that he is the only person, indeed the only Reverend, I have ever drunk beer with in a pub without a toilet, a fact he receives with rather less rapturous interest than I had expected.

The pints are, even at today's prices, very good indeed. Graham and I are seated on a wooden pew at a pine table underneath the frosted window, and we pass a pleasant hour discussing the Lake District, my ancestral research and an eclectic mix of worldly and less worldly subjects. At some point Graham declared the beer worthy of further appraisal, and the time passed by most agreeably.

And then, after a precautionary visit to the facilities at the bus station, we take a tram back to the reception building. It is rare to encounter, quite out of the blue, another soul with whom one has such a natural affiliation as I have had with Graham. If I had not delayed in the car park to change my boots, if he had not dallied for a coffee on the way in, as he tells me he did, we would not have met. That we pass such thought between us is, in itself, enough to tell me that the feeling is mutual. I have a thought that when my time comes, when a Higher Authority calls my name, I would be very pleased to have Graham "*do my funeral*".

We part with a firm handshake, an exchange of email addresses, and a mutual declaration that meeting up has enhanced the day for both of us. If there were to come a time when I have the opportunity to take a pint or two with the Reverend Graham again, I shall embrace it gladly.

***

Although it's by now late afternoon, I'm in no hurry as the Black Horse is just down the road, so I have a nose around the expansive gift shop where you can buy anything from a replica miner's shovel to a jar of genuine Beamish chutney, whatever that might be. I settle on the chutney and a small woolly sheep for my wife as she collects them, which I'm not going to go into now, and a rather fetching poster of Tynemouth from the 1920s when the rail companies sought to attract visitors to such resorts. What that has to do with Beamish and coal mines I have absolutely no idea, but it very well illustrates the history of Tynemouth in that era. It even shows the Lido in its heyday, the Plaza pre-demolition, and looking closely, pretty much the house we lived in in the background.

Back in the now deserted car park and having changed out of my boots into some comfortable shoes, I sit for a while in the car. This is, without doubt, an exceptional place. Well put together and informative as they are, the brochure and indeed the website do not do it full justice. I was ill-prepared for how authentic it is, how disconcerting it is to have the staff so continuously in role, and what a marvellous vision Frank Atkinson had to bring all this here and preserve it for generations to come. Perhaps its wonder is best appreciated by not being prepared for it.

Through the windscreen in the silence of the empty car park around me the sun is going down over the western horizon in red and yellow. I have travelled around this county and I have seen where the pits and mines used to be. I have seen the green fields, the hedgerows and the grazing cattle which have replaced them. And I will do so again tomorrow, and again I will marvel at the total, uncompromising reinstatement of the countryside, and the time, effort and money which has been expended to achieve it.

Yet here, it's been rebuilt. It's as if all the industry, the fabric and the very way of life has been scooped up, given a wash, and set down for anyone with 20 quid to come and look round. Which it has, and of course it's a museum, and that's what it's here for. We do this sort of thing all over the place. Railway museums, Saxon villages, Roman forts are all reproduced here and there with varying degrees of authenticity. It's all entirely commendable, and far better we have these things than we don't.

But although I have wandered around here today in Graham's genial company, have been genuinely impressed at the way it's all been assembled and how it's managed, and I have really felt what it might have been like to crouch in a narrow coal seam, I haven't had the sense of George's presence, or Arthur's, or Albert's. Even though the street, the shops, the little cottages are all as they would have been pretty much down to the last detail, it somehow hasn't seemed real.

Throughout this journey I have genuinely looked for them. I did have a real sense of connection when I met Albert in Grange Villa, and Arthur in his schoolhouse. But they have been absent here. I feel disappointed. For all the attention to detail, for all the deserved commendations and accolades, for all the actors and their genuinely impressive performances, there are no people, no spirits, no diaphanous wafts. The past has been well represented, but it has not, as advertised, been brought to life.

I could wander this place until the cows come home and I won't meet a genetic memory. I shouldn't have expected it, really. It is, after all, only a film set. Just a very good one

THIRTEEN

Esh, Cornsay Colliery

The Black Horse is part of a former enclave of 10 cottages, known as Red Row after their red tiled roofs. It was built in the mid-1700s on the estate of Bobby Shafto, MP for County Durham between 1760 and 1768. The largest of the cottages forms the main building of the hotel, now vastly extended at the rear with conservatories and suchlike. Some of the original buildings have been demolished, but several remaining have been converted into bedroom accommodation, and some new ones built in the same style and in keeping with the originals. The property became a pub in about 1850, although it is said to have been an illegal drinking and gambling den for many years before that.

Red Row is located very remotely, deep in the Durham countryside about 4 miles equidistant from Stanley and Beamish. Tanfield, where Uncle Arthur is buried, is about a mile away. It's a long, narrow winding country lane to reach it from Beamish Museum, but eventually I turn off the lane between the hedgerows and onto a wide driveway at the end of which is set the attractive, light stone façade of the pub, a small porch with a pitched slate roof offering a welcome for guests.

I have to check in at the bar, which gives me an opportunity to assess the place. A hearty roaring log fire, big flagstones, assorted heavy pine and oak tables, subtle amber lighting and a long bar with stools are very welcome sights, and after a few steps across the driveway to my boutique room, a shower and a freshen up, I'm back and ready to see what the Black Horse has to offer by way of reviving the weary traveller.

***

The sun has long gone down by the time I find myself in the warm bar, a few customers already sitting and standing around chatting. The barman in black tie busies himself pouring and wiping. Once I have recovered from a disarming encounter with an Oriental gentleman speaking effortless, natural Geordie, I have a pint before me and the expectation of a most agreeable evening.

Apart from interesting information about the history of Red Row and the motley assortment of characters who seem to have occupied it over the years, and some stuff about Bonny Bobby Shafto and his wavering political allegiances, the hotel brochure which I'm leafing through tells me about its ghost. Apparently, George Ridley who worked down a mine and was an occupant of the property together with his family of 9 children, went missing in 1803 and was never found. No one knows what happened to him, but I suspect that a family of 9 children and a job down the pit might have had something to do with it. He turned up some years later looking somewhat diaphanous, and has been spotted on numerous occasions since, rattling about the corridors of the pub. According to some reports, he has been known to smash glasses, leave muddy footprints and slam doors, but I imagine that these events probably happened shortly after closing time and the informants might be less than wholly reliable.

Nevertheless, and although one has to take these things seriously, George Ridley is not to my knowledge an ancestor of mine, and his is not the ghost I'm looking for.

Geordie speaking Chinamen and tales of ghosts are nothing on the spectrum of surprise compared to the short discourse which wafts across the room to me from the table a few yards away. Two middle-aged gentlemen sitting very close, almost head to head and deep in talk, have attracted my undivided attention with the words "*Newcastle Bank*", and "*Johnsons*". It could hardly have been more arresting if they had added "*Grandma Elliott*" to the conversation.

I'm getting used to imposing on total strangers by now, and Bob and Tony receive my interruption kindly. Tony turns out to be profoundly deaf, but nevertheless I'm able to determine that the garage, the garage my mother was born in, was where Bob had his cars serviced and mended for many years. And not for the first time, I find myself hoping that the subject of Ben Aunger doesn't come up, and I'm relieved when it doesn't.

They are an interesting couple, Bob in a patterned golf sweater, light beige slacks, jovial, chatty, constantly pushing his gold rimmed spectacles back up his nose. Tony, almost identically dressed, intently listening, leaning forward, head cocked slightly to one side. They are two, late middle-aged men who could be old established friends enjoying their regular pint, or a couple who have been quietly living together for years and whose relationship can now enjoy the freedom modern society has brought to their affection for each other. Who knows?

And who cares? The conversation is easy and amiable, but although I am yet again surprised to find a memory of Aunger's in a complete stranger, they would have to be at least 85 years old to have any chance of remembering my mother, so I enjoyed a pleasant pint in their company, during which time Bob told me lots about Chester-le-Street and his memories of this and that.

Tomorrow I have plans to get back on the road and travel some 15 miles south of here to visit Esh Winning where Thomas and Francis Ritchie, Harry's parents, lived in 1901, and then to Cornsay which was built around a massive colliery and brickworks and where lived William Bates, my father's great-grandfather on his mother's side, also in 1901. According to my researches, both of their houses are still standing, which is an excellent opportunity for pursuing my quest for genetic memories, I would have thought. So I forsake the brandy in case its repercussions keep me awake, and retire to my comfortable, boutique room.

***

Next morning I have to make a decision, for breakfast is Not Included. The dilemma is always between the temptation of loading up with the Full Works again, or shelling out a silly 15 quid for an orange juice and a piece of toast, which after the Lambton Worm's excessive breakfast platefuls is all I really want. So I settle for just a coffee, which is also silly because I could have had that in my room for free, but I harboured the idea that I might get something more appealing than a thin tube of Nescafe and a plastic tub of heat treated milk. I simply don't understand hotels, especially decent ones like this, and why they cannot offer anything more than a dreadful, thin, bitter filter coffee at breakfast time. It's been sitting on the hotplate since the staff opened up at 6 a.m., and tastes like dissolved coal. It's even more perplexing when there is a perfectly good Italian machine that probably cost as much as my car just sitting idle behind the bar. The suggestions box, should there be one, is destined for a stern note on the subject.

***

The expansive blue skies and sunshine of yesterday have given way to a rather dull, overcast day, but at least it's not raining. My drive takes me through the pretty, light stone buildings of Lanchester, a place known as much for its Roman heritage as its coal mining. We're as far south as Durham city here but well west of it, and the rolling countryside is dotted with short lines of isolated terraced houses, popping up in the middle of nowhere and which served, no doubt, some small industry of long ago.

Esh Winning was founded as recently as 1850 to serve a mine on the Esh Estate. "*Esh*" is an Old Saxon word for Ash, and "*Winning*" was appended by the Victorians to describe a place where coal was to be found and "*won*" by labour and industry. Here was the huge Waterhouses colliery, a brickworks, the line of the waggonway which carried coal, freight and passengers, and even a station, although of course I don't expect to find any of that today. What I do expect to find is the home of my great-grandparents at 11, Station Avenue.

Esh Winning is another drab, shabby place, not old enough to be worthy of salvation, not young enough to have any feeling of freshness. The road into the town passes grey rendered convenience stores and steel roller blinds on closed shop fronts. There is hardly anyone about and I would not have been surprised to see a ball of tumbleweed rolling across the road. At what passes as the centre, it widens as if it had been intended to install a roundabout but it was forgotten or the plans abandoned. There is a modern Co-op store, an oily looking garage, and a large unwelcoming pub, The Stag's Head. Four roads spoke away, one of which is Station Avenue.

There's nothing "*Avenue*" about it. On one side there is a short row of 11 terrace houses, and on the other behind a grey steel fence the oily storage yard of the garage full of tyres and old cars. At the end where there used to be the station and the rail line there is now just a muddy strip of land, a wooden fence, and the green of shrubs, bushes and trees. A grey winter woodland covers rising land to the distance. I park the car near the pub, and take a stroll down the road.

The short line of terraces is of an obviously better quality than most I've seen in the mining villages of Durham. The houses are bigger, the windows and doors have solid stone lintels and the brickwork has decorative detail under the roof line. Number 11 is at the end, only the pitched gable of a small adjoining cottage separating the house from where the station and the railway line would have been.

Thomas Ritchie lived here in 1901. He is described then as a colliery joiner, which the Durham Mining Museum tells us means "*general joinery work in shops*", so we can guess that he did not work underground. He would have been qualified by apprenticeship, training or experience, and would have worked on repairing and rebuilding railway wagons, and "*making woodwork for all kinds of building structures*". As a skilled worker he would have been entitled to the rather better quality of housing we see here in Station Avenue.

Thomas lived here with his wife Frances and their 3 sons, Harry's older brothers, then aged 6, 2 and 1. Harry was born 7 years later at nearby Lanchester. Frances was Uncle Arthur Hinckley's sister and her line takes us back to the north east coast of Northumberland where I shall be visiting on the next stage of this journey.

It's very quiet in Station Avenue. Hardly a car passes on the main road behind me where the roundabout ought to be. A few souls wander in and out of the Co-op store, but the pub looks closed. I pull my coat a little tighter around me in the cold, damp air, and try to imagine Thomas, Frances and their family here nearly 120 years ago.

But the images don't come easily. I had hoped for more of a sense of the past here, but it seems to be eluding me. The Ritchie family would have come and gone from that front door, Thomas in his work clothes to walk down to the colliery, Frances and the children off to school or the shop, neighbours calling in. People would have been up and down this street to and from the station. I can imagine their period clothes, dark colours, long skirts, bonnets and hats, wing collar shirts and stout boots. I can hear their northern accents and their conversations. I even try to call up images from Beamish to overlay this place with some sense of the period. But even with all that in my mind I still can't see them. It feels a bit of a failure after hoping this might be a place where memories would readily arise, and having come all this way in the hope of discovering them. Oh well, maybe next time. I turn with a sigh and walk down towards the old waggonway and the station from which the Avenue takes its name.

***

Just past the end cottage there is a muddy patch which looks as if a herd of cows has been trampling around, and I wish I had put my boots on as my shoes squelch and suck in it. Over that there is a walkers' gate in a wooden fence where a sign tells me that this is the Deerness Valley Walkway, and the site of the Deerness Valley Railway which led to the Waterhouses Colliery a few hundred yards to the west.

The walkway is now a well maintained, metalled path which curves gently away from me in both directions through bordering trees and bushes. Beyond the path a tussocky field gives way to the grey woodland which rises to the horizon. There was a station here, somewhere.

A short, elderly gentleman in a coat and cap approaches down the path. He has with him a small, shorthaired brown and white dog with a pointy nose and thin tail, which darts from one side of the path to the other. A ratter I expect, the sort that is often favoured by large, muscled men. As they draw close the old man stops and the dog wanders off into the undergrowth to sniff around some other animal's business.

"Morning", says the old man. I'm just about to offer a cordial response, but in that instant as I turn to face him I am caught off guard and hesitate, probably for just an instant too long.

There's a thing in psychology called The High Place Phenomenon. When confronted with a high up place like a bridge, or a cliff, sufferers like me have an irrational but profound anxiety that they are going to throw themselves off. It's not vertigo, or a fear of heights, and it's certainly not connected with suicidal thoughts. You know perfectly well that you are not going to do it, but nevertheless the fear that you will, or might, or could, is overwhelming. A footbridge over a road, for example, causes me great distress, seized with the thought that I might just clamber over the railings and jump. In short, it is an anxiety that you will be unable to control yourself from doing something horribly self-destructive.

Which is what grips me now with the terrible fear that I am going to blurt out, "Oh my God, what happened to your nose?"

For the poor man doesn't have one. Whether by defect of birth, disease, or just a terrible shaving accident I don't know, but in the place a nose ought to be is just a small, upturned, nodule. And I know, in that instant, the one thing I must not do is stare at it, or talk about it. Yet I am, by reason of The Phenomenon, petrified that I might.

"Morning", I manage, and instantly find myself in the grip of that other Worst Thing to be faced with in this situation, which might also be a thing in psychology and should be if it isn't, which is the I'm Really Not Looking At Your Breasts Syndrome, a condition encountered when finding yourself unexpectedly in conversation with a woman displaying an exceptionally large chest. It's usually someone you have never met before, at a conference or a dinner party. You must not, under any circumstances, stare at them. The effort of not staring at them is overwhelming.

You ought to be able to open the conversation with something along the lines of "Good Lord, you have the most tremendous bosom," to which she would respond "Well thank you, that's very kind," and then the conversation could continue without the ridiculous charade that you hadn't noticed them.

So I'm struggling here. I'm frightened I'm going to mention it, and I'm frightened he will think I'm looking at it.

I manage to tell him about my great-grandfather and that he lived just over there in number 11, and that I've come all this way from down south to look for memories and all that sort of thing. "Wasn't there a station here?" I ask him.

"Aye, you're standing on it. Station Master's house right over there." He points at a pile of logs. "Line came right through here past them houses and down to the colliery," which sets him off on a description of the railway, the trains, the colliery and everything. In order to show interest in his recollections, which I genuinely have, I try not to be rude by looking slightly over his shoulder, and occasionally feigning interest in my shoe.

He speaks with a disarmingly normal voice, given that you would expect it to have, at the least, a nasal inflection. "Do you remember it all being here?" I ask him.

"Remember it? Why Aye," which sets him off again. He doesn't seem to be at all bothered by it. The ridiculous idea briefly crosses my mind that he may not even know about it, since he can't see it himself and perhaps he has a deep mistrust of mirrors. Or perhaps like the lady with the bosoms, rather than cover it up it's as well to show it off. Deal with it, is what it says, which I think would be quite admirable.

The dog returns and snuffles at his feet. I have the completely uncalled for thought that here is a dog which could fart with impunity.

"And down there," he says, waving his arm down the track in direction of Waterhouses, "was the colliery. Massive great place, all noise and smoke," and I hope he isn't going to tell me what a smell it made. "And there was always a terrible smell in the air," testing my presence of mind to its limit.

***

The old man sauntered off up the path, his little dog trotting behind, occasionally stopping briefly to sniff at something or check for rats. I'm left with the disappointment of not having been able to give his recollections my full attention, distracted as I was, because he was genuinely knowledgeable and had seen it all with his own eyes. And I do feel sorry for him, as you would for someone with that sort of disfigurement, but I honestly think I don't need to. I think he'd come to terms with it long ago. Good for him. And I have the slightly uncomfortable feeling that it is me who has the problem, not him.

I squelch back through the mud and take a last look at number 11 as I walk back up the road to the car, but it's as empty as it was half an hour ago. The Stag's Head looks vaguely as if it might be open now, not in any inviting or appealing way but open nevertheless, and with the thought of giving Thomas Ritchie another opportunity to make himself known, I decide to go in and see.

The large bar is quiet and totally empty except for a man leaning on the counter reading a newspaper. He seems quite surprised to see me and unsure what to do about it, even though he turns out to be the landlord. When I ask about a coffee he apologises that he can't do a proper one because the till isn't set up to take payment for coffee yet, but he says he'll make me one out the back, which seems both odd and decent of him all at the same time.

While he's away I wait at the bar and gaze around at the awful patterned carpet, the fruit machines, and the big sports screens even now flickering with American league basketball. A pool table with a tear in the cloth and brown stains on the blue baize sits on bare floorboards in a charmless side room. If this place has an atmosphere, it's taken the day off.

A minute or two later the landlord returns with a blue builder's mug of something that tastes little better than the stuff the Black Horse passed off on me this morning. He can't take payment for it on account of the till not understanding what coffee is, so at least it's free.

He's come up here from down south, retired from the Metropolitan Police, so he tells me, and has only been here 3 weeks. That's another one from the Met., thinking of Malcolm from the Chester-le-Street Heritage Group. Perhaps when London coppers retire they have some uncontrollable urge to head north and get as far away as possible. Anyway, he has taken this on as a personal project to revive and reinstate to some sort of former glory, but deep down I'm not sure it ever had one. I'm about to ask him when he will get to start work on it when he tells me that he's pleased with the way it's shaping up.

He's actually a very engaging man, and as he doesn't have any customers or anything much else to do, he tells me how this place has had a bad reputation for trouble, drunkenness and drugs, which privately doesn't surprise me. He's determined to change all that and make it more family friendly. I offer him good luck with that. Esh Winning probably doesn't have the sort of family he's got in mind.

I haven't had much luck on my search for memories here in Esh Winning. Number 11, interesting as it was to see the old house, didn't offer up much in that way. And this pub, with its fruit machines and sports screens, pool table and lager pumps, is about as reminiscent of my great-grandfather's life here as the modern Co-op store across the street. It feels as if the mining community, when they left this place, took away with them all its soul.

I feel a bit sorry for the new landlord. He seems like a good bloke and he has worthy ambitions for this place. It can't be very agreeable taking on a run down, disreputable pub in a place as depressing as this. I hope he hasn't misjudged it and taken on something beyond his enthusiasm and expectations. As I bid my farewell and head out the door I find I'm wishing him good luck and hoping it all goes well for him, and actually meaning it.

***

It says much for the county's landscape that so many places actually have "*colliery*" as part of their name. There's Cornsay Colliery where I'm headed now, and not far away you can find Boldon Colliery, Shotton Colliery, Hamsterley Colliery, Easington Colliery, Trimdon Colliery and many others if you look hard enough.

The word "*colliery*" itself was only coined as recently as the 1630s, and most of the towns and villages which incorporate it in their name date only from the late 18th and early 19th centuries, so in historical terms it's all quite recent. Until the mid-17th century this was a land of agriculture by hand and horse, of estates and great swathes of woodland. The Protectorate of the Prince Bishops which gave Durham virtual self-rule as a barrier between the King's lands in the south and the unpleasantly rude Scots in the north and which was threatened by Henry VIII in the 16th century, was re-instated by Charles II in 1660 when Cromwell met his end. With the Merry Monarch came the Restoration and at about the same time England's appetite for coal emerged and grew, and the landscape began to change.

The Industrial Revolution in the UK is generally thought to have begun around 1760, which seems a bit specific to me but that seems to be the expert view. It was a gradual change at first. Drift mines cut haphazardly here and there, but the exponential advance of coal towards the end of the 18th century and into the early 19th created a landscape in which the actual names of towns and villages bore the identity of the industry. And so for a time it dominated. It dominated the view. It changed the skyline. It dominated lifestyles and the economy. It belched pollution and it made some men rich, and some poor. But really, in the scheme of things, it lasted for a short time. In the blink of an evolutionary eye, within 300 years it had served its time, served its purpose, and was gone, and then nature and the hand of man gave it a new shape, the shape we see today.

The shape of Cornsay Colliery now is just a single line of terrace houses, Commercial Street, which climbs a few hundred yards up a country hill. There's a pub at the bottom at the end of the houses where I now stop the car, and looking up the hill the terrace stretches up on the right hand side of the road. On the other side over a fence is a large field leading onto woodland.

In 1901 number 44 Commercial Street was the home of my great, great-grandparents William and Isabella Bates. William was my father's mother's grandfather, and in 1901 is described as a labourer in the mine. That simple description does not, in itself, tell us whether he worked above or below ground here in Cornsay, but he has been described in earlier records as a miner so he probably did spend some time below. He was, like many of his time and station, illiterate.

Walking up Commercial Street from the pub where I've left the car and with the terrace to my right, on my left over the fence in the fields were row upon row of more terraces with names like High Street, Chadwick Street, Liddel Street, Office Street and Stable Street, and the huge colliery and brickworks looming over them. This would have not been a quiet country road but the middle of a bustling town.

I don't know if Cornsay was the biggest, or just one of the biggest, works in the area, but it was certainly huge. To give some context to that, the following facts are taken from an 1894 paper published by Francis Whellan and Company. The mine was opened in 1868, and in 1894 produced 750 tons of coal a day, over a quarter of a million tons a year, all hewn by hand. It worked several seams, some accessed by drifts cut into the land and two shafts down to 35 fathoms – over 200 feet. The seams were narrow, hardly 2 - 4 feet in depth and often less. Much was converted into coke on site, with 270 coke ovens in operation. The colliery employed about 700 men and boys.

The mine also produced high quality fire clay which was used for manufacture of bricks, tiles and sanitary pipes. Bricks and pipes were fired in ovens on site. The scale of industry is hard to imagine.

Commercial Street is a pleasant looking row of houses now, well cared for and with obvious updating. I find number 44 about halfway up the hill. It's a small terrace, built of light coloured, beige brick. A small extension appears to have been recently added at the front, with a new front door and UPVC windows. A new front wall encloses a modest front garden. There is but one single window in the first floor. It doesn't seem to me as if there will be a great deal of room inside.

William and Isabella lived here with their 3 grown up children, William aged 27 also a mine labourer, Mary aged 23, and James, 21, an ironmonger's assistant. James had been born in Cornsay which tells us the family had probably lived here since at least 1880. They were still here in 1911, over 30 years at the same address when William is described as being retired. He died in 1917 of pneumoconiosis, the legacy of a lifetime in the pits.

Like Esh Winning it's very quiet. And like Esh, I'm finding it hard to evoke much of a sense of personal history here. The house, the geography, the whole environment offer nothing of the past. A young man in jeans and a tee shirt is washing a small car a few doors away, and I can see from its registration that it's hardly 5 years old. With a final look at the plastic front door of number 44, I stroll slowly back down the hill to see if the pub is open.

***

The door to the Royal Oak pushes open, but it's dim inside. Only by the glow of a light on the shelf of bottles behind the bar do I detect the burly figure of a man leaning over it from inside peering at some papers on the bar top. He's dressed so casually it looks as if he's just got out of bed which, as it turns out, he probably has. He looks up at me without so much as a word.

"Are you open?" I enquire, hopefully.

"No," he says, in a way that actually means who the hell are you? "Not till three o'clock." I feel like asking why the door was open then.

"Oh, sorry. I was just having a look round because I have family who used to live here. Miners. They lived up the road in 44."

The landlord straightens up behind the bar, disclosing his heavy torso, a grey singlet straining a bit at the front, strong arms and a fleshy face in its fifties. Beery I would say, if I was being uncharitable. "We get lots of people here looking for that sort of thing. Coachloads of them sometimes. And from all over the world, Canada, Australia usually." He has a strong northern accent, not Geordie but the softer, almost mellifluous, sound of Durham.

"Australia?"

"All over the place." He flicks a light switch on and I can see glasses on tables yet to be washed up. "There's a lot of mining history here and a lot of people who want to come and see it. Relatives and ancestors and that." He starts moving around with some effort and then ducks down behind the bar so I can see nothing of him except the back of his bent over bottom, which appears to be making an attempt to escape from his pants. "We've got a load of stuff about it here somewhere. Old photos and that." He pops back up again with a folder, full of clippings, articles and photographs. "Here, have a leaf through that."

I'm grateful he hasn't chucked me out and told me to come back at 3 o'clock when he's got out of his pyjamas, and he seems happy enough to let me stand at the bar with the papers while he shuffles about with a cloth, wiping things. He is wearing his slippers.

He talks as he potters about. There's an old lady who comes every year from somewhere abroad, Canada he thinks, to lay a wreath of flowers in the woodland where the colliery and brickworks used to be. He doesn't know why or the story behind it, but he thinks a relative was probably killed in the pit.

He's been here at the pub for many years and remembers it all before it was demolished. He waves a hand at the window towards the field and the woodland. "All over there were the houses, lines and lines of them." He tells me about the brickworks, the quality of the clay and the pipes which made high class ware for export.

He eventually gives up on the cleaning and joins me at the bar, leaning over and taking up some of the papers. He thumbs through them, now and again extracting a photograph and laying it aside on the bar. Pictures of the lines of houses, chimneys and rail tracks. In one, a Zeppelin floats above the roofs of the brickworks. He gazes at each of them and I notice his fascination even though he must have done this hundreds of times.

"Aye, it all happened here." There is a wistful note in his voice as he points beyond the bar and says the miners' pay office used to be here, in the back of the pub.

As I leaf through the old photos and clippings I glance out of the window into the green space beyond. It's not just the rows of houses, the chimneys and the winding wheels of the colliery that are missing, but the people. This place would have had movement. It would never have been still. The street would have been a throng of business, workers to and fro, carts, horses and wagons. And sound. There might have been the high pitched whistle of a train above the chatter of voices, shouts and the rattle of wheels on the road. There would have been the shouts and cries of children. The sounds of industry would be heard from the colliery and the brickworks, bangs and clatters, the screech of metal on metal, the hiss of steam, all heard above the clamour of the street.

The Landlord has gone off into the back of the pub, or gone back to bed, and I'm alone in the bar. I lean back with my elbows on the counter, gazing out of the window at the quiet, motionless landscape outside.

***

Across the road from the pub there is a gateway in the fence which leads to a track into the woodland, now known as Steeley Hill Woods, the name taken from the Steeley Hill Plantation that existed before coal came along. Now they've put it back again. It's one of a number of projects by which former colliery sites are transformed and returned to nature providing recreation walks and natural habitats. This one is part of Durham County Council's Woodland and Wildlife Project. It's approved as a Local Nature Reserve by English Nature and has received support from the Heritage Lottery fund, so it has a prestigious patronage.

I mention this because I have come across so many old mining sites which have been given back to nature. So many times in the past few days I have stood before a quiet field and wondered at the industry which claimed it not so long ago. And this one, here at Cornsay, is the last I shall visit before heading further north, so I think it fitting I should give it a little extra attention.

There is a heritage board next to the gate, which displays an old photograph of the works. It looks like something you would expect to see in a centre of industry like Birmingham or Manchester, so extensive are the buildings, chimneys and railway tracks and yards, overwhelming the surrounding landscape. There are also a couple of maps showing how the colliery and brickworks were laid out.

It's worth repeating what the heritage board tells us about this place:

"Looking at the woods ahead, would you think that there was once a brick works here? In the field to your right, workers and their families lived in terrace houses. The County Council and the local community have transformed the area into woodlands and fields, since the works closed down and was landscaped in the 1980's.
The Ferens and Love brick works and associated drift mines were worked over a 94 year period from 1868 to 1963. The bricks were used in the building of 2,000 homes in the west Durham coalfield. In Victorian times the bricks were used as ballast in the whaling ships and are found as far as the Falkland Islands. Later in its life it specialised in ceramic ware and pipes.
As you walk through the woods, you will find clues to its previous use. If you follow the 'yellow brick road' you will enter the woods and find the lines of the rail sidings, bricks and coke ovens in the woods"

Finally there is a rather fetching photo of an old lady with a spade planting one of the first saplings. Doris Harrison, the legend on the sign tells us, lived all her life here in Cornsay, and had family working in the brickworks. Her words at the time are recorded on the board.

"Having lived and worked all my life in the village, it is a wonderful feeling........The works used to scare away the birds, but they enjoy coming here now, and I love watching them".

The birds have returned. Buildings can be demolished, and trees can be planted, but birds won't return unless they want to. I wonder where they've been, perhaps waiting offstage somewhere for these times to come. Perhaps they knew. Nature has a wisdom of its own.

I have no idea where "*Yellow Brick Road*" comes from. I can't for a moment imagine that Elton John had anything to do with it, or The Wizard of Oz come to that, and as a track into a smoke-belching brickworks it hardly seems to accord with the Oxford Dictionary's explanation that it "*suggests a course of action expected to lead to good things*". And it's not yellow anyway, so we'll leave that aside as I push through the gate onto what is, in fact, a red brick roadway leading to the beginning of the woodland only 100 yards or so away.

The brick is broken and uneven underfoot with wisps and clumps of grass growing through it. Approaching the trees the brick road narrows to a path and gives way to a black, hard, gritty surface of clinker, or crunched coal or coke, packed down by the passage of feet. Soon I am beneath a canopy of trees, silent and slightly misty in the damp of the afternoon. There is no one else around. It is very still. I am quite alone.

I don't know how far the path wanders through the trees, but from the map and the extent of the old works I guess at about 300 yards. The trees are a mix of conifer and natural species. I can identify Ash and Oak, all closely packed, tangled undergrowth at their feet.

It's totally silent, apart from the occasional "*chuck chuck*" of a bird somewhere. Drips fall lightly from the canopy. There is no wind at all. If I didn't know better, I would say that I am standing in an ancient, natural woodland. There is nothing to give away its past.

There are no clues that I can see, as the heritage board told me there would be. There is no evidence of rail lines, or bricks or coke ovens. It's perplexing, and I'm determined to find something. Perhaps beneath the tangled undergrowth of brambles lies the proof, and so I step cautiously off the path. It's tricky going, ducking under and pushing aside the branches that bar my way, stepping carefully through the clawing, thorny brambles.

I even stamp around a bit, as best I can, in case my foot comes across something hidden and which will provide the clue, the evidence I would so much like to see. But there's nothing. Not so much as a solitary brick.

Resolved to dispatch a note to the heritage people with the suggestion that they get their facts right, I head back to the path. I take great care in the clutching undergrowth, stepping cautiously, keeping my knees up like John Cleese on a silly walk. But they say that woodland like this is a living entity with a mind of its own, which is obviously true because it was waiting for me. I had almost reached the safety of the path when one of the creepers, which I must have angered by stepping on it or something on the way in, got hold of my foot and held it firmly as I slowly went down like a felled tree. It took about 10 minutes, or seemed to, as I collapsed to the ground in slow motion with absolutely nothing I could do to prevent it. I had my hands in my pockets and couldn't get them out in time, so I went down nose first. My hat came off, my glasses and my phone flew off into the undergrowth, and how my shoe came off as well I have no idea.

It took me a moment or two, lying face down in the wet weeds, to be sure I hadn't done myself a serious injury, then to recover my hat, my phone and everything else that had been detached from me. Back on the path I patted everything down, decided there wasn't anything I could do about my wet sock, and wiped ineffectively at my coat, wet and muddy all down the front. It felt as if I had a blob of something on my nose too, but I didn't have a mirror so I took a selfie on my phone and looked at that, which disclosed a muddy streak but no blood.

After a moment two thoughts crossed my mind. The first was a feeling of enormous relief that there was no one about to witness my dyspraxic floundering in the woodland undergrowth, but secondly and far more important than that and even though I had noticed it before, just how utterly peaceful it was among these trees. I stood there on the path, my hands in my pockets and just gazed around. Drip, drip. Chuck chuck. It was wonderful.

***

The path meanders through the trees for another couple of hundred yards, when the woodland gives way to fields, and the path doubles back to take a route returning towards Cornsay by a chuckling stream, the Hedleyhope Burn.

The burn is quite a decent size for a stream, about 4 or 5 feet across and bubbling over rocks and stones, fallen logs and encroaching undergrowth. What surprises me about it is that it's milky and cloudy. I don't know if this is a consequence of some sort of seepage from what has been left below the surface, or whether it is some natural chalkiness in the ground, but it gives it a polluted, industrial feel, and actually doesn't look very nice at all.

As the path along the stream returns towards the road, there begins to form some obvious ground disturbance, some heave in the earth. Mounds now covered in creeper and lichen arise, and fallen branches and logs rest against humps and hollows that seem far from natural. The path weaves around all this, and consulting my old map this is exactly where the brick and coke ovens were situated. I have a nose about among these unnatural features, taking very considerable care of my footing. Some low brickwork can be seen underneath the blanket of green undergrowth, occasional loose bricks and one, but only one, large piece of glazed pipe. Evidence then, at last, of what was here. But that's all, and the silence still prevails.

***

Back at the car and while I get out of my wet coat and shoes and change my sock, I can see back over the road at the woodland I have just walked through, and I think to myself, that's it, that's Durham done. There are no more places to visit, at least not on this journey. It's back to the Black Horse now, a dinner and a pint or two, then it will be a long drive tomorrow up to the north east coast.

But of course, it's not going to let go that easily. I find myself, not for the first time, lingering a moment at the wheel before I press the starter. I feel rather sad that this stage of my journey is almost over. I think over the ancestors I've met, and those I haven't. The grey-green of the woodland over the road hanging motionless in the still air seems to hold many more secrets than I have uncovered today. No spirits arose from the mounds and the undergrowth, but I don't think that means they weren't there.

There have been occasions on this part of my journey through Durham when I have felt a connection beyond mere imagination. Albert was an example. I could really feel his presence there in Grange Villa. But there have also been times when I have thought that the stage might be perfectly set and nothing has come of it. In Esh Winning and here in Cornsay the very houses where my ancestors lived have stood coldly empty, as has the woodland over the road, heavy as it is with atmosphere and history.

And what of memory? Where are the real images, the flashes of instant recognition? If I had been born with "*the experiences of my parents and ancestors imprinted on my DNA*" as Carl Jung tells us they are, and which are the very essence of a genetic memory, surely I ought to have *seen* the colliery, *seen* the people, and *seen* the history. Perhaps I still might. If they're imprinted, they're always there.

Imagination, connection, memory - it all seems very complicated. Perhaps everything will come together in time, as this journey progresses. I need to give this more thought, and some liquid encouragement might help. I'm very much looking forward to a seat before the blazing log fire.

FOURTEEN

The Black Horse, Beamish

The man sitting at the bar of The Black Horse has to position his stool about 3 miles away because his stomach is so enormous that it sits between him and the bar counter like a great, wobbly blancmange. His wide thighs splay out from beneath it encased in grey trousers that might be mistaken for a pair of inflated windsocks. His age, I would guess, is about the same as his weight, 55. That's in stones, in case you were wondering. He has tight curly grey hair over a fleshy, florid face, and I notice that he has unexpectedly small feet.

There are two pint glasses before him, one half full which is receiving his current attention, the other full and ordered in advance to ensure there is no difficult hiatus between the one pint and the next. He holds forth among two or three at the bar, jovial whether by beer or personality I cannot tell. He was here when I came in, and I fully expect he will still be here when I leave.

I'm taking some advice from Pete McCarthy just now, and sitting doing nothing. He believed that this was a helpful tactic to employ when idly awaiting inspiration. It's usually called "*people watching*" and although the main view I've got is the impressive backside at the bar which engulfs the stool seat like a marshmallow on a pencil, it's an opportunity to sit and enjoy my beer in peace and wait for something to catch my ear, or my eye.

It is indeed a very comfortable way to pass the time, and I doff my hat to Pete for the tip, and with the warmth of the fire, the pleasant ambience of the bar and my third pint, I could almost nod off when the door opens with a blast of cold air and in strides a sports jacket, cap and moleskin trousers looking altogether as if they own the place, which they might.

What is it with people who breeze into a bar and up to the counter while their spaniel bounds around the place, tongue lolling and tail wagging furiously, sticking its snout into one crotch after the other distributing copious amounts of drool? Why do they think this is acceptable? Well it isn't. And the next time some loose animal sticks its slobbering face in my groin I'm going to shoot it. But I haven't got a gun on me at the moment, so I try to look nonchalantly into the distance as I take a surreptitious kick at its balls.

***

The Black Horse has fallen victim to that trend for writing sayings and ditties on the walls, intended to be humorous and to offer thought provoking inspiration. Examples might be "*Even great oaks begin with small acorns*", "*You haven't failed until you quit trying*", and that sort of tripe. Bill Bryson found some of this drivel on bits of wood in a souvenir shop in Askrigg when he was wandering around the country in "*The Road to Little Dribbling*", and he called them "*Inspirational Sentiments*", which I think was Bill being sarcastic. I've always taken the same view, and can't understand why the management of a place like this would think they confer any benefit on customers who can usually summon up their own twaddle. Mind you, I can think of one or two that might suit the likes of our oversized friend at the bar. "*The beer you have before you is but a prelude to the next*", is one I'm quite proud of.

But amongst all this claptrap there is one that holds my attention. It is, I know, as equally banal and crass as the others, but somehow it resonates with me after these days tramping around Durham after things long gone.

> *"Life isn't about waiting for the storm to pass. It's learning to dance in the rain"*

I know, it's appallingly soppy, unctuous, sentimental bollocks, and I expect that no one would be more surprised than its author to hear that someone actually finds it genuinely powerful. Yet as I was idly scanning all this nonsense on the walls, when I came to this one it did make me pause, catching a thought that within it dwelt a message I think I've received a number of times over the past few days.

I saw it in the eyes of the shipyard workers in the art at The Laing. I saw it in Albert in Grange Villa, in Uncle Arthur, and in the miners I stood amongst at the Alma Pit. It was what George was trying to tell me when he stuck his finger in my chest as I stood before his grave two days ago. I even saw it in the old man I met with his dog on the path at Esh Winning, a man with as good a cause as any to grumble about the hand he'd been dealt in life. These and the many others I have met, or thought I'd met, would have understood this perfectly. If I was being sentimental, I would have said that they had learned to dance in the rain.

***

The spaniel lies quietly at the feet of its brogue-shoed owner, brown eyes gazing up at him longingly like a spring trap waiting for the lightest tickle on its catch. The big man holds forth among his companions at the bar but the voices seem distant, and my gaze falters with the warmth of the room, the passing of time and the comforting fuzziness of just slightly too much ale.

I idly reflect that even the quiet, atmospheric woodland of Cornsay Colliery held its spirits in check this afternoon. The past has been a quiet place today.

PART THREE

THE NORTH EAST
NORTHUMBERLAND COAST

"But it's in the land that I belong
In its castles, hills and sand
Forever will abide with me
This great kingdom, Northumberland"

Robson Green

FIFTEEN

North from Newcastle, Northumberlandia, Longhoughton, Boulmer, Low Newton

Sometimes you have to say something just to make a point, even if it's obvious that you're just making a point. And so, when the young breakfast waiter in black trousers and a white shirt, both of which bear witness to yesterday's bacon and egg, offers me coffee from the flask stewing on the hotplate, I ask him why can't I have a nice one from the machine behind the bar.

"I'm afraid it's not switched on, Sir."

Obviously, what I want to say is "Then why don't you switch it on, you fool? Or is that above your pay grade?" But in fact I say "Oh, I see," which conveys the regrettable impression that I accept this as a perfectly reasonable explanation.

"I don't suppose we could switch it on, could we? Please?"

"I'm sorry, Sir. It's hotel policy."

Policy? Who makes a policy about when to switch on a coffee machine? Who've they got on the management team, Henry Kissinger? I'd go back to my room and have a paper tube of Nescafe, but I've checked out, paid the bill and handed back the key.

It all makes me rather grumpy, which is a shame because The Black Horse at Beamish is, when all is said and done, a very good hotel indeed, and I wouldn't hesitate to visit again should I be in the area. But I do harbour a hope that one day soon there will be a management meeting at which it will be agreed to add "*Switch on the Coffee Machine*" to the checklist of things to do when opening up the breakfast room of a morning. But I know I might as well hope for a complimentary Swedish massage or a "*Sorry No Dogs*" sign on the door, so I heave the bags into the car and head off for the North East coast.

***

I'm looking forward to this. The North East has some of the most breath-taking seascapes I have ever seen, anywhere. Whether in fresh, dazzling sunlight or under threatening storm clouds, sparkling blue water or white horses on a gunmetal grey, gale-swept sea, it's a place which never fails to enthral me.

And inland away from the coast the land of Northumberland rolls and sometimes rears in a vast, sparsely-populated countryside of villages, farms, woodland, rivers and high heathery moorland. There's history here, of course. Battles and political shenanigans have always been features of Northumberland, but unlike the industry of Durham they didn't scar the landscape, at least not this far north. What I will see is much as it always was, down to the little cottage I'll be staying in.

The coastguard cottage at Low Newton sits on the top of a small hill at the north end of Embleton Bay, one of my favourite places in the world. The great crescent of sand arcs south to the distant headland where the craggy ruins of Dunstanburgh Castle stand silhouetted against the skyline. And it's so wide, so expansive, so empty. If there are more than about three people on the beach it's a busy day, and at this time of year I don't expect to see many souls at all, apart from the few beards and binoculars that come here to watch the seabirds.

It's an area I know well, not only from trips here in my adult life, but from my childhood too when Mum and Dad would bring Little John and me for a day out from Tyneside to explore the beaches and the Castle at Alnwick, long before Harry Potter and the Philosopher's Bollocks was even a twinkle in Ms. Rowling's eye. And with the added frisson of an ancestral connection, I'm hoping for a melting pot of memories.

The cottage was built in the early 19th century at the very beginnings of the coastguard service. My great, great, great-grandfather John Hinkley, who for the sake of expediency I shall from now on call Grandpa John, was stationed here for 20 years between 1826 and 1846 during his posting to Low Newton by the Sea, or Newton Seahouses as it was then known, for the purpose of thwarting the activities of smugglers on this wild, remote coastline. The little hill overlooks the surf, sand and the hamlet of Low Newton where its three-sided enclave of low, white cottages remains much as it was over 200 years ago. It's stunning country, and I can't wait.

For some years now the cottage has been in the hands of the National Trust, maintained and offered for let to those prepared to endure its meagre amenities. Their website, which offers details of what to expect when staying at the cottage, emphasises that the facilities are basic. For a start, access is across a field, up a hill, and vehicular access is said to be "limited". The car may have to be left at the bottom of the hill, a daunting prospect with my bags, shopping, laptop, all weather kit, boots, snorkel etc. to be hauled up by hand. Many of the fittings are original and the wooden bunks might be on the short side for modern man – apparently we've got longer since the likes of Grandpa John lived here. The toilet is situated outside in a separate detached brick closet.

It also says there's a room tacked on the end which HM Coastguard have retained to house radio equipment and from which "*sounds may be heard*". The National Trust are not forthcoming about what sort of sounds there might be, and the range of possibilities is intriguing.

The booking blurb provides a short list of modern services which have been installed for the convenience of the 21st century visitor, including electricity, running water and that sort of thing. It even promises Wi Fi. Or at least, it might do. In the list of facilities offered in the cottage it includes Wi Fi*, the asterisk presumably employing the common convention that there is a note, some qualification to be found elsewhere in the text. But nowhere, not even in a footnote where you might expect to find it, is a corresponding * to explain what the first * meant. So I don't know if it means there's Wi Fi *"if you're lucky"*, or *"for 50 quid a minute"*, or *"when the moon is in its first quarter"*, or *"if Kevin has fixed it"*. So all I know is that it has Wi Fi*. There is much to be discovered.

***

Leaving Beamish I take the road back past Chester-le-Street to the A1(M), familiar now after my travels around the county, then north on the Newcastle Western Bypass. The road loses its motorway status here, but it's a new dual carriageway opened only in 1990. If not exactly rural, its urbanity is disguised by the green hills of north Durham and Northumberland arising to the west.

I offer a nod of acknowledgment to the Angel of the North as the road takes me back past its outstretched wings, then over the Tyne by the new, concrete Blaydon Bridge and northwards west of Newcastle. The city squeezes in here and the traffic carries me by deep concrete cuttings, grey flyovers and steel warehouses, the flat metal roofs of light industry and superstores.

At Denton, the road signs mark the junction with the A69, the road west towards Corbridge, Hexham and on through Alston, Penrith and The Lakes. My thoughts pause here, the place names offering up memories of long, exciting journeys in the back of Dad's Jag in the days of Seagull and the caravan on the hill.

It takes me back to those Friday evenings when Dad came home from work and we piled into the car for a weekend in the Lakes. It was an adventure which never paled however often we did it. The passing country always held a magic, and it seemed such a long way. Back then in the 1950s and 1960s there were no dual carriageways, no bypasses, and we would often travel miles without seeing another car.

The Jag had a big bench seat in the back. My brother and I snuggled down underneath a tartan car rug pulled up around us to the chin, not for warmth particularly, but for the simple comfort of it. It was our space for the journey, "*like bugs in a rug*" as my mother would describe us, from where we could play games, giggle at some mischief, gaze at the world passing by, or just doze.

In the summer we watched the countryside, woodlands and farmland, villages of Northumberland stone, the high moorland as we crossed the Pennines, dry stone walls and sheep gathered in fields by the roadside or dotted on more distant hillsides. And as the journey progressed we saw the sun going down over the hills and mountains of the Lake District before us in the West, streaks of red and yellow in the darkening sky, hillsides painted with purple, valleys fading into shadow.

But in the spring or autumn, by the time we had escaped the brightness of Newcastle and the suburbs to the west the lights became scarcer, fading into mysterious twilight as we crossed from the city to the magical lands out beyond the windows of the car. Dusk fell quickly, shadows gathering across the landscape, growing deeper until darkness enveloped us.

Sometimes, we entertained ourselves by playing pub cricket, which was a simple enough game but could be contentious. "*Runs*" were scored according to the number of limbs attributed to the names of passing pubs. So "*The Red Lion*" scored 4 runs, "*The Duck*" 2, and so on. If there were no limbs, as in "*The Kings Head*", the batsman was out, to which point it's all clear enough. But names like "*The Household Cavalry*", or "*The Nine Cows*" produced outrageously unrealistic batting scores, and pubs like "*The Northumberland Arms*" gave rise to complex semantic argument. Eventually, over time, we knew every pub on the road and the order in which we would meet them, and the game lost its appeal. Or Dad banned it in the interests of keeping the peace, I don't remember which.

Dad liked to suck boiled sweets or mints when he was driving, which mother fed to him from the passenger seat. Occasionally my brother would nudge me softly under the rug, and we watched the silhouette of Dad's head turned half towards her keeping one eye on the road. His lips extended in a long pucker as a fruit pastille or a Polo mint, held delicately between mother's thumb and forefinger, was offered gingerly towards his prehensile profile. His lips would envelope the sweet and it would disappear. Little John and I sniggered and puckered our lips at each other in gleeful mockery.

But when we weren't playing cricket, watching Dad being fed or poking each other for nothing but the mischief of it, we fell silent. The car rolled on through the countryside, only the dull rumble of the road and the light rush of wind above the quiet, calm of the car. I rested my head on the side window and from under the comfort of the rug watched the silhouettes of the countryside passing by.

Nearside stone walls, trees and fences flashed past. Dark middle-distance shapes, the black outlined stands of trees, crossed the land more slowly, and the solitary light of a distant farmhouse tracked with slow progress across the horizon, as if hanging in the sky. Suddenly the yellow lights of a village would twinkle around us, then disappear as we plunged back into the night.

The road snaked over the desolate moorland of the Pennines, through villages such as Alston where the lights would appear briefly and then vanish. I gazed through the car window as the journey silently progressed, mesmerised by the magic of the moors and the outlines of dark hills, wondering what was out there. Strange creatures and figures who emerged from rocky lairs at night roamed out there in the darkness. Sorcery, witchcraft and mysterious rituals were practised. There might be dances and sacrifices to the Gods of fire. Sometimes I believed I could hear the regular, distant beating of drums. Immersed in my own, secret imagination all these things were possible, brought to life in a child's mind and a blank, dark landscape. A fearless curiosity drew me out there, beyond the windows of the car.

***

The junction with the A69 recedes behind me as the traffic takes me further north. Past Gosforth the countryside opens up a little and about 15 miles north of Newcastle I turn off the A1 at Cramlington where I pass a "*Welcome to Northumberland*" sign. There is no corresponding sign on the opposite side of the road saying "*Welcome to the Metropolitan Borough of North Tyneside*", which probably says a lot. In the old days I would have been in Northumberland for about the last 20 miles since I passed over the river Tyne, but since 1974 the boroughs have been amalgamated into the bureaucratic bird's nest that obviously doesn't want to offer visitors a welcome, even with a cheap road sign. Or perhaps they would rather you didn't know.

The reason I've come off at Cramlington is because I read that Bill Bryson discovered, in the course of his wanderings in "*The Road to Little Dribbling*", the giant piece of earth sculpture known as "*Northumberlandia*", which I didn't know about either until I recently re-read his book. It's quite new, opened only in 2012. It's a figure of a recumbent woman, built of a staggering 1.5 million tons of earth and spoil from the surface mines on the adjacent Blagdon Estate which donated the land and partly funded it. It's a full quarter of a mile long and a hundred feet high, set in 46 acres of community land, all grassed over and with pathways over and around its curves. The sculpture is also known as "*The Lady of the North*" and since I've devoted a little time to The Angel, it seems fitting that I should take a look at what The Lady has to offer.

***

Like the Angel, the Lady's heritage lies in the mining industry. The adjacent Shotton Surface Mine, the spoil from which was used to build her, is operated by the Banks Group and The Blagdon Estate, the seat of the 5th Viscount Ridley. The mine is a short-term project, developed as recently as 2007 and due to be restored to nature once its operations are concluded in the near future. Land management and conservation have been essential elements in the Estate's plans and the Lady was commissioned, at a cost of £3 million, in accordance with that vision.

The sculpture was designed by Charles Jencks who describes himself as a postmodernist architect. He says that he took his inspiration for the rounded, green contours from the backdrop of the Cheviot Hills. It's the largest land structure in the world depicting the human form. The Royal Family made another trek to the North East to open it in 2012, HRH Anne the Princess Royal again, 43 years after she dispatched the Esso Northumbrian from the slipway at Swan Hunter, just 20 miles south of here, back in 1969. The names of the ship and the sculpture are pleasingly similar.

The Shotton mine is really just a big hole in the ground. There are no shafts or deep, dark tunnels here, and in that sense it bears little resemblance to the mining I've been looking at over the last few days. But this part of the north east was as much a slave to deep mining as was my ancestral Durham. The Northumberland coalfield was just as littered with pits, and its heritage is just as staunchly held in the hearts of local communities. So with all that in mind, I pull into the car park to take a look around.

It's a large, earthy car park with only a few occupants when I arrive and sit on the open boot of the car to change into walking boots. A strip of woodland separates the car park from Northumberlandia herself, with a boxy modern café at the entrance. This turns out to be a very pleasant place to take a break and a coffee before exploring the sculpture in the chilly dampness of the morning. There are no other customers in the place, but it's warm and the two extremely welcoming Geordie ladies in blue checked pinafores manning the counter seem to be delighted to see me, and offer to make me a cheese and ham toastie. This reminds me that I haven't had any breakfast yet and seems like a very good idea.

While I stand at the counter and one lady busies herself with my sandwich, the other chats away to me. She is slim with short blonde hair, and I am genuinely surprised when she tells me that she is a grandmother. She is also very knowledgeable about Northumberlandia and is keen to tell that it's all in a state of development while it matures and awaits the return of wildlife.

"Did you know," I say to her, "that Bill Bryson came here?" of course expecting her to say "Bill who?" But "Oh yes," she beams as if I had asked her if she likes chocolate, "lovely man," which rather takes the wind out of my sails. She also tells me that Janet Street-Porter visited, so I suppose they get all sorts.

From the café the path takes me through a narrow strip of fir trees, the ground thick and soft with their discarded, brown needles, into the open green of Northumberlandia herself. Walking into the sculpture – you really do walk into it – I am surprised by its massive dimensions, in spite of having read all about it. It's quite bare and immature looking, with no trees or bushes anywhere to check the wind which whistles about the green mounds. Bow-shaped lakes appear around the bases, and paths meander through and up around it. The highest part is the head, which I climb by a series of gravel pathways and find myself 100 feet up standing on the Lady's nose with a view around me that extends for tens of miles in all directions. And it's cold up here, the wind physically buffeting me, pulling at my coat and I have to keep my hand pressed down on my head to stop my hat blowing off.

All around the western aspect of the sculpture, and which I look down on from my viewpoint up here, is the wide, grey and black hole in the ground which is the Shotton mine. The crater descends in wide, tiered terraces.

Dozens of huge wheeled vehicles move about, tiny against the enormity of the mine. It is so massive it's hard to imagine how it will all be put back to nature when it's done.

An information board next to me standing on the nose describes how the surface is peeled back and retained, then rolled back when the extraction work is complete. It's a wonder that this great black maw of a hole could ever be returned to nature, but according to everything I've read and been told, that is exactly what will happen. The future of the landscape wasn't much considered when they were digging it up in my grandparents' time. Yet today the management of the land and its repair are all planned in advance. Which of course must be a good thing, but as I stand and look at it I can see nothing but an awful great wound, a colossal black blot on the landscape.

While Northumberlandia is an impressive piece of sculpture it is, at least for now, a rather wild and bare feeling place. Only about three or four other souls wander about with their dogs. Perhaps it's just the weather, and I expect that when the land matures and the wildlife does return then it will have a very different feel to that which it offers today. But for now I'm getting cold and feeling the bleakness of it, so I descend from the Lady's nose and walk back to the car, offering a wave to the ladies in the café. Perhaps one day someone will say to them *Did you know that Stephen Wood visited here?*", and no doubt they will say "*Stephen who?*"

***

Leaving Northumberlandia it's only a few minutes before I'm back on the A1 and heading north again. After a quick stop and a coffee at The Ridley Arms at Stannington, a lovely country pub we used to call in to when Mum and Dad drove us up into Northumberland for our days out, the traffic thins as I get deeper into the county. The road bypasses Morpeth and Druridge Bay further east, and on past Alnwick where I turn off to head east to the coast. Immediately off the dual carriageway the roads are narrow lanes, snaking between hedgerows. If you were to take away the A1 you'd be left with hundreds of square miles of timeless countryside, just farmland and a few scattered villages.

I'm headed for the village of Longhoughton. It's pretty much on the way to Low Newton, and I need to stop there for provisions. I don't want to hang around too long because I have to get to Low Newton in daylight. I'm anxious about getting the best part of two tons of car with an automatic gearbox and rear wheel drive up the grassy, possibly muddy hill. But apart from the town of Alnwick which I don't want to get caught up in right now, it's the only place for miles around that I know of that has a shop for this sort of thing. From the indulgence of the Black Horse I'm now descending into the world of self-catering, and the one thing I'm determined not to do is find myself without coffee, milk or, heaven forbid, toilet paper.

Longhoughton used to be a small, stone village with nothing much there except a church and a pub. Over the years modern housing has grown up around the original village, but in quite a restrained and tasteful way. Small enclaves of housing and bungalows line the road in a pleasing manner. By the time I came to know the village some 20 years ago it had a pub and a convenience store which was also a community space with a proper Post Office, a meeting room and a playroom with toys and bouncy things where the kids could amuse themselves while gossip was exchanged with Gladys on the till.

Then along came one of the big-name supermarket retailers. I can't say which in case they put a black mark on my loyalty card or stop sending me discount vouchers, but it established one of its *Express* or *Metro* or *Daily* outlets which did two things. One, they knocked down the pub to make way for the shop, and two the old convenience store had to close along with its Post Office, playroom, community facilities and gossiping opportunities. I dare say that Gladys may well be employed at the till in the new shop, and may still be available for titbits of local news, but the pub has gone, along with the old shop and its facilities, and Longhoughton has become just a little less of what it used to be.

***

There's a track leading out of Longhoughton down to the sea, about a mile away. It's well hidden and only a weather-beaten, old wooden signpost suggests its existence. My wife and I discovered it only when I was idly peering at an ordnance survey map in the bar of The Sun Inn in Alnmouth some years ago, and it turned out to be a gem. The track is wide enough for a car, but only just, and winds down to the coast. It's the sort of road that has grass growing in the middle, and you have to go through an actual farm to reach the dunes at the end. Where the road stops a gate opens to a place where the car can be left and the coast path winds off along the low cliffs in each direction, to Craster in the north and Boulmer in the south.

Over the dunes are the gems which make this place, the unspoiled, small sandy bays of Howdiemont Sands and Sugar Sands. The two crescent bays are separated by a rocky promontory, and since this place can be reached only on foot from Craster some three miles to the north, or Boulmer a mile and half to the south, or by the little-known track down from Longhoughton, there is rarely anyone here. Walkers on the coast path with their backpacks pass by, but being walkers they press on and don't tend to linger much. Seagulls cry overhead or sit with cormorants on the rocks. Wading birds forage among the seaweed at the water's edge, and occasionally seals bob about just offshore. We sat here not long ago on a beautiful sunny day, bare feet in the warm sand just gazing about at the sheer unspoiled nature of the place, and there wasn't another soul to be seen.

When Pete wandered about the west of Ireland, so he tells us, he visited many remote and secluded places that he didn't write about because he thought that if he did then other people would come and discover them for themselves and then they wouldn't be wonderfully remote and secluded anymore and the magic would be lost. I think he probably had a good point, and in a way I'm taking a risk here with Sugar Sands and its neighbour Howdiemont Sands. So please don't go there.

***

When I last came here my wife and I walked up to the sands from Boulmer which is a very small seashore hamlet where the Fishing Boat Inn is the main, if not the only, attraction apart from the views over the coastal rock formations jutting out into the surf. They have wonderful names like *Boulmer Steel, Berwick Stone, The Torrs,* and *Marmouth Scars.* Boulmer is also noted for its RAF station, just half a mile outside the village. There are no runways here. There used to be a huge white golf ball which housed, no doubt, complicated radar and surveillance equipment, but that's gone now and the station receives its signals from another facility near Alnwick. The station's website tells us something about it:

"a critical component of the RAF Battlespace Management Force and home to the Air Surveillance and Control System (ASACS).
The Control and Reporting Centre (CRC) at RAF Boulmer uses ground-based military and civilian radars to monitor, detect and identify all aircraft in and around UK airspace - 24/7, 365 days a year. This is called the Recognised Air Picture (RAP). The Quick Reaction Alert Typhoons at RAF Lossiemouth and RAF Coningsby can be scrambled to intercept unidentified aircraft.
RAF Boulmer is also home to the RAF School of Aerospace Battle Management (SABM), a worldwide centre of excellence on leading-edge battlespace management training and education for the UK Armed Forces, NATO and other foreign national military personnel"

So it's a pretty significant facility in the country's security and warfare management, which makes it all the more surprising that when we were driving into Boulmer that day we were stopped as we passed the gates of the station by an officer in Military Police uniform waving in literally hundreds of leather clad, tasselled bikers. The line of them went on and on, growling Harleys, Kawasakis, Hondas, Triumphs and BMWs, all making an awful lot of noise.

The spectacle was so extraordinary that I was still wondering what it was all about as I sat in the bar of the Fishing Boat a short while later enjoying a pint of Fisherman's Nob, when suddenly the bar emptied onto the wooden veranda at the back overlooking the coastline. Like a sheep I followed to see what the fuss was about and for a short while no one gave any hint of what was going on. About a dozen people just stood and gazed out to sea, and for the life of me I couldn't see anything of interest. I thought they might be twitchers or whatever they call over-enthusiastic bird watchers, and perhaps someone had seen a lesser spotted brown mudshitter or something.

But after a minute or so, someone pointed out into the distant sky to the south and a small dot appeared, just off the coast and low on the horizon. It grew as it approached us developing a long triangular shape. It seemed so slow in the sky, so silent, as the wings grew into a familiar delta. Then with the thunderous roar of four Rolls Royce Olympus engines the mighty Vulcan bomber flew low overhead, banking towards the Boulmer RAF station on one of its farewell flypasts before decommissioning.

As it happened, I'd known that day was one of the last flights of this iconic aircraft, and I had told my wife how disappointed I was that we would miss it over Norwich which was part of its route. So it was an unexpected and very welcome surprise to find it overhead today. It probably took it only about 20 minutes flying time from Norwich I should think, as opposed to the best part of 7 hours in the car.

And the bikers, so it would seem, had been invited to watch the event from the RAF station itself, which explains why they had been given an official welcome. How they managed that I don't know. Perhaps they threatened to trash the place.

***

Boulmer (pronounced *"Boomer"* if you wish to integrate) is on the way to Low Newton by the coastal route, and I have time to drop in before the light goes.

The village is a single row of houses, hardly more than a dozen, lining the seaward side of the road above the rocks and shingle below the low cliff. The Fishing Boat Inn is in the middle of the row, back from the road with a small stone walled car park in front. Beyond, slabs of rocky fingers stretch out into the sea forming a horseshoe allowing a treacherous entrance to the small bay at the southern end of the village. A few boats are dragged onto the sandy, stony shore on rusty trailers and an old tractor sits among broken wooden boxes and crates. Cages, buoys and rope lie strewn about. The crescent of sand is piled with heaps of brown seaweed. The sky is grey and blustery, the sea whipped with white, and the dune grasses sway wildly. There is not another soul to be seen.

Boulmer is an important place on this journey because the tiny village is noted for having been the smuggling capital of Northumberland, no doubt because of its remote, inaccessible location. I can imagine a dark night, silhouetted figures moving about slowly in secret silence, hauling boxes, crates and barrels up the shore from light boats wallowing in the shallows. This would have been a place of great interest to Grandpa John and his colleagues stationed only just up the coast. Perhaps he pushed open the door of this pub with relief to be out of the biting wind, as I do now and take my place at the bar.

Although it's deserted outside, the pub is busy with customers at tables in the bar, and in the restaurant area to the rear where big glass windows offer panoramic views over the coastline. Beyond the glass is the wooden veranda from which I watched the Vulcan bomber, although the outdoors is forsaken today, even by the birdwatchers. The wind seems to be increasing by the hour.

I like to try the local beers and at first glance a pint of "*Dirty Tackle*" looks attractive (I'm not making that one up, it's from the Wychwood Brewery) but it's brewed in Oxfordshire and I'm driving anyway so I settle for a coffee, served by a pretty blonde young lady who turns out to be from Leeds and doesn't really know anything about the history of the pub or its status as the smugglers' headquarters. However, she does point out a very elderly gentleman sitting alone at a table close by and next to an enormous plate of fish and chips. George, she tells me, is the man I need to speak to. Ordinarily, I would hesitate to disturb a man in front of his food, but George has already noticed our conversation, and looking up he nods at me in a way I take to be an invitation.

George was born here in Boulmer, and worked all his life in the area, fishing and as he got older in a tackle shop in Alnwick. He seems happy to talk to me about it, and tell me why he loves it here on the coast, and why he never left. The problem is that he speaks in a strong Northumbrian accent, he seems to have left his teeth at home and his mouth is constantly full of fish. As a consequence, I can understand very little of anything he says. I nod and smile at intervals when it seems appropriate to do so, such as when he pauses to fork another portion of battered cod through his gums. He might also be a bit deaf, as what I do understand him to say is never directly connected with my questions.

George is, I would guess, about 85 years old which puts his early memories in the 1940s or thereabouts. This coastline was then prepared for invasion but not by smugglers. It was Nazi Germany against whom the guard was kept. Even today, the sands and beaches for miles up and down this coastline are littered with the heavy concrete blocks of anti-tank traps, set angled into the sand.

The Fishing Boat is a warm, comfortable place, but there is nothing to suggest what it might have been like 100 years ago, never mind 200 in the days of Grandpa John. The pine furniture, the glazing of the dining area, even the wooden floor planking and the stone fireplace have a contemporary feel. But though the history of the building may be disguised by modernisation, around the walls are dozens of pictures of days gone by. Old framed photographs depict seafaring men with long beards, oilskin hats and coats. One large painting portrays a lifeboat filled with men straining at oars in a tumultuous sea. And I note, women. Women pulling at oars in a lifeboat alongside the men. Women standing with them beside a boat posing for an early camera. Women hauling on a rope to get a boat out of the surf.

I spend some time gazing at the photographs wondering at the physical and mental strengths of those women. I find myself reflecting on the differences between the lives of the mine workers I've been exploring back in Durham, and the lives of those who made their livings here, by the sea.

It is true that women and very young children worked down the pits before the mid-19th century, in all parts of the country. It was common for whole families to be employed in the mines. But due to concern over accidents and fatalities, The Mines and Collieries Act of 1842 prohibited the employment of boys under 10 years of age and women of any age from working underground in a mine. The prohibition did cause some economic hardship to families whose income was curtailed, and the law was sometimes not strictly heeded. There were examples of women dressing as men as and less than law-abiding employers, but with those qualifications by the middle of the 19th century women were not working down the pits alongside the men. They cooked, cleaned, looked after the bairns, made a home for the men to return to, or found some other work more suited to their gender. Hard work, relentless no doubt, but they did not encroach on the work of men. The divide was pretty absolute, enshrined in law.

Yet here, the seafaring folk imposed no such restrictions, and women contributed their efforts just the same, hauling and mending nets, even getting into boats in dangerous seas to save lives, or indeed to haul in illicit barrels and booty. It makes me think of this as a more lawless place, away from the industrial revolution and the laws and enactments that were beginning to impose some regulation on industry. Dark nights, stealthy goings on, smuggling and piracy seem a long way from the relative management of the mines. Yet they were both going on, at the same time, within a few miles of each other. They both had their dangers, and their hardships, but how different they were.

I am quietly thinking about this, the role of women then, and the stratospheric changes to the role of women in society that we see today. It's a massive subject, and frankly not one I expected to be giving much thought to on this journey, but my attention is drawn from it when the young blonde girl who served me coffee suggests I speak to the landlord and points out a gentleman across the bar. He's a middle-aged man, younger than me, dressed in a light blue wool pullover and jeans. He has grey hair and a pallid look about him that implies all may not be entirely well. He walks uncomfortably with a stick, in a way that conveys something permanent rather than having just fallen off his bicycle. Nevertheless, when I ask him about his tenure here at The Fishing Boat and the smuggling trade associated with the pub, he invites me to sit down with him, and he tells me he's been here 16 years and has collected information about the history of the pub, and the photographs displayed on the walls.

Mike the landlord sticks his bad leg straight out in front of him, stick by its side, and shuffles slightly in his chair to find a comfortable shape. The pub was, he confirms, known as the smuggling centre of Northumberland. In the 19th century the landlord here had a boat called "*Ides*", which he and his compatriots would row out to meet Dutch trading ships. They took on their booty at sea, often Dutch gin, and brought it to shore. Once landed it would be loaded onto packhorses, wagons or simply manually carried, to be transported over the Scottish borders, all under cover of night, all in stealthy silence. There was a famous gypsy smuggler named William Faa, who ruled from The Fishing Boat but travelled between here and his natural lair in the borders to the west. His story is a fascinating one.

William Faa II was gypsy royalty, the King of the Gypsies. Born in 1794 he inherited his title from his father. Innkeeper, fisherman and footballer of some note, he had his home in Kirk Yetholm, just over the border with Scotland some 50 miles to the west. He was also a prodigious smuggler, adept with pistol and cutlass, and he travelled to the Fishing Boat with his "*Boomer Men*" to recover barrels of illicit gin, taken away duty free at great profit.

Violence came with the territory. Mike tells me that in one altercation here in Boulmer a customs officer was shot dead, but such was the authority and notoriety of William Faa that no local justice would convict him of any crime. The repercussions which a man like Faa could visit upon those who sought to interfere with his activities, Customs men included, were regarded with considerable apprehension.

Eventually, however, Faa received a severe cutlass injury to his wrist courtesy of a skirmish with a Customs Man, and his smuggling activities were curtailed. He lived the rest of his life peacefully back over the border, and died in 1847.

In fact, William Faa led rather a double life. His royal title was no gypsy flippancy. He was highly regarded amongst his own clan and nobility alike. He could boast that he had never been to gaol, the Marquis of Tweeddale gave him fishing and shooting rights, and on his death many tributes were paid to him and newspapers ran glowing obituaries. Such was the man who held court here in the Fishing Boat, no doubt striking glasses with the landlord while Grandpa John and his fellow officers regarded them from afar and planned and pondered over ways to apprehend them.

I'm sure that once I get to Low Newton I will learn much more about the pirates and smugglers on this coastline, and the role played by the officers and men of the Admiralty's Coastguard Service, like Grandpa John, charged with disrupting their activities and bringing them to justice.

I can't ask what may be ailing him, and he ventures no explanation, but Mike is a genial man and as he continually shuffles in his chair I find myself sorry that whatever it is appears to be so debilitating. With that rather sad feeling, I shake him by the hand, bid him farewell, and head back to the car for Low Newton, as time is pressing.

***

Low Newton lies about 10 miles up the coast from Boulmer, and the country, hedgerow-lined road winds a mile or so inland passing through hamlets and farmsteads. Shortly after the village of Embleton a signpost directs me coastward to the village of High Newton where I pass the Joiners Arms, an old pub now transformed into a boutique bar and restaurant, and then onto the road down to Low Newton, a road to nowhere other than the hamlet above which sits my destination, the coastguard cottage on the hill, now known as Lookout Cottage.

Only a few hundred yards out of High Newton, the narrow road broaches a rise and then sharply descends to the tiny hamlet at the bottom of the hill, where it ends abruptly at the shore. The coastline is suddenly revealed before me, stretching out beyond the village, the great bay of Embleton and the ruins of Dunstanburgh Castle on the far headland. As I drive slowly down the hill, to my left beyond a stone wall the grassy hill rises with the squat, square white cottage and its 60 feet radio pylon sitting right at the top. It is, as I feared, not looking good for the car.

Halfway down the hill to the hamlet there is a gate in the wall leading into the field from which the hill arises, and a grassy track leads away and upwards in the direction of the cottage, as the National Trust told me there would be. They also told me that there is a combination lock on the gate, so

I sit in the car and fish out the paperwork, locate the combination, and steel myself.

Even the car shakes slightly in the buffeting wind, and I have to hold onto the car door firmly as I open it to step out into the road. I stumble round the front of the car, my coat flapping and my trousers pinned to my legs. I get to the gate which turns out to be a rickety affair, through which is threaded a chain and a padlock. Bent down at the gate it takes me forever to line up the numbers on the lock, my fingers getting stiff and numb. Eventually the lock pops open and I pull out the chain leaving it dangling. The gate is loose and saggy on its hinges and won't open without me physically lifting it off the ground, but eventually with a great deal of heaving and blasphemy it's open and wedged securely. I haul myself back to the car, falling in gratefully out of the wind.

I reverse a bit back up the road to get an angle on the gate, nudging forward over the kerb then through the opening into the field. I take the car in a few yards and stop, then I get out again into the howling gale. I lift the gate and heave it closed, find the chain and thread it through the gate. I clamp the padlock shut and reset the combination. My face contorted by the wind pressure I haul myself back to the car and fall into the calm of the driving seat. I sit and regard the grassy, rutted track rising before me.

I select drive and move forward slowly. The car bumps and there's a bang from somewhere below. I hope that hasn't done any damage. For the first few yards it's level but badly rutted, then the track takes a left and starts to ascend. For another few yards the car climbs, and I can see Lookout Cottage high above me on the hill. Then I feel the back wheels start to spin. I nudge the accelerator adjusting the revs, but the tyres won't grip and the rear end slides away. The car comes to a halt slewed across the track.

Slowly, very slowly, I reverse back to the flat bit, then stop. I select anti-skid traction control and set off again, slowly. I bump around the left-hand bend and start to climb again. It doesn't feel much better, and surely enough the wheels spin and the rear slides again. Again I reverse back to the flat bit.

I sit and think for a moment, regarding the various buttons and things the car manufacturer has provided to assist in situations like this. I remember that Jeremy Clarkson, when appraising some vehicle, noted a button he said put the car into "*mad bastard mode*", which I think meant it turned everything on at once and should be used with caution. I wonder if that sort of thing might help here, but look as I might I can't see such a button and I don't think my car is capable of being turned into a mad bastard. I, on the other hand, might be.

I have one more go at the hill during which I simply make the track worse with my spinning, slewing wheels, and I give up. Carefully, very carefully, I reverse bumpily back to the gate. I sit there, the wind whistling around the car, and regard the cottage sitting smugly at the top of the hill with increasing disaffection.

Now I've got to get my stuff up there, so I try to work out if I can do this in one go. I have to accept that I can't, not if I want my laptop, case of Important Belongings, food, toilet paper etc., which I do. Two trips, I decide, should do it.

I also know that having fought with the combination lock on the gate, I have another combination to defeat to get the cottage key out of the key-safe box on the wall. Again I fish out the paperwork, check the combination required, and open the car door into the gale. I manage to hang onto it to prevent it being torn off, and then struggle around to the boot where I gather up the first load. Then, beleaguered with my stuff, heavy straps over both shoulders, hugging all the bags about me, I set off along the track, head down, and up the hill.

It's only about 200 yards, but my feet slip and slide. I stumble on rocks, and I have to keep my eyes half closed, my body leaning forward as I fight against the wind. Eventually I reach a white picket gate in the heavy stone wall which surrounds the cottage. It's irritatingly difficult to open the gate because the latch sticks and the mechanism seems to be misaligned. As I struggle with it I wonder to myself, between oaths, whether Grandpa John cursed as much as me at this hill, the weather and this wretched, obstinate gate. Eventually, with an extra yank on the bolt I get through and find myself before the door of the cottage, and mercifully slightly shielded from the gale.

The key box is the sort where you have to line up the combination rollers, then the box should snap open revealing the house key. I line up the numbers with difficulty. My fingers are numb and fumbly and won't work properly. Does the box pop open? No it doesn't. I reset the numbers and pull on the release catch. Nothing. I try again. I must have battled with that box for at least ten minutes going from irritated to angry to really quite worried, thinking about what I could do if I really couldn't get in. Who would I call? How would I call? What could anyone do even if I did get through to the National Trust helpline in Swindon? Will the Joiners Arms have any rooms?

Eventually, on the millionth attempt, the key box pops open with a click that seems to say "*Hey, wasn't that fun?*" Thankfully, the key works in the door lock, I fall into the sanctuary of the cottage with my bags and stuff, and get the door closed onto the wind, the cold and the noise behind me. I collapse onto a sofa to take a look around me, and at what all this effort has brought me to.

***

My first impression is that it's very light blue. The timber walls and woodwork are light blue. The room is small, about twelve feet by ten. There's a light blue bay window at the far end with bench seating and cushions, a fireplace with a wood burner and a supply of wood and coal. There's a modern electric cooker, a toaster and a kettle, a sink and some light blue cupboards. To the side of the fireplace is a small electric heater, and a small television hangs on the wall. Above it on a light blue shelf coloured lights blink in a couple of small boxes, and I think of Wi Fi*. The wooden floor is half covered by a light brown, hessian mat. There's a two-seater sofa, a small round table in the bay, but no chairs. That's it.

There are two doors, the one I came in through and which leads to wind, and another which opens to an even smaller room, about ten feet by eight, which is also very light blue. A double bed is squeezed in before wooden, light blue built in bunks occupying the other wall. The bunks look very small, as advertised, and I'm glad I'm not going to sleep in them. I notice another small electric heater. I sit on the bed and am relieved to find it soft and comfortable.

I open some cupboard doors next to the bed expecting to find some hanging space, but the cupboard accommodates a small basin and a shower. So there is no hanging space, and notably but not unexpectedly, no toilet either.

But it's not over. I can't put my feet up yet. Back down in the car is my toilet paper, my coffee, my Other Stuff, and my bottle of brandy which I can't help but feel is going to be necessary. Back out the door I battle into the worsening gale. I notice a small, lean-to brick shed built into the wall which surrounds the cottage. I assume that must be the toilet, and make a mental note not to need the lavatory for the next 2 days. Then it's back down the hill to the car, collect the stuff, and battle back up again. At least there are no combination locks to fight with this time. Eventually I push the door closed against the weather for the final time, at least for now.

I'm frankly exhausted. And it's not very warm. It's not exactly cold, but it's not cosy either. What is good is that there is an excellent mobile signal, which may or may not have something to do with the 60 feet pylon right outside the door. And there is Wi Fi* working and free. So I still wonder what the * means in the brochure. I think I'll send the National Trust a note* about it.

***

I've taken off my muddy shoes and heavy coat, turned the little heater up to full, and sitting in the bay window on the cushioned wooden bench with a cup of tea, a delicious and thoughtfully provided National Trust chocolate cookie, at last I can relax and take in what I've arrived at. The view from the window down over the coast is stupendous, long and wide over the sandy, rocky coastline, just as I imagined it would be. I could sit here for hours, out of the weather, and gaze out there. Listening to the howling noise outside, it may come to that.

I wonder that Grandpa John actually lived here 200 years ago. Not with these furnishings, these facilities, perhaps not even with the light blue, but nevertheless here, within these walls. I wonder what it was like, back then.

SIXTEEN

Coastguards and Smugglers

So, who was John Hinkley?

Grandpa John was born in Rye, Sussex in May 1800 to parents who had lived there all their lives. His father, Thomas, was also in the Coastguard Service, or the Preventative Water Guard as it was known before the amalgamation of services in the 1820s.

John followed his father into the Service as soon as he was old enough to do so. He had various postings around the south coast including Selsey Bill, Shoreham, and Jury's Gap at Dungeness. In 1821 he married Mary Stone at East Preston in Sussex. John's rank then was Boatman, the bottom rung of the ladder, an oarsman, a pair of hands, an extra fist and a cutlass when required.

By 1823 he had been promoted to Commissioned Boatman with higher responsibilities, commanding a boat and planning operations. On 8th July 1826 he was posted up to Low Newton on the Northumberland coast, more than 300 miles from home. He spent 20 years here at that rank before being transferred back to the south coast in June 1846.

John was still a young man when he came to Low Newton, only just 26, and he was leaving his family behind to travel almost as far as one could while remaining in the same country. He was probably thinking of starting a family of his own at that time too, married to Mary for 5 years by then. I've wondered whether the posting was a voluntary one, but it was probably just part of the job, going where he was told. The coastguard service was expanding rapidly at the time, and the need to man remote stations was pressing. As a commissioned man John's experience would have been valuable.

During those 20 years here in Low Newton John Hinkley engaged with the landscape of the north east, he lived alongside colleagues and local folk alike, he pursued the miscreants and vagabonds of the smuggling community, and he raised a family including his eldest son, James William, the next name on the family tree which will ultimately lead to me. By spending some time in this place I hope to discover something of his life here, his experiences and perhaps memories which he laid down in my genes.

***

Low Newton was a long-established, working fishing village. Seaweed littered the rocky shoreline, boats were hauled up onto the sand, nets, buoys and all the paraphernalia of the sea would be scattered around, as indeed it is today. Fishermen in sea boots and thick, heavy clothing would have been milling about. It would have all been sandy, muddy, and certainly dishevelled. There were no tourist rosettes in the cottage windows. Deserted coastline stretched as far as the eye could see in both directions, and the village would have been rude, dirty, and smelly from the communal pit in the middle of the square.

John would have made the journey north by sea, in a Coastguard Cutter or a Revenue Cruiser, taking perhaps two or three days with stops at various stations on the way up the coast. Once here and disembarked from the landing boat John would have found himself before those cottages on the shoreline, perhaps with a sailor's kitbag slung over his shoulder. The first thing he would have noticed was the wide splendour of the coastline. Although John would have been well used to the sea, magnificent coastlines and wild weather, the remoteness here must have astonished him. He might have stood for a moment there on the shore and just gazed at the seascape and the eccentric spikes of ruined Dunstanburgh Castle on the distant horizon.

No doubt John would have been welcomed by the men and the Chief Officer of the station, perhaps crowding round to meet the newcomers off the boat - handshakes, warm greetings exchanged, perhaps a pat on the back or a hand on the shoulder. There were about 6 coastguards stationed at Low Newton and it was usual for the Chief Officer, the man in command, to be a Navy Lieutenant. I don't know who that was when John arrived, but in 1841 it was a man called John Brunton. Brunton had commanded a number of navy ships including frigates, had seen action on the high seas, and had been involved in the 1824 search for the North West Passage under Captain E. W. Parry, so he had an impressive pedigree, especially as he was, in 1841, only 45 years old. Was he a stern, unforgiving commander? Or was he a soft touch? I have no idea.

Just outside the village there was a low row of 5 houses called *"Coastguard Buildings"* which accommodated the men, including the Chief Officer. As government buildings these were substantial, well-ordered and well-provided dwellings, far from the fishing folks' cottages which at that time were little more than hovels. There was also the little cottage on the top of the hill then called *"The Watch House"*, today known as *"Lookout Cottage"*. This commanded a view right up and down the coast, and it was to this little place that John and Mary were billeted when they got there. I don't know for how long they occupied The Watch House, but there came a time when they moved down into one of the Coastguard Buildings. Perhaps it was when James William came along in 1828, or when Mary was expecting him.

***

Smuggling had become a major problem on all coastlines in the country. This area was no exception although it was, and is, especially remote and its protection required special resources.

From the 13th century taxes had been imposed to protect industry from foreign imports, wool in particular in the early days. By the mid-18th century taxes had been extended to a much wider range of goods, and duty was charged at a staggering 119% on tea by the later part of that century. There was scope for great profits for those prepared to risk the penalties.

It was organised crime, and gangs used secluded coastlines to land their booty. In collusion with Dutch trading ships barrels of gin, tobacco, linens, spices and tea would be loaded onto small boats offshore and spirited away from the coast by carts and wagons. Smuggling was such a serious problem that it had the attention of the Government. In 1794 the Prime Minister William Pitt the Younger said that hardly one third of the tea drunk in England had been legally imported. The loss to the Treasury was enormous.

The end of the Napoleonic wars in 1815 released 300,000 men and sailors back into society. With no trade to go to, many fell to smuggling. But it also provided a pool of men from which more Revenue Officers could be recruited. Which side to support must have been a dilemma for some. The potentially substantial spoils of crime, or the security of the Service must have been a question that tested many moralities. Or perhaps, in some cases it didn't.

Over the latter part of the 18th century and as the problem became more acute, sophisticated and organised, the government agencies to counteract smuggling developed and the Coastguard Service was formed in 1822 from an amalgamation and restructuring of existing services.

The prolific smuggling trade was often endowed with a false romanticism. Rudyard Kipling wrote "*A Smuggler's Song*" in 1906. It's a tale, told too sympathetically in truth, of advice to a child to avert her eyes from the "*Gentlemen*" of the trade. I can't avoid reciting it in full here as it so perfectly encapsulates the relationship between the criminality, the romance, the complicity and the corruption. The words do vary slightly between versions, but this one is taken from the Kipling Society and so I respect its authenticity.

IF you wake at midnight, and hear a horse's feet,
Don't go drawing back the blind, or looking in the street,
Them that ask no questions isn't told a lie.
Watch the wall my darling while the Gentlemen go by.

Five and twenty ponies,
Trotting through the dark -
Brandy for the Parson, 'Baccy for the Clerk.
Laces for a lady; letters for a spy,
Watch the wall my darling while the Gentlemen go by!

Running round the woodlump if you chance to find
Little barrels, roped and tarred, all full of brandy-wine,
Don't you shout to come and look, nor use 'em for your
play.
Put the brishwood back again - and they'll be gone next
day!

If you see the stable-door setting open wide;
If you see a tired horse lying down inside;
If your mother mends a coat cut about and tore;
If the lining's wet and warm - don't you ask no more!

If you meet King George's men, dressed in blue and red,
You be careful what you say, and mindful what is said.
If they call you "pretty maid," and chuck you 'neath the
chin,
Don't you tell where no one is, nor yet where no one's
been!

*Knocks and footsteps round the house - whistles after
dark -
You've no call for running out till the house-dogs bark.
Trusty's here, and Pincher's here, and see how dumb they
lie
They don't fret to follow when the Gentlemen go by!*

*'If You do as you've been told, 'likely there's a chance,
You'll be give a dainty doll, all the way from France,
With a cap of Valenciennes, and a velvet hood -
A present from the Gentlemen, along 'o being good!*

*Five and twenty ponies,
Trotting through the dark -
Brandy for the Parson, 'Baccy for the Clerk.
Them that asks no questions isn't told a lie -
Watch the wall my darling while the Gentlemen go by*

It's a quietly stirring tale that endows the "*Gentlemen*" of
the trade with an almost heroic quality. But moonlit nights
and tall ships wallowing at anchor were far from the truth.
It wasn't just a few barrels of rum rolled up a sandy beach
and a bunch of jolly, red cheeked scallywags, mischievous
but otherwise likeable fellows going quietly about a
victimless crime. The reality was violent and brutal. Local
people lived in fear, and reprisals on informers were
abrupt.

Complicity and corruption were not limited to local
people but engaged in by officials, business owners and
politicians. The collusion that went on behind closed doors
erupted onto the shorelines in a clash of interests. It
became a running battle, a game of catch me if you can with
cutlasses and pistols.

The Guards kept watch offshore in boats at night, and
along the coast The Riding Officers patrolled on horseback.
A constant watch was kept by those patrols and from The
Watch House on the hill. There were informers, local people
who didn't welcome the intimidation and the disruption to

their law-abiding lives. The Coastguards kept a watch on known offenders, a look out for shipping activity off the coast, and a constant surveillance over their ward, day and night. Especially at night.

It was dangerous work. Weapons were carried on both sides, and confrontations involved blades and firearms. Injuries and even death could, and did, ensue. When arrests were made offenders were hauled off before a local justice whose allegiance might be unpredictable. If convicted, a prisoner would be taken off to Alnwick gaol. Hanging was a common penalty. It was a dangerous environment to inhabit, and John lived with this day in, day out, for 20 years here.

***

There were several coastguard stations on this coastline. Alnmouth, Amble, Bamburgh, Berwick, Boulmer, Budle, Craster, Holy Island, Newbiggin and Seahouses all maintained their own stations at one time or another. Although communications would have been no better than hand to hand or by signal over line of sight, one can assume that the stations worked as closely together as possible, and John would have travelled regularly by sea up and down the coast between them. He would have been familiar with Boulmer, for example, and the notorious William Faa. I wonder if John rued the fact that Faa was never punished for his crimes. I wonder, indeed, if he ever came face to face with him.

Over time the coastguards took on more and more of a role in search and rescue, coastal navigation, and assisting the navy. Their role expanded beyond revenue protection as taxes were relaxed on imported goods and smuggling became a less profitable trade. By the time John was well settled in Low Newton, as well as patrolling the shore and coastline, he would have been on the lookout for vessels in distress, maintaining navigation equipment, providing signalling and telegraphy, reporting ship movements, search and rescue, the discharge of cargoes and taking on the more civilian role we think of in the coastguard service today.

***

I've wondered that John and his family stayed here for 20 years. Coastguards were discouraged from becoming too acquainted with local people to avoid both collusion and reprisal, and so they were transferred frequently. This didn't happen with Grandpa John, but I have been unable to find any reason for that.

John and Mary's first child, my great, great-grandfather James William was born in Low Newton in 1828. A number of other children followed, and by 1841 he and Mary were caring for 7, ranging from a new-born to James William, by then aged 13.

When he left Low Newton, posted back to the south coast in 1846, John took his wife and children back down south with him, apart from James William who stayed behind. I wonder how John felt about leaving after making a life for himself and his family here. Was it a relief to return home to Sussex, or had 20 years installed a new sense of home? I wonder, after all that time, where John felt he belonged.

But James William did stay behind. He must have developed quite a connection with the area to watch his family leave, aged only 18. He joined the Coastguards too, at least for a while before leaving for a life on the land. We find him later in nearby Ellingham working with horses on the estate, and he will later leave for the coalfields of Durham, to Esh and to Cornsay Colliery. In due course James William would father Uncle Arthur the schoolmaster of Tanfield, and Francis who would become Harry's grandmother. And so the circle is completed.

John retired from the coastguard service in Sussex in 1852 on a pension of £35 p.a., about £3,400 today. He died in Dover in 1861, by then widowed for 10 years.

Thus was the man from whom I am descended. I feel quite privileged to have in my heritage a man who, I fully expect, had great courage and endured no small hardships. I feel he would have discharged his place in the community with a strong sense of duty and responsibility. I think of him as a reliable man, trustworthy among his colleagues and friends, the head of his family and a protector of them. He was, I feel, a kindly man, religious in a personal and moderate way, not taken to excess or vice, and a confident hand whether on the tiller of his boat or on the shoulders of his family.

But in all honesty who knows? John's was a world that we today can imagine only in its wide panorama, and hardly at all in its detail. Perhaps my time here in Low Newton will add some colour to my picture of his world.

SEVENTEEN

The Ship, Low Newton

It's remarkable how a cup of tea, a long linger over a stupendous view and a National Trust biscuit can dispel exhaustion and feelings of glumness. I can't feel the wind here sitting in the bay window of the cottage looking out over the coast, but I can see it. It's the sum of things, the scudding clouds, the ragged white horses on the sea and the movement of grasses on the hill. It's quite hypnotic, and as I thought earlier it would be no disaster to do little more than sit here and watch the sea. But now the light is fading quickly. I'm going to have plenty of time to feel John's presence, if it's here, in the course of the next couple of days. I think I'll go to the pub.

***

I stumble into the tiny porch of The Ship as if a hand on my back is pushing me through the door. I turn to heave it closed and it feels like a leaf blower is being held in my face. Eventually the door latches shut and suddenly the noise stops. The slippery, windswept, combination-lock encumbered trudge down the hill in the fading light is shut out and calm descends.

I step into the bar and push the hood of my coat back off my head (if I had worn a hat it would be halfway across the North Sea by now) and take a moment to unzip my coat.

I recognise the bar from when I've been here before, although I haven't visited for some time. It's only one room, a small place with a low ceiling, walls of big, irregular stones, timber plank floor, high-backed pews around the walls, pine-topped tables and chairs, and a semi-circular wood-fronted bar at one end making the best use of the small space.

Figures sit at tables amidst low chatter. There's no music, an agreeable feature of nearly all pubs up here. I daresay there are those in towns like Alnwick and Morpeth, seaside resorts like Amble and Seahouses, which still insist on assaulting their customers with the disagreeable background thump of the latest plastic boy band, but they are a far cry from these coastal village pubs where serenity tends to prevail and conversation is possible at the low murmur I find myself amidst here. A couple of dogs lie low and quietly underneath tables, their only movement big brown eyes following some sound or interest in the bar. Good dogs.

An array of pumps on the counter offers only the beers brewed here on the premises, in what was a stable next door. They've been given the names "*Ship Shape*", "*Emblestones*" and "*Sandcastles at Dawn*". Appropriate, I think.

I'm the only customer standing at the bar, and I have a pint of the Ship Shape which is hoppy and fresh. Alex, the young, slim lady who serves me, has long fair hair over a grey long sleeved top and jeans, no make-up that I can see and the casual look of youth that suggests she might be on a holiday job while at University. She has an easy smile and I'm surprised to hear that she came here from Bristol 6 years ago intending to work at the pub for just one season, but found she liked it and stayed. She now lives in the village and can't see herself leaving anytime soon.

Alex is telling me that all the cottages in the village have stories to tell, tales of fisher-folk, smugglers, coastguards and dark deeds perhaps, but before she can elaborate we're disturbed by an unreasonable customer who wants to be served, so I find a vacant seat from which to enjoy my beer.

Middle-aged and elderly couples sit quietly at tables. The dress code is outdoor wear, pullovers, sturdy trousers and walking boots. The low talk is of people whose natural inclination is towards the restrained. There don't seem, at first glance, to be any pirates or smugglers lurking in the shadows, only holidaymakers who are probably renting one of the former fishing cottages in the hamlet or nearby, cottages renovated and equipped with the services of the 21st century and a rosette stuck on the front porch window. They are people who tomorrow will walk the wide beaches, take a crab sandwich at lunchtime, and in a day or two will drive back home. I seem to be the only solitary traveller, as usual.

The pub has a very small kitchen. I can see through an open door beside the bar that two or three people are busy in a space that would be small for a coat cupboard. Accordingly, the menu is also limited, so I order crab with a side of crab and another pint of Ship Shape.

I find amusement in the wine list which advises that "*Wines on this list may contain eggs or fish*", which makes me chortle. In fact, I mention it to the waitress. I think I might have used expressions like "*Chateau Bloater*" or "*Herring Bordeaux*. She firmly reminds me, before pointedly removing the menu from my fingers, that people have allergies and that egg and fish products are used in the fining process of some wines, and that puts me in my place. I really must read up on things like this before making ill-considered jokes, and a proper fool of myself.

***

Being alone allows me the benefit of being able to sit, sip, watch and imagine in a way that would be impossible in company. My thoughts are allowed to wander without the encumbrance of conversation, without the distraction of having to listen. My eyes can explore the surroundings without being accused of not paying attention, and I can absorb a place in my own time. There is no better way to admit a place to one's mind than in one's own company.

If the mists of time rolled back right now and the people here, the low chatter and all the tables and chairs faded away, what would I see? A stone floor perhaps, rough tables, and only a doorway through to some back room from which tankards and pots of ale are brought by a rough sleeved landlord or a rosy faced serving girl. Perhaps blue waves of smoke waft in the airless room, the sweet smell of tobacco and the strong, slightly acrid reek of ale. Would there have been heavy set, bearded men, raggedy ruffians with less than a full complement of yellow teeth, a cutlass and crude loud laughter? Or men in red doublets, three cornered hats and buckled boots, the colours of the Service, men just off duty, or about to set off on patrol? What was their conversation here of an evening? Was this a place where the Chief Officer would gather his men for the planning of operations and patrols, to take a tally or to exchange intelligence? Did they meet collaborators and informants here? Were words exchanged quietly, a name here and there, men to be watched?

I wonder if John Hinkley might have been one of these men in red. I wonder at the manner of his speech, the manner of his dress. As I look about the bar and my surroundings from my solitary chair I wonder if he might be sitting over there in the corner regarding me with curiosity, my three-times great grandfather.

Then again, perhaps this was a place where ponies, slung with quarter barrels and cases, were led quietly and unseen past the darkened windows, and where a barrel of gin might be left at the back door to secure the landlord. Perhaps this was where a young girl sat quietly and watched the wall, as the Gentlemen went by.

But like The Fishing Boat at Boulmer when I open my eyes and return to the present it's impossible to get a sense of real history from the fabric of the place. The wooden ceiling beams are suspiciously shiny and smooth. The modern floor planking and all the new fixtures and fittings about the bar are an impenetrable disguise. Yet that said, the shape, the heavy set windows and the yellow flames in the grate all allow some sense of what this place might have been like, if not down to the detail then perhaps just a taste of the atmosphere, the talk and the comings and goings through the door.

***

The Royal Family have left traces of their visits to the North East in a number of places I've passed through on this journey, but I didn't expect to find their footprints here, in The Ship. But I can't help notice on a windowsill prominently displayed underneath a not very authentic looking depiction of the heraldic feathers of the Prince of Wales' Badge, the words

"By Appointment to HRH the Prince of Wales
Suppliers of fine ales – for one afternoon 24 July 2012"

And next to it, as if proof were needed, is a photograph of Charles smiling broadly and looking exceptionally content with a pint of ale of some sort, presumably one brewed here at the pub. Whether he actually drank it is, of course, not recorded, but it does seem that the Royal tradition of getting up north whenever possible was observed by our King in waiting not many years ago. Whether the Royal Warrant is displayed with The Prince's formal patronage is probably a matter best not looked into.

I confess to holding some affection for Charles. He may well talk to plants, and I don't much care if he does, but he holds solid and well-reasoned views on many subjects from architecture to climate change, and he's not afraid to express them. I nearly always find myself nodding in agreement with him. I'm not a monarchist by any means. I always grimace when the cost of the Royal Purse is mentioned, and I am as aghast as most at some of the more dysfunctional behaviour displayed by some of them. But Charles runs the Duchy of Cornwall with an admirable hands-on, practical and altruistic approach and, unlike most of his corporate counterparts, the Duchy's profits are re-invested in projects like housing, land regeneration, conservation and a host of other decent causes. I like Charles. I'd like to have a pint with him. I think he would make a good King, when and if his time comes.

***

The couple sitting at the table next to me are in late middle-age. They have the slim shape of people active in retirement, professional I would think, with the time to enjoy a more leisurely lifestyle. They are growing old gracefully, comfortably off but not staid, casual but smartly dressed, and I happen to notice they have immaculate teeth. They talk quietly and directly to each other over a pint for him, a glass of white wine for her. They are a couple who listen to what each other says and they look at each other with a genuine interest when they speak. Or it could be, of course, that she's his secretary and that he's actually at a conference in Nottingham. But I don't think so. It looks to me like a longstanding, solid relationship, an inseparable connection, and it makes me want to meet them.

I'm an old hand at this sort of thing by now and I lean towards them, only slightly so as not to cause alarm, and ask if they are enjoying Low Newton. "Oh yes," she says, "we always do."

Always? Yes, they've been coming here every year for the last 15 years, which takes me aback and she must have noticed my surprise. "Oh we're not unadventurous," she says with a smile, "we go to other places too. But we love coming here for the walks and the sea. We love the quiet of it. Sometimes there's hardly anyone about, almost no one else on the beach. We wouldn't miss a year, would we?" looking across the table at her husband, or her boss. Who cares?

It turns out that David and Catherine, who is David's wife after all, come here from their home near Sheffield every year to enjoy the walks, the scenery, the history and just to get away from Sheffield, which seems reasonable. He's a retired dentist which explains Catherine's teeth, and they always stay in the same cottage if they can, one of those in the row of Coastguard Buildings just up the hill.

"My three times great-grandfather," I tell them, with an unexpected note of pride, "used to live there, 200 years ago. In one of them anyway, I don't know which," at which David offers to get a round in. He smiles broadly, and startlingly brightly. The glint of a star accompanied by a light "ping" would not have seemed out of place. I try to smile like my father, with my lips.

We manage to have a laugh about the weather and my predicament in Lookout Cottage, but it doesn't seem to have deterred David and Catherine who have walked all the way to Craster and back today, a walk of about 6 miles along the beach, the dunes and around Dunstanburgh Castle. Eventually I have to give some attention to my crab, and they are ready to head back to their cosy, warm cottage, but not before they offer the very kind invitation to drop in to see them in the Coastguard Building where Grandpa John spent some of his time, which naturally I accept, tomorrow before the pub, which seems perfect.

***

By nine the pub is emptying and most of the tables are unoccupied. Two or three couples linger, perhaps delaying the battle that lies outside, the brief struggle until the sanctuary of the rented cottage is reached, and where boots can be exchanged for slippers, the television tuned to the weather forecast, the ordnance survey map studied for tomorrow's walk, and then a warm duvet and a cloud soft pillow. I doubt Grandpa John had such expectations.

Nor do I, and I sip my pint of Ship Shape contemplating my first night in Lookout Cottage. The flames in the hearth are no longer replenished and are dying to a red, ember glow. Alex is quietly busy as she moves about wiping down tables and setting the chairs into place. As the last couple stand and move towards the door I zip up my jacket and pull up my hood. The walkers, bird watchers and lone travellers don't carouse into the night in Low Newton.

***

As I leave the pub the square is lit only dimly by the lights of curtained windows in the rosette cottages, and beyond them the shoreline and the sea beyond is pitch, impenetrable black

Next to Low Newton's one streetlight at the bottom of the hill next to the square, there is a glow from a telephone box and a dim, green light on a defibrillator. Those are the only public lights in the village, and as I make my way beyond them, up the road to the gate in the wall and then on up the hill to the cottage it is inky black. I'm grateful that I had the presence of mind to bring a torch, and for the existence of the defibrillator come to that, wondering if anyone knows how to use it should I expire on the way. The wind has eased a little, but I'm still buffeted, head down up the hill. There is neither moon nor stars to offer even a glimmer tonight. I can't see the sea, but I can hear it out there in the darkness, crashing on the shore.

There may be those who have reached the sanctuary of their rental cottage and are even now toasting their socks before a fire with a glass of something warming, but I am not one of them. It's not warm enough in the cottage to take off my outdoor gear. Grimly I run the basin for a wash and to warm my hands, but the hot tap runs persistently cold. I can't believe there's no hot water. With cold fingers I fumble through the National Trust Welcome folder. There is an immersion heater for hot water, it tells me. It even tells me where the switch is, which is in a cupboard below the sign that says "*Beware of the Leopard*". It's switched off. With a resigned discontent I switch it on and wonder how long it will take.

Both the little heaters are on, turned up full, but they're fighting a battle that can't be won. I've never had a wood burner, and haven't ever regarded them as being of much use when it comes to heating a room as opposed to just aesthetically, but needs must. The burner is already loaded with split logs and paper, so all I need to do is put a match to it, which I do. Immediately comforting flames and little crackles erupt around the wood. I squat before it for a moment watching the licking tongues and feeling the gathering warmth on my hands before it, and I wonder whether Grandpa John felt such comfort within these walls.

While I'm waiting for the wood burner to have whatever effect it is capable of, I need to explore the toilet. I've not been looking forward to this, and I'm not going to describe it all in detail, for the sake of decency if nothing else. Save to say I nearly got blown off the hill, the door to the shed slammed on my fingers, and I couldn't find the light switch. But curiously there is a heater switched on in there and it was warmer than the cottage by a good bit. It briefly occurred to me that if push came to shove I could always squirrel myself in here for the night. The sanitary ware is modern, flushing and there are copious supplies of toilet paper. It seems they'd been expecting me.

To my great surprise, when I return from the outside shed, the effect of the wood burner is even now apparent. The temperature of the room has increased already by several degrees, and it seems to me that if this carries on then "*cosy*" just might be a word I could apply to this little space. And thus it is. By the time I have poured myself a generous brandy I can take off my boots, heavy outerwear and settle down on the sofa to watch the flickering Wi Fi* lights in a much more comfortable frame of mind.

***

After the last embers of the wood burner have died away behind its glass door and my brandy has warmed my inside in the way that the fire has warmed the outside, I lie in the bed before switching off the light listening to the howling of the wind about the cottage, whistling in the struts and wires of the pylon outside the window, and thoughtfully I regard the light blue, wooden bunks built into the opposite wall. The National Trust assure me that the bunks are the originals, installed here when the cottage was built not long before Grandpa John arrived with his wife Mary.

This is where they slept. And it occurs to me that on one day, or on one night, in June 1827, and assuming they weren't into anything unconventional, here in one of these bunks they expressed their love for each other in a way that had the most profound consequences, for their son James William, and ultimately for me. I drift off into a comfortable sleep idly wondering which bunk it was, and whether Grandpa John took his boots off.

EIGHTEEN

Low Newton, Embleton, Craster

I wake up to brightness seeping through the closed curtains, and a sound I did not expect: nothing. For a full minute I lie listening to the silence, wondering whether the world has gone off somewhere else for the morning and left me alone in some quiet, temporary limbo land. Then I ease myself up, and my legs over the side of the bed. My bare feet don't find the floorboards cold, nor do I feel much of a chill in the air of the room, and I pad suspiciously through to the sitting room. Kneeling on the bench seat of the bay window, cautiously I pull the curtains aside.

The sky is translucent blue with the bright white luminescence of the sun over the horizon in the east. Small cotton cumulus hang dotted around with not much to do, feathery tails of cirrus streaked high above them. The sea, once torn with white spray, lies calm and glistening. Small waves lap at the hard sand below the seaweed line. A clump of wild grass growing in the wall six feet from my eyes occasionally flutters, but otherwise is still. The sunshine bathes a calm, benign landscape. My car, I am relieved to note, is still where I left it beside the gate at the bottom of the hill.

The wind has gone. Overnight, the storm has blown itself out or wandered off over the North Sea to bother the Dutch. It has left behind an effortless day. Hats, umbrellas and small animals will not bowl along the sands, coats will not flap and flail, faces will not be contorted into cadaverous grimace.

It's not exactly tee-shirt and shorts. The north east coast rarely lets you get away with that sort of thing, not at this time of year. But at least the day will be unencumbered by the persistent struggle of simply trying to go about ordinary business in the face of a gale. It's amazing I think, as I gaze out over the coast from my little window, how the weather has such ability to affect us, not only in the way we behave and go about our day, but in the way we feel. I wonder if Grandpa John would have looked out at this new day with approval and the prospect of a day without struggle against the elements, or if he would have ruefully observed that there would be little trade today. Fishermen will gladly launch their boats onto a benevolent sea, but the Gentlemen will wait for the storm, darkness and the mists and fog of cover.

This is probably the best day, weather-wise, that I've had since I left Norfolk all that time ago. I've had some pleasant spells, certainly. My day wandering about Cullercoats and Whitley Bay was most benign, and the sun shone very comfortably on Beamish Museum. But this looks to be the best. And what a place to have it.

As if to mark further how much difference a day makes, the tap runs with copious hot water, the toaster and the kettle provide me with all the sustenance I need for the morning, and the outside toilet seems almost welcoming to me as I step outside the front door into nothing more than the warmth of sunshine on my face. I feel ready for a day exploring. Jaunty, I might say.

***

At the bottom of the hill I glance over my car to check it hasn't been dented by some flying dustbin or flailing seagull, then step through the gate onto the road and head down towards the village, the sun glinting off the whitewashed walls and quartered windows.

Almost immediately on my right is the gable end of the row of Coastguard Buildings, five of them white-painted and all with tiled roof porches. It's a very solid, well-built row and I find it quite hard to believe it's more than 200 years old. The windows may well be replacements, and the porches are probably not original, but they have big, multi-pot chimneys and a depth to the row that suggests plenty of room inside, fireplaces and a level of quality that was certainly not enjoyed by the fishing cottages down the hill in the village. I am looking forward to meeting David and Catherine later to see for myself what they're like inside.

Down the hill, between the Coastguard Buildings and the village, is a stretch of about 200 yards of houses which are later additions to the village and were not here in Grandpa John's day. Here there were only grasses and sandy clumps, perhaps with the odd shed, stone walls enclosing goats and horses. Then the road ends at the sandy haven, and the white enclave of cottages opens onto the shore. The Ship - known as "*The Smack Inn*" to Grandpa John - nestles in one corner, a green square in the middle. It's extraordinary to think that over the past few days I have been exploring the history of Durham as it was 100 years ago, and here before me is history 100 years older than that. Just that thought brings forth images that offer a glimpse of those times. I can imagine fishermen tending their boats at the shore, men in duffel coats and huge boots striding about or sitting with a pipe of tobacco, women, shawled and long skirted, scrubbing things and shrilling at the menfolk. Why do I always see them as old people? I don't know why, but I do. Old, poor and roughly dressed. I wonder what the truth was.

It's quaint now, and clean. Other than the few cars belonging to residents, vehicles are not allowed down here in the village. The cottages may be small, like dolls houses, but they look cosy, comfortable and welcoming. It was not always so, and I slip the straps of my day pack off my shoulders, and sit down on a low wall at the front of the cottages. I look around me trying to imagine what the truth was 200 years ago, and what John Hinkley might have seen had he sat here with his tobacco and taken a rest.

Before me is the green square in the middle of the enclave. Today the grass is mown and its perimeter is defined by attractive white painted stones. Tables and benches are placed on the grass outside the pub, and I know from previous experience that in summer colourful umbrellas will be raised. There is no litter that I can see, and the smell in the air is faintly of the sea. 200 years ago this place was the midden, the pit into which the detritus of the village was emptied, all the rubbish, the fish heads, the leftover bones, and the effluence of the privies.

On 18th October 1873 the Alnwick Rural Sanitary Authority published a report about Low Newton, the housing and the conditions here. That's nearly 30 years after Grandpa John left, so the conditions that he witnessed here were no better, and possibly worse if that can be imagined, than those described in the report.

The cottages comprised one room, the report tells us, with a loft in the high tiled roof. In the fishing season extra men were drafted in, "*Yarmouth Men*" they were called for whatever reason I don't know. Perhaps they came up from East Anglia, like me. They were accommodated by the fisher families. One dwelling included three such extra men and, according to the report, a pig, all squeezed in together. The dwellings were low, crowded and deficient in light like ship cabins or berths. They were also "*deficient in sanitary contrivance*". The windowless lofts were crowded with "*all things useable at sea, for our fishing work gear takes a large garret*", sails and masts, creels, tarpaulins, ropes and lanterns.

The author of the report states that the contents of the houses were "*made out of the materials of wrecks*", coals were piled up at the back of beds, everything covered with fish scales. The common refuse tip, the midden in the centre of the square, was dependent on the care of a farmer tenant to "*remove and keep it low*". It seems he was less than reliable in his duty. Another report from the Alnwick Medical Officer dated January 1882 noted cases of smallpox and diphtheria, and recommended that the pit "*from which noxious effluvia arises*" be removed weekly, although even that doesn't sound nearly enough when you think of what went into it.

Water, the 1873 report tells us, had to be brought a considerable distance, from an "*arched cavern below some basalted rocks*", wherever that was, which tells us that there was no running water anywhere in the village.

There's a lot of imagining going on in my mind, but you can't argue with a record like that. Sitting here on my wall I am looking at the pretty white holiday cottages, the fresh green grass in the middle of the square, and the walkers enjoying the morning sunshine in brightly coloured Gortex and Velcro, carbon fibre walking poles and reflective sunglasses. A cameo flits briefly across my mind, the bizarre image of tourists in pink jogging pants, trainers and baseball caps picking their way cautiously amidst the squalid, noxious arena of the midden while shabbily clad, unsmiling figures in grubby shawls and black boots eye them suspiciously from the cottage doorsteps. Two alien worlds occupying the same space, separated only by the passing of time. They see no recognition in each other's eyes, yet they are connected by the tendons and ligaments of humanity, stretching through the decades and centuries, the past and the present. And there will come a future too, when someone not entirely unlike me might sit on this wall and consider the past, which is my present, and I wonder if he will feel a connection to it, as I think I do on this wall where John Hinkley sat 200 years ago.

***

The coastguards' accommodation receives quite a different appraisal. The Sanitary Authority's 1873 report describes the Coastguard Buildings just up the hill as "*models of order, smart with black and white wash, taut and trim and possessing every sanitary contrivance including earth closet and commode*" which makes me feel rather relieved on Grandpa John's behalf, perhaps in more senses than one. If he were sitting here on this wall regarding the business of the village he might shake his head slowly at what he saw. Or perhaps it no longer surprised him, and given the midden pit which would have been right here in front of him, he wouldn't sit here at all but move on to the more fragrant wafts of salt and seaweed at the shore.

Easing myself up off the wall and pulling the straps of my day pack up over my shoulders, I walk up the narrow lane that leads behind the cottages, around the back of The Ship, and between the rear of the buildings and a row of outhouses, now converted into mini holiday accommodation. Further on a gate leads onto a path out of the village between the dunes. The sandy grasses rise high to my left, shielding me from a view of the sea, until hardly more than 200 yards from the enclave of cottages is a house, low-set and alone nestling in the dunes. This is Risemoor Cottage, now a holiday let but in days gone by The Fisherman's Arms. This former inn is set apart from the village, yet only by a minute's walk. It amazes me that this place could support two pubs, even taking into account the wider, agricultural catchment area, and given there is also The Joiners Arms just up the road at High Newton.

I wonder if there was a demarcation of factions, with the Gentlemen, the ruffians, the petty and the not so petty criminals in the Fisherman's Arms, and the good folk of the village, the Admiralty Men and those who gave their allegiance to them up the path in The Ship. I imagine the short distance between the two a sort of no man's land, each side watching the other, waiting for the first move.

***

From Risemoor Cottage I clamber back through the dunes and in a few short steps I feel the soft, loose sand beneath my boots. Then a few yards on, stepping over the straggly brown seaweed at the high water mark I reach the hard, damp sand near the water's edge where a boot, a bare foot or a paw print leaves only a shallow, wet indentation to mark the passing of a walker or some bounding animal.

Slowly I saunter along the sand, the water lazily lapping up to my feet, and then, as if it can't be bothered with the effort, receding slowly back with a gurgle, leaving white streaks of foam behind against the brown sand. Although Low Newton is usually referred to as being at the north end of Embleton Bay, the village actually has a small bay of its own, Newton Haven or St Mary's Haven as it is sometimes known. A small headland a few hundred yards down the beach separates this little crescent from the main, long stretch. Here the coastguard boats would be put to sea and is where Grandpa John would have gathered with his colleagues when they set off to patrol the coast. Even today boats and tackle are drawn up, lying idle among the sand and shingle. And here I remember as a child playing in the sands building castles with Little John, throwing stones into the sea and gambolling about with the energy of childhood while Mum and Dad sat watching from the soft sand by the dunes. It was a long drive for a day out, but a change from The Lido or the boating lake.

There are but a few walkers on the sands as I walk around the headland onto the long crescent of Embleton Bay. Dogs gambol about after balls or sticks. Wading birds strut stiffly and bob in the shallows. On the rocky outcrops offshore a pair of sentinel cormorants sit at guard. Overhead, seagulls make their raucous calls hovering effortlessly against the gentle breeze. I have this place very much to myself.

Halfway down the beach I haul myself up through the high dunes to find a path which crosses a hundred yards of marshy reeds and then reaches the mown grass of the golf course, only the width of the first tee at this point, where in busier times men in diamond pullovers, check trousers and spiked shoes wait impatiently for walkers to pass by on their right of way. I cross by the tee to the low, sprawling cabin that is their clubhouse with its car park. From there a long, narrow lane winds between high hedges for about half a mile to the village of Embleton, where Grandpa John's son, James William, was baptised in the Church of the Holy Trinity on 27th April 1828.

Embleton is a quiet, peaceful, informally structured village. Historic development has followed the lines of roads and lanes rather than in any planned pattern. Thus it is pleasantly irregular, well-spaced, and it's endowed with three pubs: the Greys Inn which is a particular favourite of mine with a small but steeply terraced garden abundant with flowers and greenery, The Blue Bell which I have never been in, and the incongruous Dunstanburgh Castle Hotel, the purpose of which I have never understood. It's a large hotel of no discernible character sitting rather out of place in this quiet little village. It would be better suited in the high street of some county town. I dropped in for a drink one afternoon some years ago and I was the only one in the small, refined, cocktail style bar. In fact, I was the only one in the hotel so far as I could tell, other than a barman who on that day had better things to do than offer me a welcome.

Retracing my steps back down the lane, past the golf course and the dunes, I'm back on the beach looking up at the looming remains of the castle, sitting on the headland formed by the northernmost outcrop of the Great Whin Sill, a layer of igneous rock featured through the counties of Cumbria, Durham and Northumberland. Hadrian's Wall takes advantage of its high, rocky outlines, and here at Dunstanburgh in the 13th century it offered a promising defensive location, although as it turned out not an impregnable one.

The spiky ruins remind me of the eccentric shapes left by the World Trade Centre towers, holding in its outline against the sky a depiction of conflict and war. But unlike the grim consequences of 9/11 these ruins possess a romantic, stirring spirit, a place resonant of knights in armour, heraldic pennants, heroic deeds and bravery. Yet the battles which were witnessed here were just as brutal and just as ill-conceived as the atrocity perpetrated against the citizens of the United States in 2001, and I wonder to myself what it is that allows Dunstanburgh such deception. It seems to me that in its ruinous condition it manages to maintain an almost majestic defiance, as if to say "*in spite of all I've been through, I'm still here, and in another 100 years I still will be. Will you?*"

My route takes me from the beach up through stones and rocks onto the grassy coastal path to the castle itself. Ruined it may be, but the brown stones rise dramatically above me as the path takes me around its feet. The great gatehouse, towers and battlements have withstood the storms of this coast for hundreds of years, but they could not withstand the assault and battery occasioned by the conflict between the Yorkists and the Lancastrians, the Wars of the Roses, in the 15th century. It was so badly damaged that the castle then fell into disrepair and was derelict soon afterwards, never to be restored.

So when Grandpa John looked at this iconic and defiant place it was exactly as I see it now, as if with his eyes, as if in his boots on this the same grassy ground. Landmark, navigation aid, place of refuge or ambush, this was a stark sentinel on a coastline of rocky promontories and sandy bays, the one thing that could be seen for miles around, and John would have seen it every day of the 20 years he spent here. I feel his heavy coat, his stout boots, and his careful eye as he surveys the coast.

From the castle my route follows the edge of an unfenced field of cows along a grassy path above the low, rocky cliff, and the village of Craster advances ever closer with each step. Eventually, a mile on from the castle, a gate opens onto the end of the village road, a line of white cottages, all with rosettes in the porch windows of course, and then the road curves around the short, stubby piers that enclose a rather muddy little harbour, strewn with brown seaweed, lines of rope, chains and sturdy working boats moored at the quay, boats for fishing and for day trips to the Farne Islands and Coquet Island off the coast where seals and seabirds colonise the rocks. It has the feel of business, of quiet activity.

Craster has two features I am particularly anxious to explore, the Jolly Fisherman and the smoke house where, so I was led to believe by the van on the Newcastle quayside, kippers are "*manufactured*".

The smokehouse on the main street overlooking the harbour has old, big, wooden gates set into the front of a heavy, stone building. It has a greasy, oily feel to it, and the appearance of having been here for centuries, smoking kippers since time immemorial. In fact, it was built here as recently as 1856 and sadly Grandpa John had long left the area by then, so would have been unable to partake of a manufactured kipper even if he had a mind to. The Robson family have it now, since 1890 in fact, and I'm keen to find out what it's all about.

I walk in through the big gates to a yard where there is a kipper restaurant - closed to me today - and a door which leads to a kipper shop. I wander in, where I find modern cold counters displaying not only kippers but crab, lobster, wet fish and things in shells. There are also freezers, and shelves of bottles and jars of fish pastes, terrines, and oddly to my mind, jam preserves. I'm the only customer, and so have the attention of the young lady in a striped apron behind the kipper counter.

The lady is a Robson herself she tells me, the daughter, or maybe it was a niece but some relative anyway, of the owner Mr Robson, Neil son of Alan, the Kipper Master of the current generation. She is immensely proud of this, and affectionately fondles the forked tail of a kipper on the cold counter. The air in the shop is eye-wateringly fishy.

I have a poke around the shelves while she chats away, whether to me or herself I'm not sure, and I manage to find a pot of crab terrine which I guess will last till I get home and will make a gift for my wife. Not very romantic, I accept, but a present nevertheless, and a counterpart to the Beamish preserve I bought for her back at Beamish Museum.

At the kipper counter with my purchase, I ask her if the van I saw in Newcastle, the one with the legend "*Manufacturers of the Famous Craster Kippers*", was likely to have been one of hers. Oh yes, she confirms, they deliver kippers all over, to restaurants, shops, supermarkets, all over the county and beyond. They even have an international clientele who receive their kippers by post, securely packaged I hope.

Unfortunately, I'm encouraged by her enthusiasm and easy conversation to pursue this. Adopting a jocular tone I offer the suggestion that to describe a kipper as "*manufactured*", is highly humorous and deserving of a chuckle. This is not, as I probably ought to have foreseen, as funny as all that. A kipper she tells me, having dispensed with the smiley face, requires significant production from raw material to plate. Herrings are imported from Norway, then they have to be soaked in brine, gutted and then split into kipper shape. Then they are hung in a smoker of whitewood shavings and oak sawdust for up to 16 hours. Although the splitting is done by a machine all the rest is done by hand. And, she tells me in a tone I detect as less than wholly approving, there is only one woman involved in the whole process, and that's her aunt.

As I retreat from the shop, across the yard and out of the wooden gates towards the Jolly Fisherman over the road, clutching my jar of crab terrine, I think to myself that, as ever, I should have done some research first, which might have avoided the feeling that I've made myself look a damn fool, again.

***

The Jolly Fisherman has a fine and deserved reputation for its seafood, served in the compact, oak bar or in the conservatory which stretches along the back of the pub overlooking the coast, not unlike the Fishing Boat at Boulmer. Little John and I were often brought here by Mum and Dad on one of our day trips up to this part of the county. We sat at one of the high tables on stools, our legs dangling while we forked nuggets of crispy breaded scampi from a shared bowl. Mum and Dad always had prawn sandwiches.

Prawn sandwiches were Dad's favourite, second only to prunes. Dad had prunes in sweet syrup out of a tin for breakfast every day. He spooned them onto a bowl of All Bran in the expectation that the fibre in the bran would counter the laxative effect of the prunes. He was wrong, and so would supplement his breakfast with Immodium or Senokot depending on where he was on the spectrum of bowel function. Sometimes he would sit at the breakfast table, pause, stick his chin forward, open his mouth and emit a noise like a cow giving birth. Why he didn't just have a bowl of cornflakes like the rest of us I will never know.

After our scampi and chips Little John and I would scuttle out of the pub and down the harbour steps to the seaweed and hard, brown sand where we cautiously lifted the slimy fronds in the hope that a crab might scuttle out. Sometimes we ran along one of the short stubby piers and peered down onto the boats moored below us, fascinated by the boxes and nets, brightly coloured buoys and ropes. I longed to clamber down one of the steel ladders to a boat, but they were slippery with green weed and the drop was at least 15 feet, so I was never allowed to do that.

***

I do like a pub. I always have done, ever since I made my first expeditions to The Broadway and then braver forays to The Rex and The Chain Locker. Later I followed in the footsteps of the likes of Kevin Whately and discovered the dark, back-alley bars of Darlington and Barnard Castle and the quieter country pubs of Durham and Yorkshire cluttered with horse brasses, Toby jugs and red-faced gentlemen in brown brogue shoes and dark green tweed jackets. It's not just the beer, it's the social interaction, the anticipation of unexpected meetings, the wonderful experience of coming across someone just slightly but harmlessly bonkers. I love that.

These days I like a pub which is just a little fussy. I like to be able to sit at a stool with my elbows on the bar, beer towels and an array of pumps before me, and at the back of the bar an excessive display of bottles and mirrors. I like wood panelling, heavy oak tables, real beams and low ceilings. I like the low chatter of people around me, and I do like an open log fire. In all these respects, The Jolly Fisherman is fully compliant. The diners in the conservatory are keeping most of the staff occupied, and the barman has time to chat to me, feigning labour by wiping a glass with a tea towel as he does so. Naturally, I tell him about my journey and why I'm here, in the vain assumption that he will be at all interested. I didn't realise I was being overheard.

"Did you say Tynemouth?" is the way Steve introduces himself from the next barstool. He's about my age, and my sort of shape which I like to think of as not slim but not heavy. He dresses in a similar way to me when I'm not in walking gear, which is pullover and casual trousers. I think he may have been here a little while already today. "Yes," I respond turning on my stool towards him, "I was born there. I live in the south now though. I'm here on memory lane, if you like." And so the conversation progresses as it becomes clear that we were born within yards of each other. We discover our mutual acquaintance with the Spanish City, Whitley Bay, The Broadway, and Steve reaches the certain conclusion that at some point we surely sat next to each other at the bar of the Broadway pub. Well, possibly. But not only that, Steve knew Alan Hull, of the band Lindisfarne who bought me a pint in that bar. Alan Hull lived in Tynemouth he says, which I didn't know but it makes sense as to why he was there that day when I made my adolescent self known to him.

The landlady, Jan, perhaps drawn by the conversation between me and Steve and talk of Tynemouth and Whitley Bay, joins us with a glass of white wine or prosecco held lightly in her fingers at shoulder height. She introduces her husband, Steve, and I'm beginning to feel as if I have stumbled into a convention. Jan is, like the Steves, about my age. She has styled light grey hair, artistically applied make up and a smile that reveals just a touch of red lipstick on her white teeth. She wears cashmere and fine linen. She is quite clearly the pub's gregarious hostess.

Jan grew up in her parents' hotel, The Grafton, right next to The Rex where I spent my teenage evenings listening to loud rock bands. When I mention the High Point Hotel which overlooked the Whitley Bay promenade and where my father's company held dinner dances and conferences, Jan says "that would have been MacGregor's then." It begins to feel as if Douglas Adams' Infinite Improbability Drive that transported Arthur Dent and Ford Prefect into more and more unlikely situations has just activated as she relates that her parents regularly attended those events, and would undoubtedly have known my own mother and father.

As I've left the car back in Low Newton I'm pleased to accept Jan's offer of another beer. We are all indulgent in our reminiscences, indulgence that becomes more earnest as one or other of the Steves attends to another round, and before very long we are all very good friends indeed and email addresses and phone numbers are exchanged with vows to stay in touch, drop in any time, and possibly we will all set up home and move in together.

***

I do enjoy the long walk back along the grassy clifftop, past the castle and along the sands, although I stayed at The Jolly Fisherman longer than I had intended and I'm not sure my route along the beach was quite as direct as it would otherwise have been.

Through the gate in the wall and up the hill, before I go inside I take a walk around the heavy stone wall that surrounds Lookout Cottage. The grass is long and hummocky, falling away towards the coast and I can feel the gentle breeze of late afternoon. The sun is falling towards the horizon in the west, but the sea still sparkles under a light blue sky.

I have a photograph, taken by me from this exact spot, sometime in the late 1960s. In it my father and my mother are standing against the cottage wall in weatherproof clothing, my father in a grey checked cloth cap. My mother has her arm through my father's. They are both smiling at the camera with the coastline curving away behind them, the ruins of Dunstanburgh in the background. This was long before we knew that the white cottage had anything to do with our family history, and long before any of us had even heard of John Hinkley or our connection with Low Newton and the Coastguard Service. But years later when my father was still well, I was able to talk to him about my researches into our ancestry, and tell him about the cottage we stood next to in Low Newton in that photograph. Dad was genuinely fascinated as we both pored over the notes I had made and the lines of the family tree I had drawn, and he smiled as he traced a finger over the names and places. I have always been glad that I had the opportunity to share this part of our history together.

As I stand here in the cooling air as the light starts to go down, I have a sense of my father standing here with me, his dark green coat with burgundy red shoulder pieces, brown-laced walking shoes and cap, gazing out to sea with slightly rheumy eyes. For a moment I can see John Hinkley standing there next to him, a heavier man in heavier clothing, beard and black cloth hat. Two Johns, two men who bear the same blood as me. I try to hold the scene before me but although I linger there on the grass beside the cottage wall, it fades. I walk back round the wall, through the picket gate and into the light blue room.

***

David and Catherine welcome me into their holiday let cottage in the middle of the row of Coastguard Buildings. A bottle of wine is already uncorked on the fashionable glass coffee table. Three tall flutes await a toast, and David ushers me to sit down on a smartly upholstered sofa. "Well," he says, "do you think this is where your great-grandfather lived?"

I shake my head slowly. "Three times great," I correct him. "I've no idea, but it could well have been." Looking about me, I seem to have entered a magazine of contemporary home design. The room is spacious with glossy varnished timber flooring, immaculately plastered white walls, recessed lighting and subtle pastel fabrics. Prints in white frames hang with exactly the right distances between them. The open plan design leads to a kitchen area bright with sparkling white, brushed steel and swivel stools at a breakfast bar. A curving, light wood open staircase leads to the upper floor where, I fully expect, will be found a bathroom that a quality hotel would be pleased to offer, and bedrooms equipped for the comfort of the discerning.

I know, because I looked it up, that the on-line brochure for this cottage speaks of "*original features*". There is a fireplace, quite small with a heavy stone lintel, which I suppose could be original, but it has a large vase of flowers in it. Both the front and the back doors are made of battened timber with latch fittings and the 6 pane sash windows are wood frames, but they aren't strikingly original. If I was a tourist, a holidaymaker seeking comfortable, warm accommodation, fully equipped with every modern convenience, this place would fit the bill in every respect. But Grandpa John would not recognise an inch of it. There is not a hint of how he lived here, how he cooked or slept, how he washed or relaxed, how he even existed. Beneath the new, unblemished plaster there may well be the brickwork that enclosed him then as it does me now, beneath the varnished floor boards there may be the foundations that were built 200 years ago, and the hole in the ceiling may well be the hole that gave him access to the upstairs as it does now. But then, it may not.

"It's really lovely," I say to David and Catherine, as David fills a glass with a good measure. "Really comfortable. But I think it's changed a bit since he was here."

David chuckles and sets a glass down on the table in front of me. "I don't think we'd be here if it hadn't. Imagine it in the weather we've had over the last few days."

"You should have been up the hill," I remind him, and take a sip, "but really, there's nothing left in here that he would recognise. There must have been a cooking range, open fireplaces, God knows what sort of furnishings and bedding. You've got a full hob and a built in oven. You've got a bathroom upstairs I expect?" David nods. "The trouble is, there are all sorts of records to tell you where they lived, and to a certain extent what they did and how they did it, but there's hardly any domestic detail. There's very little to tell us about their daily life. I've got a whole sheaf of coastguard records, which is how I know he was here and when, but I have no idea what life was really like for them, what they did from day to day. I don't know how they cooked or ate, or even what they ate come to that."

"Fish," says Catherine with a smile that brightens nearby glassware. "I bet they ate a lot of fish. So they were probably very healthy."

"Except for smallpox and diphtheria," I say, "which I do know they had here."

"And cutlass and gunshot wounds," David adds. "You can't imagine it, can you?"

And that wise observation is a point. I'm not sure you *can* imagine it. You can *imagine* that you imagine it, but it's a best guess, which might be close to the truth or it might not. There are some things that were never recorded, and never could be, but were things which would have shaped their lives. What was John's relationship with his fellow men? Did he enjoy his work? Was he fearful, brave or cowardly? Was he a rough irascible man, or kindly and soft spoken? Was he a scrawny little fellow, or a beast of a man?

I have wondered too at John's manner of speech. As a man born and brought up on the south coast, what accent or dialect did he bring with him to this remote northern outpost where the local people spoke in a way that he may well have been hard-pressed to understand, and they him? Did he take on a northern brogue over time? Did his son, James William, born here and raised in the village adopt the Northumbrian tongue?

There is no way of knowing the truth of such things. But 200 years from now those who follow my generation will have no such trouble. They will have no need for imagination. Through film and video, archives, databases, all the incessant recording of the daily lives of every one of us, by governments, service and utility providers, police and security agencies, even our local supermarket, every detail, every nuance of our lives is recorded and preserved, with or without our consent and whether we like it or not. Our descendants will know what television shows we watched, what we bought at the store, where we went on holiday and when. They will know of every cough and sneeze for which we sought medical attention, our pleasures and our pains, every stroke on our keyboards parked in some memory bank.

To be honest, I don't like it. I don't like the invasion of my privacy, and I don't like it that I can't turn it off, or be certain that I have done so. I'm not a criminal and I have nothing worse to hide than my taste in shirts and my appalling golf swing, but I'm deeply unhappy about wholesale covert surveillance. So was George Orwell, and he knew a thing or two.

Anyway, I do now harbour the idea that perhaps my imagination is not as unreliable as I think it might be. If Carl Jung is right then *"we're born with the experiences of our parents and ancestors imprinted on our DNA"*. That is the Genetic Memory I've been looking for since I set out on this journey. Perhaps I've been looking in the wrong place. I wonder if I am closer to the truth in my visions than I sometimes think I am.

Hans Christian Andersen wrote *"Out of reality are our tales of imagination founded"*, recalled by Graham Greene in his spy creation *"The Human Factor"*. The imaginations which formed those authors' narratives had their genesis in the real world. They drew on their experiences, their emotions, what they had read, seen and heard, all consigned to that deeply complex place in their mind, their memory.

A genetic memory is a hidden, latent file of images and data that have their origins in the experiences of one's ancestors, and if imagination can access that then maybe those imaginations are not as wild or as speculative as you think they are. Perhaps they are, by virtue of that genetic memory, more real and more accurate than you might think.

Perhaps the images I have been seeing in what I have called my imagination, unknown to my consciousness, are in fact born of the genetic memory I have been looking for. Perhaps it's been there all the time, helping me along quietly in the background, offering me those images and feelings I have had so often on this journey. Perhaps that's what it is.

***

By the time we adjourn to The Ship for dinner, we've finished the bottle and darkness has fallen. For some reason the streetlight at the bottom of the hill has failed to come on, and we are guided to the pub by the green light of the defibrillator like a ship drawn to shore by the lights of a harbour.

Dinner has the genial composition of new friends with fresh conversation. Our talk moves from shoes to kings, taking in the ships, sealing wax and candlesticks along the way. But tomorrow David and Catherine are leaving, to return to Sheffield and crowded streets, supermarkets and gas bills. With smiles and handshakes we thank each other for the company we have enjoyed. We do exchange addresses and we may well use them. I bid them farewell, then leave them to continue on my journey.

Back in Lookout Cottage I spend some time sitting in the bay window, gazing out at the reflection of the moon in the dark water, the lights of two ships far out to sea. The air is still, the seagulls have gone to sleep, and the wood burner is dying away to a dull, ember glow.

Sipping my nightcap brandy I have my notebook before me on the table in the bay window. Leafing through to a new page, I write a heading at the top - "*Bamburgh*", then "*Alnwick*" and "*Ellingham*", places which will take me in new directions in the search for my Northern Soul.

NINETEEN

Night Ambush

The night was moonless. A damp mist hung in the still air and obscured much of the shore. John Hinkley leaned against the high, grassy dune in front of him and shifted his feet on the sand. Through the reeds he could make out the water's edge fifty yards away. He could hear the regular light splash and see the fleeting thin white line of foam. Beyond the beach, far out, a faint horizon marked where the heavy sky met the sea.

John peered more intently over the dune, his eyes half closed for focus. The needles of three masts outlined against the sky were moving very slowly south. The ship showed no lights. Dutch, he thought.

John looked sideways down the line of the dunes where five yards away a dark figure also leaned against the wall of sandy grasses. The man had his back to him, leaning sideways but watching out to sea. John could see by the figure's shape he held his pistol in his right hand, and John felt the weight of his own weapon in his belt.

John made a low hissing sound through his teeth, and the figure slowly turned towards him. With his hand John motioned out to sea and the figure followed the line of sight, then turned back. John held up three fingers, and the man nodded. John motioned again with his hand down the path behind the dunes, the man nodded again and silently they doubled low and crept another ten yards then stopped.

John took a glass to his eye and poked it through the spiky grasses. He squinted through the gloom for a moment and then without turning his head and with the glass still to his eye he whispered in a low voice, "Dutchman."

Gin runners thought John, as they had expected. That meant two, maybe three boats. A dozen men, maybe twice that with 20 or more barrels between them. He was ready for them.

John and Will, his boatman and a strong and eager lad, stayed still and waited in the dunes. They didn't speak. The only sound was a light splashing at the water's edge. The mists came and went across the shoreline. Fifty yards on, John knew, were the Lieutenant and three others. They would be waiting too, and they would have seen the ship with three masts. Two hundred yards beyond them were the men from Boulmer, eight of them probably with muskets. John's hand went to his belt again, feeling the lock of the pistol and the leather cover keeping it dry from the damp air. His left hand felt the hilt of his cutlass and the heavy leather baton at his hip.

Will's eyes were still fixed on the shoreline. They were both wearing colours, red tunics, not for authority but to show their side and keep them safe from taking a friendly ball. John's eyes turned back to the dark sea. It was the waiting that was the worst, and he felt the nervous impatience of an actor waiting for the curtain. The ship was now a little further to the south, its masts smaller to the eye. It would soon disappear from view, and John wondered how many other drops the ship had already made on its journey down the coast, and how many more it would make further south on the east coast shore until it berthed in London and duty was paid on only half the cargo it had left home with.

John held his head still and drew a breath slowly through his nose. He was seeking a sweet smell, a smell of straw, hay, the unmistakeable drift of animal, of pony. They would be there, somewhere at the back of them, two probably, and a boy. They would likely be further on down the dunes, between the Lieutenant and the Boulmer men, held back from the coast waiting, just like them, but unaware of the trap set for them. John couldn't smell the animals, but they would be there.

Will turned to him. "Where are they?" he whispered.

"Soon," said John quietly, his gaze still focused on the shore. "Very soon."

At first the boats were just shadows, then John made out their shapes. They came in silence, three of them emerging from the gloom, low in the water, oars shipped. They came to shore with a quiet crunching as the keels met the shingle, and then the dark figures of men slipped over the side into shallow water and began hauling the boats onto the sands. Silently they worked, without speech or call. Still John and Will waited, watching.

Twelve men John counted, black clad and stealthy in their work. They were quick, hauling the small, heavy barrels from the boats into the arms of men standing by next to the half-beached boats. They rolled the barrels up onto the hard sand, ten John counted, then fifteen, then twenty as hard calloused hands heaved them off the boats. Any moment now.

"Stand there!"

A shout from 50 yards away, the Lieutenant's shout. Then a flash from the shoreline just before the crack of a pistol. The ball must have missed its mark for there was no cry. Two shots came in reply and a shout from the shoreline. John scrambled up and over the dune in front of him and then he was running forward, feet sliding in the soft sand until he felt the grip of harder ground beyond the tideline. Will ran beside him breathing heavily. Black figures were scattering down the beach. Some scrambled for the boats. Shouts erupted all down the shore, angry shouts, shouts of authority and shouts of panic. The Boulmer men were coming up from their position in the south. John could see a figure on the sand, cursing loudly. He kept running.

Two men were running up the beach to the north. They had some distance on John and Will and the better of them. "With me!" John shouted to Will and they headed at a run towards the beached boats. John held his pistol forward in his right hand, his cutlass unsheathed in his left. Figures moved in confusion, some up the beach, some to the south and others into the dunes. The red tunics were dull in the misty darkness, but sufficient to identify an Admiralty Man. John heard no more shots but he could see the shapes of cutlasses drawn and as he neared the boats two men ran at them hard. Will took one to the ground with a hefty punch to the side of the head and John held one with his cutlass, point to the chest. It was but a boy of sixteen, and scared. John shook his head and took the boy's arms behind him, roughly but expertly securing them with twine from his pocket.

"Mind these two," John said to Will who had them both now. The frantic shouting had stopped. Men on the shore moved slowly, and a few torches had been lit, lanterns casting flickering shadows. John walked down the hard sand past the barrels lying on the beach to a huddle of red-clad figures thirty yards away. "Two of them," he said to his Lieutenant who was standing with several men one of whom John saw was the other Lieutenant from Boulmer. "Plus the one with a ball in his shoulder. Yours I think." John grinned but no one saw in the darkness.

"Aye," said the Lieutenant. "The others off like rabbits. They'll be half-way to the border by now."

"Ponies?" said John.

"Never saw them," the Lieutenant replied. "They'll be away too by now. Get the barrels loaded and up to the lock house. The three we've got will go with the Boulmer men. They'll have them up to Alnwick in the morning."

Two men in red from Boulmer stepped forward. "Aye," said John, and walked back to where Will was standing over two figures, cross-legged on the sand, heads down, arms tied with twine. A few yards away another man in red was standing over a figure lying on the ground, who he kicked sharply when a curse or some blasphemy was uttered, which was frequently.

"Find Tom and Alfred," John said to Will, "and get the cart. Get all this up to the lock house and pull these boats up."

"Aye," Will replied. "You could have saved the trouble and ran that one through." He nodded down at the boy. It was more a question than a statement.

"No, Will, you know the rules. Killing's for the magistrate, not us. Not if it can be avoided." Will grunted and walked off down the beach. The two Boulmer men hauled the prisoners to their feet and pushed them off down the sands to where their company was waiting. The man with the shoulder wound was being roughly treated at the hands of the Boulmer men, dragged on his feet towards the dunes where a cart and a horse waited.

John walked back to where his Lieutenant was standing. For a moment the two men stood together and regarded what lay around them. Three ship's boats, bows on the shingle and sterns wallowing softly in the shallows. Barrels lay haphazardly on the sand where they had been dropped. Men in red tunics moved slowly about, a couple roughly shoving their prisoners up the beach.

"Well done, John," the Lieutenant said to his second in command. He stroked his beard. "We ought to have had more of them though."

John nodded. "Some will always slip through," he said. "They know the land as well as we do. Better, some of them." He pointed the tip of his cutlass in the direction of the barrels lying on the shore. "There's a few gallons of gin that won't make it to where it shouldn't be."

He trudged back up the sands to the dunes and the path up the coast. He left the men at the shore to haul up the boats and secure them, and to load the barrels to the lock house in the village where they will wait to be taken to The Authority in Alnwick.

Twenty barrels. John idly wondered how many would make it to the excise store in the town. Brandy for the parson, baccy for the clerk. Even the excise men had to live.

TWENTY

Bamburgh, Alnwick

This is the second morning that I wake up in Lookout Cottage and it holds neither angry storm nor luminescent sunshine. As I kneel on the window bench in the bay window I'm looking out at curtains of rain moving slowly across the landscape from the west, dulling the outlines of the land, supressing any colour beyond blended shades of grey.

The sky is a monochrome patchwork of slate and ash which moves slowly from west to east. Slanting diagonals blend into the colour of the sea where showers fall from darker clouds. From time to time a squall of rain hits the window of the bay with an urgent patter, then fizzles out. The ruins of Dunstanburgh are all but hidden, occasionally poking through the gloom like little fingers in the distance before retreating behind the cover of the misty haze.

It's not unpleasant actually. I'm content to sit with a mug of coffee and watch the weather, the landscape slowly coming and going as the stands of slanting rain pass through. I'm in no hurry to go out in it. Bamburgh will wait for me.

***

By the time I have attended to the matters of the morning, which included having lukewarm water dripped on me by the shower and making a brief and damp excursion to the outside closet, I take myself and a fresh mug of coffee to the window seat again. I'm still in my socks and tee shirt, not expecting any outdoors action anytime soon and thinking I might just spend the morning tootling about the cottage and maybe write up some of my notes onto the laptop. Then a hint of blue appears in the western sky, nervously at first then with more confidence as the minutes tick by. For half an hour I watch it growing and drawing further eastwards, pushing away the greyness of the early morning, allowing stripes of brightness onto the landscape and the hillsides.

As the dark clouds head further off out to sea, glimmers of light on the ruffled water turn into sparkles and then into shimmer. The heavy skies are replaced by clear blue and dots of white. The rain ceases and I can see all the marks on the window pane as the light of the sun catches it. The regular drip from a gutter outside marks the passing of the rain.

By the time I have got myself ready, boots on and day pack sorted, the day outside the door of the cottage is bright and clear. The air has the slightly damp freshness that the rain has left behind, and a smell of wet grass and earth mingles with the salty ozone of the coast. Happily, I tramp down the hill to the car.

***

I'm going to Bamburgh for a purpose. Although it's only some 15 miles north of Low Newton and is very probably a place Grandpa John would have visited in the course of his time here, Bamburgh is the source of an entirely different line of my ancestry. Through my father's line two generations spent their lives in Bamburgh before they, like the line of the Hinkleys and others, came south to county Durham and work in the mines. It intrigues me that, if they had been seeking work in the collieries, none of them stopped in the coalfields of Northumberland, on the way and much closer. I have no idea why that was. It's the sort of detail that would take me so much closer to their lives, and I feel some frustration that this sort of particular so often remains beyond my grasp, no matter how much research I do.

These people were my four times great-grandparents, William Beveridge and Ann MacDougal. They were born in Bamburgh, William in 1770, and Ann in 1774. I've wondered at her maiden name, so obviously Scottish, and that this is the closest I've ever come to uncovering a family connection north of the border. Perhaps further back in time her line would explain the light, gingery hue I noticed in my father's hair when he was a young man, but I haven't been able to explore that far.

William and Ann had a daughter, Isabella, in 1797. She was married in 1825 to William Agar from whom one line descended to me, and another across the ocean to Utah USA where Mormonism and the tradition of taking multiple wives was enthusiastically embraced by a remote cousin of mine, many times removed. But that's another story.

***

Once I'm in the car and settled, the engine turns and fires with an unhesitating willingness that I always find most reassuring. It's not that this car has ever shown any tendency towards the unreliable, but I suppose I am of a generation which remembers all too well the apprehension experienced before turning the starter key on a second hand 1970s British Leyland, acquired for a few quid out of a student grant, or borrowed from Dad. What is not reassuring on this occasion is the warning message which appears on the dashboard, "*Smart Key Battery Low*".

A Smart Key is, to me, an example of technology doing stuff just because it can, rather than because it's useful. In the case of my car, so long as the Key is in my pocket the vehicle will unlock and I can press a button to start it, which is supposed to be an advance over putting the key in the ignition. It's in the same category as devices which enable you to shout across the room *"What's the weather like today?"* instead of looking out of the window.

There is, I'm told, also a security benefit in the Smart Key. Without its specially coded signal the vehicle will remain obstinately asleep and refuse to be stolen. Which means, so I've heard, that young men in baseball caps stand in your driveway at night with a portable device that communicates with your Smart Key indoors and enables them to nick your vehicle with far less trouble than messing about trying to pick a lock. It's technology gone too far, especially when it doesn't work.

What worries me now as I sit in the field next to the gate with the engine idling, is what happens if the Smart Key battery actually fails, as it seems to be telling me that it might. If it does, I imagine the car will neither open nor start, unthinkable prospects. I lean over and pull the manual from the glove compartment and sure enough there is a whole section about the Smart Key, pages of it, and some of it tells me what to do if it fails.

The first thing to do is dismantle the rear offside door handle, which is a screwdriver too far for me. Obviously the simple solution is a new battery. The manual tells me it's a CR2032, which so far as I know might be as rare as pink sheep in rural Northumberland. If I do manage to find one the instructions are to prise the side panels off the fob with a screwdriver and the top and bottom will separate revealing a small circuit board beneath which is the battery. I know, because this sort of thing happens to me, that if I do this the thing will spring apart in a shower of components. If I manage to put them back, which is unlikely, there will be a small but crucially important bit left over. I can't imagine Grandpa John having this sort of grief when he attended to the technology of the 19th century. A heavy hammer and a boot probably fixed most things.

I set off feeling anxious, bumping out of the gate onto the road, hoping that I'll find somewhere to get a battery before the thing gives out and I'm stranded in deepest

Northumberland with no mobile signal and the nearest dealership in Newcastle.

***

The road takes me back through High Newton and the Joiners Arms where I was going to stop for coffee and a look at the place, but which I daren't do now in case the Smart Key gives out and I can't get back in or start the car again.

Hardly five miles north the road by-passes the small coastal town of Beadnell. I've been to Beadnell before and while it has a pleasant old village centre with a couple of nice pubs and an interesting old harbour, most of it consists of post-war holiday bungalows, chalets and a couple of really awful holiday caravan parks, the like of which ought never to have been allowed by whoever is in charge of that sort of thing. So I don't bother with it and stay on the road towards Seahouses, only another two miles away.

Seahouses is not a place I intend to linger in either. It's a seaside town in the traditional fish and chips, candy floss, amusement arcade sense that I find quite out of place up here. It's a sizeable town with a main street endowed with a good smattering of decent coffee shops and I daresay a good pub or two, but there are too many gift shops selling authentic Seahouses bric-a-brac, models of Bamburgh Castle that look as if someone has dropped a turd on a plastic mount and stuck a flag in it, and all that seaside tat one expects to see in places like Blackpool, but not here, not on the wild coast of Northumberland.

However, as I approach the town I spot a garage on the outskirts. It's one of those village garages that have a shabby, faded red canopy, two oily fuel pumps endorsed with a brand name you've never heard of and a scruffy low shop with a small selection of groceries, some cans of motor oil, some crisps and a small, grubby Formica counter. The shop is manned, in this case, by Francis Rossi.

I pull in hoping to get some advice about my Smart Key, and I take it into the shop where Mr Rossi stands behind the counter with what remains of his hair pulled back tightly over his head into a small tail. He has the craggy look of a rock star whose career is largely behind him but is pressing on regardless. Status Quo were never really my taste, but I don't tell him that and ask him, without much real hope, if he has for sale a CR2032. "It's for my Smart Key," I tell him, placing it on the counter.

I don't think Mr Rossi knows what a CR2032 is, and I'm surprised to hear him speak in broad Northumbrian because I thought he was a Londoner whose father sold ice cream. "What's it for?" he enquires.

"It's the battery for the key," I tell him, and he raises an eyebrow slightly as if he very much doubts it. But he goes off into a back room and after a little while and the sound of much rummaging about, returns with a small piece of red cardboard in plastic packaging. The pack is printed with the encouraging legend "CR2032", and inside are two silver metal coin size batteries.

"£3.75," Mr Rossi says, which I say sounds very reasonable.

"I don't suppose you've got a screwdriver?" I wonder to him. "It's just I want to fit it now before it dies and I get locked out of the car."

Anyway, hunched over the counter together and with the aid of a pair of scissors, a screwdriver and a great deal of patient concentration, we do manage to get the fob apart, replace the battery, and put it all back together again. I think Mr Rossi is as relieved as I am when the final piece of the fob clicks into place, and like a true northern gentleman he charges me nothing for his time and assistance. I did discover later that if I had gone to a main dealership the battery would have cost me over 30 quid. I wouldn't have paid that even if he really had been Francis Rossi Himself, legend of rock and roll.

***

Bamburgh is only two miles on from Seahouses, and its enormous, solid brown fortress grows almost naturally from the rock above the town. It's not a pretty castle, not to my eyes, but it has the handsome bearing of an old grandee. I see it long before I reach the town and its great flanks tower above the road which curves beneath it past the wide, green cricket and recreation ground into the main, and pretty much only, street of Bamburgh.

It's a spacious place with wide green verges, and a fork in the road encloses a village green with a canopy of oak, ash and sycamore. It's also a popular place and parking spaces are hard to come by, even at this time of year, but I find a spot to leave the car right outside The Lord Crewe. It's another old pub that has been given a boutique makeover, and where my wife and I stayed some years ago. I remember its comfortable, low-key interior, and decide to pop in for coffee.

I wonder about visiting the castle, and decide against it partly because I've been in before. Outside, within the great walls, it's wide and open with space to walk around the expansive battlements, cannon placements, and enjoy unrivalled views of the coast from Dunstanburgh in the south to the lonely tower keep on the island of Lindisfarne, Holy Island, to the north. Inside, and because this is the ancestral home of the Armstrong family, access is restricted to the public rooms which are overwhelmingly museum-like with formal displays of art and collections, specially set-up galleries presenting cameos of life here in times gone by, sewing, ale storage, mannequins of guards in armour and that sort of thing.

But mainly I decide against a visit because I don't think it would have had any significance in the lives of my ancestors, William and Ann Beveridge. The long volcanic crag on which it is built has been occupied in one way or another since pre-historic times. It has been a pawn in political intrigues, witnessed many horse and sword battles, settlements and sieges, and has been assaulted by the Scots with tedious persistence. It suffered, like Dustanburgh, badly in the Wars of the Roses when in the 15th century the Yorkists besieged it and fired cannon at it until it fell to bits. By the 16th century the castle was effectively in ruin. Eventually it came into the hands of Lord Nathaniel Crewe, the Bishop of Durham and from whom the pub in which I sit with my espresso takes its name.

Under Lord Crewe the castle was used variously as a hospital, a school and a hospice for sailors. It even had a spell as a coastguard and lifeboat station, but it was not restored. It was not until 1894 that William Armstrong came along and gave it a full restoration. So when the Beveridges lived here in the late 18th century the castle would have been of little practical importance to them. The bulk of its walls would have towered over the village, but it would have sat there battle-scarred and forlorn like a disused coal mine, quietly refusing to go away.

William George Armstrong, Baron Armstrong of Cragside as he became known, bought the whole lot in its dilapidated condition for £60,000 in 1894. Armstrong was an extraordinary man, and he bears some connection to me and my family in a number of remote but positive ways. He was born in Newcastle for one thing, and after a grammar school education he embarked on a career in law for another.

But engineering, innovation and invention were at Armstrong's heart. He was a pioneer of hydro-electric power and hydraulic systems. He developed engineering businesses and based them on the river Tyne alongside the docks and shipyards that my father came to know so well. His companies became household names. Armstrong Whitworth built ships, locomotives and aircraft. Vickers Armstrong built planes and armaments, and Armstrong Siddeley built motor vehicles and aero engines. He was known as a philanthropist, a charitable benefactor, an environmentalist, innovator and a respected, all round excellent fellow.

But mainly, Armstrong was an arms dealer. He manufactured and supplied naval guns, he designed and manufactured armaments for the British Government, invented new breech loading systems, and putting business before allegiance he sold guns to both sides in the American

Civil War. If you needed some serious firepower, William Armstrong was the man who could provide it. He made a great deal of money out of it, which is how Bamburgh Castle came to be saved.

He lived for a time in Jesmond Dene, a suburb of Newcastle where he designed and built the iron bridge over the dene which I passed on my way from Tyneside to Durham so many days ago. He bought land near Rothbury north of Newcastle and built what was to become the great house and estate known as Cragside, where he constructed lakes and dams to create hydraulic and hydro-electric systems. His house was the first in the world to be lit by hydro-electric power. Cragside is now in the hands of The National Trust, an extensive domain of gardens, lakes and woodland.

But the castle held his true ambition, and brought him here to establish his family's ancestral seat. Now, long after his death but still in the hands of his descendants it has become one of the most iconic restored fortresses on any coast of England. It is, of course, also a major tourist attraction, a film location, and it offers itself as a venue for weddings, events and self-catering accommodation, all no doubt in response to the eye-watering cost of upkeep.

But in spite of all that, its connection with the great man Armstrong, and its dominant majesty overlooking the town, I don't think it would have had much relevance to the lives of my 18th century ancestors when it was a dilapidated hulk on the top of the hill, and I think I'll give it a miss today.

I don't even know where the Beveridges lived here in Bamburgh, but it must have been within a couple of hundred yards of where I'm sitting in the Lord Crewe. There are several little rows of cottages of the right vintage in and around Bamburgh. All I can do is try to take in the atmosphere of the town, and so I finish up my espresso and head out into the wide open main street, and up the road to where I know there is a museum dedicated to that legendary heroine, Grace Darling, who lived here not only around the time of William and Ann, but also when Grandpa

John was here just a little way down the coast. I feel I've got to know something of John Hinkley over the last day or two, the occasional fleeting image and sense of presence, and I don't want to lose any opportunity to learn more about this place and the lives of William and Ann.

Born and buried in Bamburgh, Grace Darling is famous for having played a principal role in the rescue of survivors from a shipwreck off the Farne Islands in September 1838. She was born in 1815, and when she was only weeks old went with her family to keep the lighthouse on Brownsman Island on the outer Farne Islands. In 1826, the very year Grandpa John came to this coast, the family moved to the lighthouse on Longstone, the furthest out of the Farnes. It was a remote existence. She took her schooling from her father, and learned domestic skills from her mother. All their provisions, including drinking water, had to be shipped in from the mainland. Even seabirds didn't live on the bare outcrop of rocks.

On 18 September 1838 the steamship Forfarshire ran aground on the rocks around the Farne Islands during a severe storm. It was in the dark, early hours, and only at first light were Grace and her father able to see the wreck and survivors clinging to the rocks awash with heavy surf. Grace, only 23 then, went with her father, just the two of them in a small boat, and in atrocious conditions managed to save a small number of lives.

For these heroic deeds Grace received many accolades, and was awarded medals for bravery from what is now the Royal National Lifeboat Institution (RNLI) and the Humane Society. Sadly, she died of tuberculosis only four years later. Her memorial is in St Aiden's Church, across the road from the museum.

The wreck of the Forfarshire took place at the time when Grandpa John was engaged as a coastguard at Low Newton, and I have sometimes wondered if the men from his station played any part in the matter. But there's no record that they did, and I doubt it. Low Newton is about 15 miles south, and much too far on a dark and stormy night in 1838. He would have heard about it later, I'm sure, but I can imagine him giving little more than a shrug at the news. Shipwrecks on this coast were far from uncommon.

The Beverages on the other hand are likely to have known all about it, soon after the event if not as the rescue unfolded. They may even have been at the shore when the survivors were landed. I'm anxious to discover what the museum dedicated to the young heroine can tell me about it, and if any unexpected connection might arise in the detail. The museum was established by the RNLI who still curate it, and it's located just on the outskirts of the village.

The RNLI is an institution which safeguards our coasts with lifeboat, lifeguard and search and rescue deployments. It performs a unique and indispensable service. And I, like many I'm sure, have often wondered why it receives no government funding. Its existence depends on legacies and donations. Its crews are unpaid volunteers. Why it isn't a fully funded public service is quite beyond me. But there it is, it's a charity.

So you would have thought that the RNLI would be among the more assiduous fundraisers. It costs a fortune to run and can't be serviced by a few collection buckets in the high street, which is why I'm baffled by the fact that today the museum is closed. It may be off season but it's a Saturday, and the village is teeming with people all prepared to give them a few quid to go in, like me, and probably spend more inside. A jar of RNLI preserve, for example, would add nicely to the collection of gifts for my wife.

Sadly, the modern, stylish, and no doubt very expensive, automatic glass doors at the entrance are resolutely closed, and it is with both disappointment and puzzlement that I turn away into the road. I am tempted to send the RNLI a note* about it.

***

The church of St Aiden is across the road from the museum. Over a stone wall in open grounds, it's surrounded on all sides by a grassy cemetery. Beyond is the low coastline and above a wide sky. Treeless, it has a bleak, elemental feeling. The present 12th century church is a heavy stone building with a squat, crenelated tower and Gothic arch windows. From the gate in the wall a long path leads to the arched portal doors, winding through ancient leaning headstones, worn and yellowed with lichen. It's a big church for a small village, and as well as being central to the foundation of Christianity in this area, it's the place where both William and Ann were baptised, married and buried.

In the year AD635 King Oswald, incumbent of these parts at the time and promoter of early Christianity, invited Aiden to come to Bamburgh from Iona on the west coast of Scotland to spread the word. I'm intrigued by that expression "*invited*", or similar ones like "*called*", used when describing Aiden's summons to Northumbria. It's not as if Oswald just picked up the phone or popped a note in the post, and I've often wondered how they overcame the logistical problems of communication and travel over vast distances back then. Nevertheless Oswald seems to have managed it and Aiden responded, to establish the church here in Bamburgh, and the Abbey on Lindisfarne.

Lindisfarne's history reads like a Who's Who of monastic Christianity, The Venerable Bede and Saint Cuthbert being the two best known of its famous inhabitants. Cuthbert, in fact, provides an interesting link with earlier parts of this story because after his death his body was revered by his monks and in fleeing from the marauding Danes they took it to Chester-le-Street where the Church of St Cuthbert remains to this day. In fact, I've heard it said that his body, or at least parts of it for they were enthusiastic relic collectors in those days, was hidden for a time at Tanfield, Uncle Arthur's parish.

***

I'm quite alone in the church. Although the doors are open and welcoming there are no visitors or even any sign of a clergyman. The trust of the clergy here must run deep as there are any number of glittering objects lying around to attract the attention of anyone less virtuous than myself.

And it is silent. The air is still, cool but not cold. I try to tread softly to avoid the echo of my footsteps on the stone floor as I wander about, taking in the arched columns, intricate figure carvings and the high vaulted roof. Stained glass, bright from the sunlight outside, casts mosaic shapes on the floor and I can see the dust glistening in shafts of light. Here lies the pale recumbent figure of Grace Darling, hands clasped at her breast, and marble memorials on the walls in remembrance of notable and respected families.

I don't know whether William and Ann Beveridge were religious people who came here to offer their prayers with due diligence every Sunday. That's another one of those details I find so frustrating in its absence, because just that small particular would provide an invaluable insight into their lives. But as is so often the case at this level of inquiry, it's missing. That said, I know for certain that they came here, into this church, no less than four times in their lives - to be baptised, to marry, to baptise their daughter Isabella, and to be put to rest. On at least two of those occasions they would have seen with their own eyes very much what I see before me today, and they would have stood on the very flagstones beneath my feet. Standing there in the cool tranquillity of the church, I wonder if I can feel their presence. Is that calm serenity I feel here a sense of them gathered around a heavy stone font cradling a new-born child, a clergyman offering the baptism in pastoral gesture and low voice?

Around the walls are tables and displays about the life and wanderings of the church's founder, St Aidan. If half of what I read is true he was a remarkable man, quiet, devout, modestly diligent and ceaseless in his toil. He gave his life to his ministry and the cause of Christianity, his only reward being a belief that he was bringing solace and salvation to the lives of others. It's hard to think of someone in today's world who would fit that description, not without the accompaniment of wealth, celebrity or self-aggrandisement. I think about Mother Teresa, or Mahatma Gandhi perhaps. Not many come to mind. But then by their nature they wouldn't. Perhaps, like my genetic memory, they're just helping along quietly in the background.

Leaving the church by the main doors, outside steps lead down into the crypt and ossuary where the bones of 110 men, women and children, originally buried in the dunes next to the castle in the 7th and 8th centuries, have recently been brought and laid to rest. The crypt accepts visitors onto a small stage at the entrance to the stone room. The platform has railings overlooking the vault, atmospherically lit with amber highlights appearing in and around fluted arches. On the railings at the front of the platform is a button labelled "*PRESS*".

I'm the only one in the crypt, and as soon as I press the button some cleverly concealed projector releases images onto the stone wall opposite me, images of the church, the crypt, the life and times of St Aiden, local people depicted in line drawings going about their domestic business. It's a storybook of St Aiden's life and the lives of his people, accompanied by a commentary in an unctuous, purring female voice which sounds as if it will break into a commercial for hair colouring at any moment. But in spite of her I'm held for the duration of the show, caught in the story of Aiden and his unstinting devotion to God and his fellow man.

I find myself trying to imagine that distance in time, nearly 1,500 years ago. It's so easy to say yet obstinately hard to comprehend. Trying to imagine the people who have passed through this space over all those years, the gradual changes in their speech, their dress, their work, their very appearance is intoxicating. I don't even notice the family of four who sidle in behind me.

***

Walking back through the graveyard to the road, I do take a casual look around for any sign of Beveridge on the gravestones, but the inscriptions are weathered, worn and hard to read. Still, I'm occupying the same space as they did, as I did in the church. Sometimes the few visitors, shuffling around the cemetery pausing now and then to look at a headstone, shimmer briefly into the shapes of roughly clad figures, clergy in white and black, people of the time.

On the road back down to the car outside the Lord Crewe, the rampart walls and long battlements of the castle dominate the view in front of me, high on the bluff above the village. It's hard to overstate its powerful dominance. It's a view that would have been before the eyes of William and Ann, and their daughter Isabella too, every day of their lives. As they walked around the town in pursuit of whatever was the business of the day, there it was. I wonder what they thought of it.

***

From Bamburgh the country road winds for 5 miles through fields and hedgerows to the A1. The Great North Road is only a single carriageway up here, although there's no shortage of traffic. The relief of a dual carriageway comes about halfway on the 20 miles south to Alnwick (*Old English for "settlement on the river Aln"*), the county town of Northumberland and where I will find the Castle, the gaol and The White Swan Hotel.

There is also the famous, if somewhat bizarre, Barter Books, which I pass on the road in. It claims to be one of the largest second-hand bookshops in Britain, and I don't doubt it for a moment. It's in part of the old Victorian railway station, an astonishingly elaborate affair in itself, built in 1887 with unusual grandeur because of Alnwick's position as the seat of the Dukes of Northumberland who felt the need to impress visiting royalty. The shop itself is cavernous. It houses work of every genre - antiquarian books, science books, history, poetry, classics, religion, philosophy, highly specialised reference works and books of great rarity. It's an Aladdin's Cave of the written word.

I can't resist spending half an hour here, lazily wandering through the maze of shelves and side rooms, peering at the vast array of literature. It's impossible not to become immersed among the packed, crowded shelves, racks and glass cases which hold the more rare and valuable examples. On top of all that, model trains continually chug around overhead at gallery level, referencing the shop's connection with the railway age. It's all quite quirky and slightly bonkers.

***

The road into the town passes through the narrow arch of the medieval Bondgate Tower into the broad street known as Bondgate Within. Among the shopfronts is the wide, impressive façade of The White Swan Hotel, two storeys of beige stone, heavy dormer windows and an imposing balustrade above the arched entrance. This 18th century coaching inn was one of the principal stages for coaches on the Great North Road, and in Grandpa John's time a meeting point with which he would have been very familiar.

I'm able to park close by, and step past the brass-framed menus on each side of the heavy revolving doors into the hushed interior of this grand, county hotel. The polished, modern reception area is deserted apart from a smartly dressed member of staff quietly engrossed in a computer screen behind an enormous rosewood desk.

The modern upgrade does not seem to have been extended yet beyond reception, and the carpet in the corridor I take towards the rear of the hotel is a little faded, the paintwork dull cream and showing the scuffs of wear. My wife and I stayed here a few years ago and I remember that upstairs the narrow corridors creaked underfoot and heavy iron radiators clanked beneath multiple coats of grey paint. But lining the walls of the corridor which is leading me through to the main dining room are the photographs which depict the source of the theme this hotel has adopted, the great S.S. Olympic, sister ship to the Titanic.

In 1936 the Olympic was dismantled at Jarrow on the river Tyne. The then owners of The White Swan, having voyaged on the ship and developed an affection for it, bought the whole of the first class lounge, a first class staircase, and the revolving doors through which I passed when I came in. The vessel's lounge was installed as the hotel's dining room where I now find myself, amidst a scattering of visitors taking morning coffee or an early lunch at white dressed tables.

Actually, it's not very nautical at all. It has more the bearing of a stateroom, a grand drawing room with oak panelling and scrolled finishing, stained glass in ornate windows. I feel a little out of place amidst the hush, interrupted only by the occasional clink of cutlery. A member of staff, stiff in black and white, enquires of me and I hold up my hand which says "*Just looking*", and retire from the waiter's slightly worn, and I suspect disapproving, look.

Outside the revolving doors the street's shape is the same as it was when John stood here, brought to Alnwick by some errand - the collection or dispatch of a Coastguard Inspector, or the delivery of prisoners to the Gaol or courthouse. Grey cobblestones at the side of the road make it easy to imagine it two centuries ago. I dwell for a moment there, hesitating, calling to my mind the sweet smell of hay and horse, the rattle of solid wheels on the cobbles, carts of people, and waggons of produce. I hear a jumble of voices, some rough sounding, gruff oaths and the shouts of vendors and drivers. A stagecoach stands in the road, a door open to the barely upholstered, red interior. Four horses stand in front tossing their heads and snorting billows of steam into the cold air. There's a clatter of metal-shod hooves as a horse stamps the ground. Among the rough sleeves and woollen coats a man in a tall hat, a winged collar and an embroidered waistcoat walks confidently through the crowd, silver tipped cane in hand. John Hinkley in the red tunic of his commission languishes by the coach, patiently observing. Amidst the people of the town who attend their business, there may be Gentlemen in disguise.

The House of Correction to which John would have delivered his charges later became the courthouse and gaol. I've read about it, but nowhere have I found an address for it, so I'm headed for the Tourist Information Bureau where I'm hoping that someone will be able to tell me. It's situated in the Playhouse, just back through the Bondgate arch.

The Playhouse has recently undergone a major refurbishment, and been given a new, modern interior. Through the shiny, new automatic doors which open with a soft swish at my approach, there's a plush carpet, a new café area, a bar, box office and a fully refurbished auditorium. There's also a wide, stylishly curving reception desk above which hangs a sign, "*Alnwick Tourist Office*". It is closed.

I'm beginning to get a strong sense of something here. I'm not sure if it's a feeling of being unlucky, or of being unwanted. It's still Saturday, the town is fairly busy, and the Playhouse café has several customers. So why the Tourist Information Office should be shut is troubling. I have a brief wander about to see if there is anyone with a badge pinned on them who I can ask, but I can find no one. The only prospect of assistance seems to be a young man with a pale complexion, blond spiky hair and a black tee shirt with "*Staff*" printed on it hovering behind the café counter, so I go and stand before him.

"Is the Tourist Information Office closed?" I ask of him, with an inflection on the last word that says, *"Why is the Tourist Information Office closed?"*

The young man is rather absently wiping a cup with a piece of cloth, and continues to do so as he rather pointedly looks over at the empty desk. "Yes," he says turning his look back to me.

"Oh," I say. "Do you know when it will be open? I'm looking for the gaol."

That gets his attention, and he stops mid wipe, his gaze lingering on me. "The jail? I don't think we have one in Alnwick. There's the prison at Acklington."

"No, I mean the old gaol. I think it also used to be the courthouse. It's somewhere in the town and I thought the Tourist Office might be able to tell me where it is."

"It's closed," the youth offers, resuming his wiping. After a pause he says "Bob might know."

"Bob?"

After a pause, during which I try to offer an expression which says "*Yes, but where do I find Bob*?" the spiky youth shrugs. "He might be up in the bar," pointing to an open spiral staircase.

I nod a reluctant thanks, and at the top of the spiral find a long, newly furbished bar, empty apart from another young man on his knees polishing low coffee tables. Bob is much more friendly than his recalcitrant colleague and looking up he offers me a genial "Hi!"

I think Bob is probably relieved to get up off his knees and take a rest from the cloth and polish. He too has "*Staff*" stencilled on his tee shirt. His hair is an unlikely blend of pink and green, falling over his eyes into quite a lot of black mascara and eyeliner. But we are in a theatre, so I give no further thought to the matter.

The old courthouse he tells me, is now the Alnwick YMCA, just a couple of hundred yards up the road called Green Batt, and no, he doesn't know why it's called that either. I'm grateful and thank him before retreating back down the spiral staircase and out past his spiky associate who eyes me suspiciously from behind his counter where I would swear he's still wiping the same cup.

***

Green Batt actually dates from the times when men were compelled by law to train in archery, "*Batt*" being a dialect version of "*Butt*", a place where archery was practised. Only a couple of hundred yards off the main street it's another wide road of heavy, stern Victorian buildings. I'm not expecting the YMCA to hold much memory of the old courthouse or gaol now, and imagine it will be encumbered with beards, rucksacks and half eaten packets of muesli and lentils, with a hint of rules and regulations thrown in. But I'm hoping that a feel of the building, the shape of the rooms and perhaps some original features will give me a sense of the place to which Grandpa John would have come to deliver those who were due to face the attention of the law.

It's an easy building to find. Heavy, blackened stone, like a country town branch of Barclay's Bank, it even has "*YMCA*" signed on the big front door, now painted institutional blue. It's closed.

I'm starting to find this perplexing. Sir Terry Wogan titled one of his autobiographies "*Is It Me?*" and I'm beginning to understand what he meant. It's still Saturday, about lunchtime, and the time I would have thought a Youth Hostel would be welcoming and open for business. In my day Youth Hostels were often used by young men on a beer pilgrimage and Hostels were convenient and cheap places to sleep it off when they could no longer see an elephant at five yards. Today I gather they are more about salvation and shelter, and I would have thought their very objective would require them to have their doors open. But they're not, and I can only conclude that this Hostel, like the Tourist Information Office and the Grace Darling Museum before it, has for some reason marked my card.

I'm not at all sure what particular eminence this building holds, or even why the YMCA in Alnwick might be especially deserving in spite of its commendable ambitions, but in 2011 HM Queen again graced the North East to open it. Against the importance of the many other places up here where she's cut a ribbon, I can't help thinking Her Majesty must have been at a loose end that year.

Eventually and with some idle speculation as to what Grandpa John would have thought had he turned up here with a cartload of ruffians and found it closed, I turn off back down Green Batt towards the town. Like Bamburgh, the dominating feature of the town of Alnwick is its castle, and since I'm here I think I'll take a look.

***

The way to the castle visitors' entrance takes me back through town and the appropriately named "*Narrowgate*" which winds closely through small, independent shops and cafes. A board outside one of them states "*Open Sunday's*". Sunday's what? I can't even think of anything that could belong to a Sunday. I suppose it could be Sunday's Evensong, or Sunday's Cup Tie, but that's not what it means. The plethora of misplaced or missing apostrophes, split infinitives, wandering adverbs and all the rest of the grammatical nonsense one sees all over the place these days is something that irritates me profoundly. Lynne Truss would be proud of me.

I probably sound pedantic, but I'm nothing compared to one of my best, dear friends who is a Master of Pedantry. Not a grammatical mishap escapes his attention. No wandering apostrophe, no misplaced modifier gets past him. If he ever happened upon The National Trust's brochure for Lookout Cottage I expect he would have something to say about the Wi Fi* as well.

Beyond the grammatical errors, a chalk board next to the entrance includes the items "*Stottie Cake*", and "*Pease Pudding*". Northumberland is not widely known for its culinary specialities but in so far as it has any, these are they. Stottie Cake is a heavy, part-leavened doughy stodge masquerading as bread that lies in your stomach like a cannon ball, and Pease Pudding is a yellow builder's putty made of split peas and tastes of almost nothing. They are both old, rustic, peasant recipes, and I expect Grandpa John would have been familiar with them both.

I can see John sitting on a three-legged wooden stool when Mary offers him a plate of Stottie Cake and Pease Pudding. I can imagine her standing back with her arms crossed over an ample, aproned bosom as she watches down on him. I wish I knew whether he enjoyed cutting chunks of the stodgy bread with a sharp working knife and spreading knobs of yellow pudding over it before pushing it past his beard into his mouth. Or, on the other hand, perhaps he looked up at her with quiet resignation from under bushy eyebrows, his plate held in heavy calloused hands, and smiled weakly at her wishing to himself that, just for once, it wasn't bloody Stottie Cake and Pease Pudding again. Another detail, another particular that would add new brushstrokes to my picture of John Hinkley and his life here, but which is beyond me, lost for want of an old shopping list or a grocer's receipt, perhaps.

***

Alnwick Castle has been in and out of the hands of the Percy family for centuries but by John Hinkley's time the Percys were permanently established here. Like Bamburgh, the castle is partly a private residence and today its incumbent is the 12th Duke of Northumberland. The fortress occupies an elevated position at the edge of the town overlooking the River Aln, and the open fields beneath its ramparts mark the site where battles were fought, cannon fired, sieges held and in more recent times the creators of Blackadder, various Robin Hoods and Harry Potter set their scenes and cameras.

The main visitors' entrance from the town is a grand archway surrounded by low, crenellated battlements. Towers and pinnacles can be seen further in, and the Union Jack or the flag of the occasion flies high above. Beyond the gates vast courtyards and public areas are perfect for exploration and games. I remember when Mum and Dad brought my brother and me here when we were quite small. We neither understood nor cared about the history. To us it was a playground where we could run about, clamber over the battlements and black cannon placements, and play hide and seek while Mum and Dad wandered about sedately in casual slacks admiring the views, and trying to look in the windows of the private quarters. Then we sat on the grass for a picnic with sandwiches, crisps and orange pop.

These days it's all about interactive displays, exhibitions and activities for excitable children. There are archery lessons, hawk handling, sword play, jousting, dressing up and medieval games. Most famously, the castle has embraced the phenomenon that is Harry Potter. In the grassy courtyard within the great ramparts of the castle children receive instruction from local youths on work experience in disciplines such as broomstick flying, dragon slaying and all that nonsense. It's contrived and devoid of spontaneous adventure. It's all no doubt a significant, if not vital, contributor to the finances and upkeep of the castle and its worthy preservation, but when I was that age I thought that wizards and all their magical fantasy were stupid, girly sissyness. When I was under four feet tall what I wanted was a gun.

My first gun was accompanied by a cowboy outfit, size small. It had brown chaps, a waistcoat with a silver sheriff's star, check shirt, cowboy hat and a holster belt. Little John had a similar outfit, but he was three years shorter than me and his chaps flapped around his legs like a loose tarpaulin. The gun was a silver revolver which fired caps, a thin green roll of paper dotted with explosives. The caps produced a realistic bang, and the resulting whiff of cordite was pretty convincing too. When Mum was engrossed in the kitchen and Dad was at work we escaped from the house and roamed the streets with menacing swaggers. Anyone who thought we looked cute was shot.

The revolver was realistic enough, but the snag was that nothing came out the end, which meant you couldn't shoot anyone properly. This problem was solved by the discovery of the Spud Gun.

Looking back, I'm surprised we were allowed such a thing. I suppose that Mum and Dad thought that a six year old boy could do little harm with a toy pistol and a potato. But boy, were they wrong about that. Loaded by pressing the barrel into a raw spud, it could fire a pellet of vegetable with an astonishing velocity. The neighbourhood became our manor. Little John and I hid behind walls and bushes, potatoes at the ready, and shot anything that moved – cats, dogs, the postman, the old lady next door. Before long every kid in the street had a spud gun and battles ensued. The pavements were littered with miniature gangsters and slippery, vegetable pellets.

I fired it at Mother once I remember, when she had her back turned in the kitchen. The gun made quite a crack when it went off, and Mum turned abruptly with a piece of potato lodged in her hairdo as I stood before her with the gun hanging limply in my hand. "How many times have I told you not to aim that thing at *people?!*"

"I didn't" I said meekly as mother made her mouth go thin and opened her eyes wide at my fib. Then I turned and fled into the garden and took a pot shot at a startled pigeon for revenge.

But one day there was an incident of some sort, not involving me or Little John directly, and a child got a spud pellet in the eye or somewhere and the baby went crying to its mother. It didn't come to any harm by it as I recall, but a stop was put to the potato wars and that was the end of the spud gun.

***

I've left Alnwick behind, and taken a final beer or two and dinner at The Ship. Now I find myself on my last night at Lookout Cottage, and with the warmth of a late evening brandy to keep me company. The sun has long gone down, and from the window in the bay the sky holds a faint light on the horizon. The streetlight at the bottom of the hill casts a yellow glow, but the night is very black up here.

I find I have grown fond of Lookout Cottage, in ways that I could not have imagined when I stumbled in through the door three nights ago. I've spent a lot of time sitting in this bay window. It's a peaceful, thoughtful place where I can sit entirely alone. I can engage my own thoughts and imagery comes easily. The grassy hill falls away to the shoreline. The dunes are dark beyond the sands. Are those dark shapes the figures of men crouched closely behind them? Do I see the shadowy outlines of boats just offshore? The bay curves away, diminishing in perspective to the ever-present outline of Dunstanburgh's spiky fingers on the horizon.

I wonder that Grandpa John and Mary spent some time within these walls. Perhaps, like me, they sat and wondered at the view. Perhaps Mary would knit or sew while John spent time in The Ship with the men, or on night patrol among the dunes or in his boat out to sea.

Perhaps sometimes they would sit here together, and after the sun went down the candles and the fire would cast shadows flickering on the walls, and as darkness fell the lamps and candles would be doused and the world given over to the night.

It's easy sitting here to empty my thoughts and allow the imagery in, letting what I now like to think of as my Genetic Memory take over, helping me along. If I half close my eyes the 21st century fades, the features in the room fade, and it becomes a space that I can fill with whatever comes to mind.

TWENTY ONE

Ellingham, Alnmouth

I have actually grown fond of the cottage, although in truth only parts of it – the curved bench seat under the bay window, the view, the wood burner even, and the silence when the wind stopped howling outside. I have not grown fond of the outside toilet and stumbling about in the darkness, the slog up and down the hill, or the heavy, sagging gate in the wall. So it's with mixed feelings that I deposit the key in the little box outside the front door and trudge down the hill with the last of my belongings.

After I have heaved the gate open, bumped the car out onto the road, got it shut again and chained and locked it, I find I'm reluctant to leave without standing here for a while to take it all in, one last time. I squint my eyes a little into the cool breeze from offshore as I gaze into the hazy morning light, down the hill past the village and the bay to the distant castle fingers.

Up the hill the squat white cottage with its sticky picket gate and radio pylon seems to look back down at me with a lonesome, wistful expression. I will probably never walk up there again, my knees protesting, the feel of slippery grass and muddy ruts under my feet. I will never again sit in that light blue room and invite John Hinkley to make his presence known.

In the car, thoughts of the things I'm leaving behind tumble around haphazardly, yet at the same time I know that I'm taking a great deal with me too. I've found some memories I didn't know I had, and added a few new ones besides. As I drive away, the village and its little haven disappear behind me as I crest the rise in the road, and as the cottage on the hill appears in the rear-view mirror it seems to bid me farewell, until it too passes out of sight.

***

I may be leaving Grandpa John behind, but not his legacy. When he left here in 1846 to return to the south coast he left his eldest son, James William, behind in Low Newton. It's James I'm following now, a generation closer to me, and he needs a close eye as his journey takes unexpected turns.

I've often wondered why James stayed. Was he enamoured of the majestic views, or was he held by the charms of some local girl? Whichever it was, it kept him here for a year or so, patrolling the coast in his red tunic as his father had done. Then whatever it was must have paled or waned or was overtaken by some other draw because before too long he upped and left and took himself to Devon. I don't know exactly when, and I don't know why.

James spent nearly 10 years in and around the Devon area, and he continued his service with the coastguards. There he met his future wife and in 1858 he married Frances Sophia Crook at Okehampton.

James then did something which, to me, is quite remarkable. He came back. I wonder if he became homesick for Northumberland, or whether he felt the draw of the land of his birth. He gave up his coastguard service and almost immediately after their marriage returned to the North East with Frances where they settled in the village of Ellingham, only a few miles from Low Newton where he was born. He took employment on the estate of Ellingham Hall as a farm steward and groom and shortly after their arrival their first son was born in 1859. This was Arthur William, Uncle Arthur of Tanfield.

And so to take up James' story, and the beginning of Uncle Arthur's, I am headed now to Ellingham, away from Low Newton and inland a few miles through country roads and lanes lined with hedgerows, fields and woodland. I pass through Christon Bank, Falloden and Preston, villages no more than hamlets, farms and outbuildings. The countryside rolls away to the horizon on both sides of the road with barely a sign of habitation. Nearing Ellingham the road turns into a lane. Weeds and loose gravel have accumulated in the centre and small muddy laybys provide the only means of passage for oncoming traffic, no more than the occasional tractor today.

As I drive into the village I pass the imposing entrance to Ellingham Hall. Stone pillars supporting iron gates open to a grand driveway and I can see the house in the middle distance. It's a grand 17th century house of impressive architecture and history which now provides wedding services and prosecco in pleated white marquees.

An overcast sky has pushed away the brightness of the early morning and it has come on to a light drizzle as I drive on through the village. The windscreen wipers flick occasionally leaving streaks across the glass. Sandy brown Northumbrian stone cottages line the road, simple houses to which the estate workers would have returned from the land. They stand proud and well cared for now, with pretty gardens and clean paint on the doors. Range Rovers and BMWs are parked outside second homes. The rosette stickers of holiday lets appear in many of the windows.

I stop near the pub at the end of the village and walk back down the road. I pass the iron-gated entrance to Ellingham Hall, then turn into a narrow, leafy lane leading to the church where I know that Uncle Arthur was baptised. The lane winds between mossy, damp stone walls enclosed by a silent canopy of trees. The drizzle has passed and the air drips with occasional patters on the road. Fallen leaves lie in mushy clumps and soon my boots are heavy with clarts of country mud. I can imagine walking down here with a small procession of villagers, dressed in whatever

Sunday best they could muster, ladies smiling, heads turned towards each other, gossiping in low voices.

The Church of St Maurice is Church of England, founded in 1150. In the mid-19th century James would have trodden this lane himself down to the church with his family, and in the spring of 1859 with his first son.

It's a long walk and I take it slowly, enjoying the ivy and lichen on the stone walls and the air absent of any sound except for birdsong and the occasional squawk of a pheasant in the woods. Eventually, the lane reaches an archway, wooden supports set on stone flanks and forming a highly pitched timber roof. It's a little odd, as I am still some way from the church itself, and the archway sits in the middle of the track. It would be quite easy just to go round it.

I spend half an hour nosing around the church, which is open and quite deserted. It's plain inside, the pews old and wooden, and echoes bounce from the white walls and high roof with every step I take. I feel the quiet ambience of the past and of lives long gone, and as I wander slowly around I'm surrounded by a place of solemnity and stillness which my presence seems to trespass upon. It makes me cautious and I tread delicately in reverence to it, almost in apology. This is a place which belongs to someone else, not me, and I don't think it belongs to James William Hinkley either. It feels weary as if bearing the weight of some past burden, discontent at interruption by the present. There's a smell of damp plaster and old stone. As I walk out through the heavy old doors the air outside feels warm, and for the first time I realise how cold it was in the church. As I head back to the village I wonder what it was that I disturbed in that place.

After some years in Ellingham, James did something even more unexpected than before. For the second time in his life he abandoned Northumberland. He took Frances, his children, his life, to a place with which, as far as I know, he had no connection. He took himself south of the river Tyne to the coalfields of County Durham.

For some reason, I know not what, James went to Esh, where I found myself a few days ago in Station Avenue and on the waggonway where I met the old man and his dog. He came and joined the throng who embraced the industrial revolution, although not down the pit itself because he worked as a gardener. He raised his family here, and his daughter Francis Mabel (Uncle Arthur's sister) married Thomas Ritchie, whose son Harry married Irene Elliott, whose daughter Moreen married John Wood, whose son is of course me. In 1889 Frances Sophia died and James himself followed a year later. He is buried in nearby Lanchester.

***

What drew James around the country, from Low Newton to Devon then back again, and then to the coalfields of Durham is a mystery. But that he made those journeys, that he brought the Hinkley line to Durham and joined with those other lines of Ritchie, Elliott and Wood is something that has often drawn me to thought. How on earth did it happen that all these ancestors were in exactly the right place, at exactly the right time, to give me the rare benefit of existence? What were the chances of that?

Perhaps it's not a matter of chance. Perhaps it was always written, preordained. Was every event that led to the circumstances of my birth an immutable inevitability? Was it always going to be so? If that were the case there can be no such thing as freedom of choice, only the illusion of it. Could that possibly be right?

None other than Winston Churchill pondered this. In his autobiography "*My Early Life*" he pronounced "*....which brings me to my conclusion upon Free Will and Predestination; namely – let the reader mark it – that they are identical*". He wrote this after explaining how a last minute decision to learn up on mathematics enabled him to get into Sandhurst and thus follow an army career, and if he had not done that then the world we live in today would be a very different place. He said that if he had not done that then "*the whole of my life would have been altered, and that I suppose would have altered a great many other lives, which in their turn, and so on.....*". He meant, of course, that he came to play a crucial part on the world stage when war came upon us, and that things may have turned out very differently if those earlier decisions had not placed him in the position to exert the influence he did in those dark times.

I would be more comfortable if Winston had said that free will is not *incompatible* with the concept of determinism, for that is a position capable of argument, rather than being *synonymous* with it. I find it difficult to accept Winston's view that predestination and free will are one and the same thing. If he was predestined to make decisions which ensured his entry to Sandhurst then he could have had no more than the illusion of free will in making them. I believe in free will, and that is why don't accept the concept of predestination, but I'd be the first to admit it's complicated.

So, if predestination isn't it, were my ancestors drawn together by an unimaginably complicated sequence of coincidences and free choices which determined every action and reaction since whenever it all started? Neither written nor pre-ordained, each result dependent on an infinite number of options, each chosen, consciously or not. Does every choice, every action however small and apparently insignificant determine the path that led to me? Am I the consequence of a long and complex sequence of free choices?

Or then again, perhaps there are an infinite number of universes, not such a daft idea some will have us believe. Within them an infinite number of possibilities exist and my being is just the result of one of them. At every crossroads the direction that will lead to me is always taken, along with an infinite number that don't. In that case I was always going to exist, and exist in an infinite number of forms and states. Perhaps in one existence I am a great philosopher, although not in this one, obviously.

There are those who think that our paths in life are shaped by the hand of God or some Supreme Authority in whatever way He sees fit from time to time. Or not shaped but simply observed, like some grotesque cosmic experiment. Am I really part of a creation in which Hope and Faith are the recommended convictions for getting through it all in one piece?

For the smaller brain, like mine, clarity of thought is difficult to come by when faced with such exquisite complexity. I cannot for the life of me grasp the science, the mathematics, and certainly not the philosophy of the question, never mind the answer. It's mind-boggling, like trying to imagine the number of objects in the universe, or the dimensions of the cosmos in feet and inches.

How did I get here? What caused me to be? And why? All this existential philosophy confounds me as it has confounded thinkers of far greater intellect than me. If you start with religion, any religion, it has the blessing of simplicity, and provides comfortably reassuring answers to impossible questions such as *"where do I come from?"* and *"what happens to me when I die?"* It provides a point of direction, a reason and the journey. But if you start with science then it's rather more complicated. The theories of evolution, genetics, chance, odds, quantum mechanics, time, space and every other scientific discipline you can think of conspire to provide the answer in a reasoned, provable way. But the Answer to Life, the Universe and Everything is inevitably going to be 42, and that, as we know, is not helpful.

What is wrong with the idea that I exist simply because a sequence of events, some random, some not, contrived to come together at a given time in a given place and produce a consequential event which, in this case, happens to me? John Hinkley is one such event. Grandma Elliott is another. So is George, Albert and all the other characters in this story, and all the things that happened to them on the way.

Our own individual, unique existence is a pretty damn amazing thing. For me to be, I needed all the pieces in the right place, at the right time. It doesn't really matter whether this happened by the causation of determinism, the chaos of indeterminism, fate, chance, or by the design of some Higher Authority. When the threads are spun, drawn from all the dimensions of all there is, the thread into which they were woven had to converge on Allotment Cottage at Aunger's Garage in Chester-le-Street where my mother was born with the blood of Ritchies, Elliotts and Hinkleys in her veins, and where my father found her and brought the blood of the Woods and the Beveridges. I am the consequence of those events. I am the sum of them all, and I am in awe that I am.

Ellingham is a part of the thread that was James' journey. Walking back up the road from the church I wish I could identify the house that he lived in, then I could put some colour on that strand. I wish I could see the detail of his life. I take an idle kick at a clod of mud in the road. It sticks to my boot and I curse under my breath. Engrossed in my thoughts, James Hinkley and my muddy boot excluding all else, I am startled by a close beep behind me and have to move sharply out of the way of a Range Rover. It passes arrogantly close and the two Labradors in the back window stare at me with grinning jowls and lolling tongues. For a moment I am James Hinkley trudging down the road, and the dogs sit above me on the social scale. I resist the temptation to doff my cap at the receding car. But only just.

*****

From Ellingham I am following James Hinkley's final journey south through Northumberland, but not all the way. He would have continued on down the Great North Road to Newcastle and over the river into County Durham, but I am profoundly conscious that my journey is coming to an end, and I think I'm entitled to an indulgence of my own. Alnmouth is about 15 miles south on the coast, and the country road takes me back through Embleton and Longhoughton. At Hipsburn, only 4 miles from Alnwick, the road into Alnmouth crosses a bridge of four low, stone arches over the estuary of the river Aln, then up a short rise called Shepherds Hill to a small roundabout. The left turn leads along the coastal route to Boulmer, and the right into Alnmouth itself. I don't know whether to describe it as a large village or a small town as either would be fitting. It's just one street, an old fishing and trading settlement which has grown in recent years with the tourist trade but has managed to sustain an agreeable mix of 19th century charm and 21st century amenity.

Like Low Newton, the village road is one way in, one way out, so there's no through traffic. It wanders through the village past pubs and restaurants, small shops and cafes, to end at the estuary where the river Aln meets the North Sea and the magnificent Alnmouth Bay. I called it an indulgence because it is probably my favourite place on the whole of the Northumbrian coast, and although it is not on my heritage trail I would be disappointed to miss it while I am up here.

My wife and I discovered Alnmouth many years ago when she persuaded me, against my natural inclinations, to have a go at self-catering. For me a holiday is where a hotel and its staff do the bed-making, cooking and the washing up. I made valiant attempts to distract her from the notion but my objections were over-ruled and to my surprise in the end I was quite converted. We took an exceptionally well-appointed cottage on the outskirts of the village, within a minute's walk of the nearest pub and less than two from the second. We've returned on at least a half a dozen occasions since, but not for two or three years, and although this time I have booked myself into one of the hotels on the street I'm looking forward to revisiting the pubs and the scenery here, all of which is, to me, the epitome of the Northumberland coast.

My hotel is The Hope and Anchor, a pub with rooms. It's an old, whitewashed building, 18th century or older like most in the village, but it's been refurbished and modernised inside to an exceptionally high standard. It's right at the beginning of the street and close to the cottage we used to stay in. Across the road is The Sun Inn, another favourite of mine. After I've parked up outside the pub, checked in and stowed my luggage in the boutique room, I stroll out of the hotel into the road to take a walk down the street.

The early afternoon sun shines brightly from a sky blotted with small, white clouds, and a cool breeze brings a salty tang to my nostrils and the slightly acrid taste of seaweed strewn on the sand by a receding tide, energising me with an eagerness to walk and explore. Deep in shadow, small side roads and alleys lead off the main street. On my right they lead to the backs of the buildings and overlook the wide Aln estuary, at low tide merely a stream with wide muddy banks where seabirds and eider ducks go about their incessant foraging. A solitary heron, the grandee of the shore, stands dead still, watching the water. Small boats are dotted about leaning on the mud, awaiting the tide which will lift them to sway slowly with the current on their mooring lines. To my left, the backs of houses lead onto the golf links, the dunes and the sands of Alnmouth Bay stretching way into the distance, north towards Boulmer.

From the Hope and Anchor and The Sun I pass a couple of small restaurants with short but attractive menus, residential cottages and holiday lets. I recall The Red Lion pub where my wife and I have often sat on the timber terrace at the back in hats and sunglasses lazily gazing over the estuary. Opposite is the tiny post office and convenience store where I remember that the proprietor manages to offer a friendly and efficient service while maintaining a demeanour that suggests his house has just burned down. Further, a couple of gift shops and a delicatessen, a café, The Schooner pub which is also a curry house, and almost at the end more cottages and the stern Hindmarsh Hall, an 18th century granary and later Anglican chapel, now used as a community centre. The street is mostly sandy Northumberland stone and whitewash, and all engagingly quirky.

At the end of the road is the wide estuary. Dunes tumble down from the road to the sands, pathways formed by the feet of visitors snaking through them. There's a place to sit just here, a small garden with a couple of bench seats and an information board, looking out over the coastline. It's called *"Dr Joy's Garden"*, a memorial to the late Dr Joy Edelman, a respected cardiologist and resident of the town.

The garden is a favourite place of mine. From the seats here the whole coastline is spread before me. Far to the south across the wide bay the low, grey shapes of the harbour wall and rooftops of the seaside town of Amble are just visible. Inland the pennant at Warkworth Castle flies high above the distant woodland, and out to sea, low on the horizon I can see Coquet Island with its lighthouse, where blue painted tourist boats take visitors to see the seals and seabirds.

I find myself wondering about Dr Joy. I know nothing about her save for what I read here on the information board. It seems to me that if the people of Alnmouth took the trouble to erect a bench dedicated to her in this engaging place, and name the garden after her, she must have been regarded with much affection. She used to sit here, apparently, for hours on end enjoying the splendour of the coast.

This part of the coastline is the most southerly part of the Northumberland coastline before the continuous ribbon of coastal development begins, the outskirts of North Tyneside. But north of here, back up through Boulmer, Craster, Embleton, Low Newton, Bamburgh and on past Lindisfarne to the border at Berwick, it's unspoiled coastline. For 100 miles or more, apart from the disappointing exception of Seahouses, there are no fish and chip shops, no amusement arcades or fun fairs. Not even a promenade encumbers the grassy dunes, sands, rocks, bays and promontories over the whole of the coast.

After a while I ease myself up from the seat. The path loops around the back of the village alongside the estuary and past the yacht station which is little more than a few sailing dinghies pulled up onto the shore, sails furled and the rigging tinkling in the breeze. The path is called *"Lovers' Walk"*, but as I'm on my own today I shall have to use my imagination. That's not hard to do while the sun glistens on the water as I wander along the edge of the estuary mud flats. A small stand of trees creates a shady grove where a wooden bench provides a perfect spot to sit and watch the wading birds and the watchful heron. Then a short stroll up the path brings me to the four-arched bridge, back up Shepherds Hill to the roundabout and the Hope and Anchor.

***

The Sun Inn is small and low inside, and will provide me with dinner. It's fussy, with fishing related paraphernalia on the walls. Seashells and driftwood are formed into candle-holders on the rustic pine tables, and comfortable high stools line the bar. The counter is adorned with an assortment of pumps, and behind it bottles, mirrors and glassware create a glistening backdrop. My first pint of the day is presented to me by welcoming, rosy-cheeked Annie, a local girl who has served me here ever since I first set a tentative foot through the door many years ago. And it's nice to be remembered. We chat a while as she twirls a strand of hair next to her chubby, smiling face.

I'm full of reflection on the last few days. After I've eaten and pushed my empty plate away I'm sitting at the pine table with my beer and a small ring-bound notebook. My mind is a complete jumble of thoughts and memories all clamouring for attention. The only way to make any sense of it all is to note it down. When I've consigned a thought to paper I can dispel it from my mind and move on to the next and in that way I can whittle down the clamour in my head. I'm sitting deep in thought, pen poised or between puckered lips for inspiration, sipping my beer occasionally and from time to time making scribbles on the pad.

"You an inspector?" comes the voice from the next table, and I look up into the eyes of a gentleman in late middle age sitting with a small woman I imagine to be his wife. He sits with a straight back, thin face and a clipped, military moustache which is greying like his neatly trimmed haircut.

He's wearing a navy blazer with gold buttons and a tie under a light grey pullover. He's looking directly at me, expectantly. His question wasn't unfriendly, but I've no idea what he's talking about.

I offer him a smile. "Sorry? Inspector?"

"You know," he says, "a reviewer." He nods towards the table where my notepad is lying open. "For one of those papers. Those internet things that have stars."

It dawns on me that he thinks I'm some sort of researcher. It never occurred to me that in all the restaurants and bars I've sat in like this, a glass and a notebook before me and a look of concentration on my face that people around me might think of me as some sort of undercover reporter. There might have been dozens of people, including proprietors and bar staff, who have assumed that I am making notes about them with a view to publishing an assessment which they will undoubtedly expect to be neither neutral nor accurate. It makes me chuckle that I might have carried around with me some measure of perceived influence all these days.

I give one of those half laughs, just a "Ha!" but he's still looking at me. "No, no, I'm not a critic. I'm writing a book."

"Are you now?" The man's mouth forms a thoughtful pucker. His wife has the permanent smile of an elderly person which says *Isn't this lovely*?" She looks at me with wide eyed interest.

"A writer then, are you?" he says, as if it's a most unsavoury thing to discover.

"Well, we're all writers when we put pen to paper," I say brightly. He looks at me as if I have just said something deeply profound.

"What's it about? Is it a thriller?"

"No, nothing like that. It's about my family history. It's a sort of travelogue following the places my ancestors lived in and I'm trying to learn a bit about them. Actually it's my last day," I tell him, holding up my pen in case he misses the point, "I'm off home in the morning and I'm just trying to get down the things I remember."

"You should have made notes as you went along," he remarks, and before I can lodge an indignant response he continues, "I don't care for that sort of thing. I like something with a good plot. I don't suppose yours has a plot, does it?"

"Well, no, it's not that sort of book. Plenty of villains though," I add with another little laugh for levity, but it doesn't seem to divert him.

"Are you from round here, then?" he persists. Next to him his wife is still beaming.

"No, I'm from down south now, but I was born up here on Tyneside."

"You don't sound like a Geordie."

"I know, I lost it when I was much younger." I so much wanted to add "*Now go away and stop bothering me*".

Out of the corner of my eye I catch Annie grinning at me from behind the bar but she doesn't come to my rescue and I have to take it on myself to make an excuse and go to the bar. I wondered whether I should buy the man a drink but thought better of it as it would probably encourage him to linger.

"Strewth," I manage to Annie as she giggles at the glass she's pouring for me. I linger at the bar longer than I need to. I can't end it here. Not like this.

When I return to the table the couple are standing to leave, pulling on their coats. He's very glad to have met me, I'm told, and I offer the best genial response I can manage, then I'm glad to sit down alone. I'm starting to wonder if I have some unfinished business.

***

I've moved on to a glass of Shiraz. I've laid down my pen and find myself staring blankly through the table top. I don't know how long I've been sitting like that, trying to disentangle my muddled thoughts. I've walked the streets and quaysides of Tyneside and Whitley Bay, I've scoured the coalfields of Durham, and I've wandered the coastal villages of Northumberland. I've discovered and learned, met people living and dead. I've accomplished all I set out to do, and I've got a full notebook to prove it.

I set out on this journey to look for two things. I've been looking for Genetic Memory, and I've been looking for a feeling of belonging. I've also wanted to find out if those two things are connected, if a feeling of belonging might arise from a memory I never knew I had. Somewhere among the pages and pages of notes I've scribbled, the feelings I've recorded and the unwritten memories that wander through my mind, lie the answers to some of this. Maybe.

The plan is to return now, sit somewhere quiet and try to disentangle the unruly ball of string that presently makes up the sum of all I have discovered up here in the North East. But somehow tomorrow doesn't seem like the day for a long drive back to Norwich, to the place that I may, or may not, call home.

Part of me is telling me to stick to my original plan. Get back, settle down and start to write it. No good can come of lingering, it will only muddle things. But there is another part of me saying, shouting actually, that I don't have the end yet.

If I go home now my journey will end not with a bang, but a whimper. I don't think that a journey like this could ever end with a bang. It's never going to close the curtain to fireworks or the popping of champagne. But I don't want a whimper either, and certainly not in the way that T S Eliot envisaged it. I need to find the catalyst, the component which will draw me closer, if not to a conclusion then at least to an understanding of all that I have learned, felt and discovered.

I think about my wife and how much I miss her. I worry that if I stay away much longer she will forget who I am and be startled by my appearance on the doorstep. I'm torn, unsure of my decision.

When it does so, it comes with unexpected clarity, possibly assisted by the brandy which follows my glass of wine. It's so obvious I'm surprised that I hadn't planned it this way. My life started there, or as near as makes no difference, and so did this journey. I must complete the circle. This has to end where it all started. It has to end in Tynemouth. I take up my phone and call The Park.

TWENTY TWO

Coming Home

The call to my wife to tell her that I was not coming home did not go quite as I had expected. I imagined rather more disappointment and less enthusiasm for me staying away a bit longer. Still, it allayed my conscience and I awoke fresh and eager at the prospect of re-visiting Tyneside.

The images of the few days I spent there only about three weeks ago come flooding back – the Longsands, the pier, the Spanish City and all the landmarks I wandered around recovering memories that had been lost or forgotten, unearthing new ones and discovering the changes that the passage of so many years had imposed on the north east landscape. I feel a frisson of excitement having made the decision to go back there.

As I step out the door of the Hope and Anchor to my car parked in the road outside, my hand goes instinctively to my eyes to shade them against the light, the sun now climbing over the rooftops to bathe the street, one side washed almost white, the other dark in shadow. I stow my things in the car, and I'm ready to go.

While I feel restless to set off on the road south I also have a reluctance to abandon this place so suddenly. I stand, hanging around looking up and down the street for a moment or two. But in spite of the hesitation and indecision, it doesn't take much to persuade myself that I have the time to stay a while and take a final walk around, a few more images to consign to memory and perhaps a few photographs to help it along.

I take a walk down the street to Dr Joy's garden and dwell a moment looking out over the coastline. Without the cover of the rooftops the sun blazes from the eastern sky, embracing the garden with light. Early roses sway before the dunes and the sea shimmers exquisitely beyond. I stroll back down Lovers' Walk, round the estuary and back into the village, and as an excuse to delay I take a coffee on the timber terrace at the back of the Red Lion. I recall sitting here so many times with my wife, and now that I have a plan I also have the anticipation of seeing her, whether she likes it or not. "*Absence makes the heart grow fonder*" is an expression I am relieved not to have used last night when I called her. It's in the same league as the sentimental claptrap I found on the walls of the bar in The Black Horse at Beamish, and I'm sure it would have gone down very badly should I have delivered that message. But it's true, I persuade myself, although with little real conviction.

I open the car door and sit behind the wheel for a moment, wistfully watching the morning walkers in the street and the village going about its daily business. But the moment can't be delayed forever, and the pressing of the starter button comes as a submission to the inevitable. Soon I'm driving out of the village, across the four arch bridge and onto the coast road south. Slowly, as the road unfolds before me thoughts of Alnmouth fade, not forgotten but reserved, and those of approaching Tyneside take over as the final stage of my journey draws closer.

***

After four miles the rural, coast road takes me through the boutique village of Warkworth with its tea shops, imposing ruined castle and pennant flying over the highest tower. Then it skirts the disappointment that is Amble. It's a large, unstructured town which has embraced commercialism in a big, brash way. Its light industrial areas, business centres, supermarkets and the steel skeletons of half-finished warehouses enclose a busy, tourist centre of gift shops, cafes, amusements and fish and chips. It's windmills on sticks, red and blue plastic buckets and fizzy, cheap lager. Tall apartment blocks built to look like grain silos overlook the functional, concrete harbour which encloses hordes of sailing boats with tinkling rigging. They crowd the marina looking jolly, but dredgers and dirty working boats are moored alongside. Converted fishing boats, tied up alongside chalk-written timetables and narrow, wooden gangplanks wait to ferry families and children in orange lifejackets across the choppy sea to the seals on Coquet Island. Captains in white, peaked sailors' caps languish, smoking, waiting for custom. It's an ill-fitting end for the rural, pastoral River Coquet which ends up here after meandering brown and slow through the leafy countryside, and around the castle at Warkworth.

As I roll on further south the unspoiled Northumberland countryside slowly merges into the urbanity that is The Metropolitan Borough of North Tyneside. Past Amble the roads become wider, there are roundabouts every few hundred yards, and new housing estates arise on either side. Ranks of pylons appear. Hedgerows, fields and cattle are replaced by retail parks and service stations. I drive on past flyovers, heavy trucks and commercial vans, and a sense of impatience in the traffic as it grows faster, denser. Although I've seen it many times before, the transition from the natural, timeless countryside of Northumberland to the horizon-wide conurbation of Tyneside within just a few miles is an unwelcome landscape to me. The birth of yet another business park in concrete and bare steel girders where not long ago sheep grazed against a backdrop of the Cheviot Hills witnesses the inevitable advance of progress, field by field. I wonder how long Northumberland has got.

At Ashington I pass the Woodhorn Colliery Museum. I've never been in before, but I've read about it and I have a feeling that Bill Bryson mentioned it, if I remember his *Little Dribbling* book correctly. It has original mining buildings, a winding engine, a narrow-gauge railway and various colliery themed exhibitions. It's a sort of mini-Beamish so far as I can tell. I can see the high winding wheel as I approach on the Ashington ring-road, and I have a mind to drop in. But it's closed, and in front of the padlocked gates my forehead falls forward onto the steering wheel. If I ever come back up here I'm going to check Northumberland's opening hours in advance.

I drive on past Blyth where MacGregor's had a fabrication facility, and where I did two or three weeks' holiday work in my late teens. I was quite unsupervised, making steel calculations on green-lined paper at a wooden desk in a prefabricated site building, shoed into a job which wasn't really a vacancy, a favour to my father. My figures were all wrong, apparently. Later my father told me that the manager said he wanted to "*pull his teeth out*", meaning mine. My father reported this to me with an amusement that surprised me, his eyes wrinkled, smiling with his lips. Maybe he didn't like the Blyth manager much, I've no idea.

Blyth is industrial in an untidy, grubby way. I pass the power station on the coast side, then after Seaton Sluice, rows of Council houses with broken cars and weeds in the front gardens. After a formidably awful static caravan park, the coast road opens out and I'm driving past St Mary's lighthouse, the Spanish City, down the promenade, past The Rex Hotel, the Longsands and the Park Hotel. I drive slowly, feeling the comfortable familiarity of these surroundings growing with every yard of tarmac.

I don't stop at The Park but drive on, around the promontory, the old, decaying Lido and King Edward's bay to Tynemouth Village. I park the car and step out next to Wood's Café where I sat and watched the street at the beginning of this journey. The road from the end of the main street takes me down to where the pier stretches out into the mouth of the Tyne.

Out on the pier I can see a few solitary figures, coats flapping, heads down, hunched, dragging themselves onwards. At the root of the pier a mere breeze ruffled my hair, but as I walk out of the lee of the land, the wind suddenly catches me, throwing me off balance and I stumble, clutching my hat. Bracing myself against the railings, I try to capture the wind by pointing the camera back down the pier to the pedestrians holding their heads, faces turned into collars and the white spray arching off the top of waves. I hold the camera with both hands trying to steady it, battling to hold it still. It's a long drop down to the waves crashing against the rocks at the bottom, and I have a sudden sense of the High Place Phenomenon. But I don't jump off, as my erratic, staggering return down the pier testifies.

Along the coast road past The Lido I walk down to the beach, feeling the hard sand beyond brown strands of seaweed which mark the tide line. I walk slowly, taking in the air off the sea, listening to the rush of waves, the rustle of shingle as the water retreats, and the rumble of breakers further offshore. At the end of the sands I walk up to The View Café. I dwell there a while as I did three weeks ago, sitting in a wide, picture window gazing out at the view of my childhood.

I have to walk all the way back to Tynemouth to collect my car from where I had left it outside Woods Café, and by the time I've done that and driven back to The Park, it's late afternoon and the sun is settling towards the horizon. The colours in the sky are taking on streaks of lilac and purple. Above me the first few stars appear in the darkening sky.

***

The bar in The Park hasn't changed since I walked out last time to set off for County Durham, and it feels as if I have been away only a couple of hours. The tall stools against high tables, brick walls and low amber lighting, the long bar with its sparkling backdrop, and Ben, standing behind the bar counter in his white shirt and black trousers, styled, metropolitan hair, confident, a glass in one hand and a cloth in the other. And Ben's colleague Lily, about 18 years old, long blonde hair, eyelashes like shop awnings and dressed in bar-staff uniform of white blouse, black tights and a black skirt so short it would have had Harry Ritchie on the edge of his seat and Gran Elliott reaching for the salts. It's all as I left it, familiar, comfortable, reliable.

There are only a few customers in the large room, some couples sitting quietly at tables, and no one at the bar as I approach for my first beer.

"How's the book?" are Ben's first words to me, which means both "*Hello,*" and "*I remember you.*"

It's nice to be remembered. I hold up my notebook. "Full of history, full of villains."

We both laugh. "And memories? Did you find those?" Ben's Geordie lilt is memory in itself, of me, my father, and a whole childhood spent with the music of the north east. He's pouring my pint, looking down as he watches the flow.

"I think I did, yes. At least I think they were memories. It's hard to tell what are memories and what's imagination. I've had a lot of both. Sometimes it's hard to know which is which."

Ben places my beer on the bar counter. "How long are you staying?"

"Just tonight. I didn't actually plan to come back here, but I had the time and, well, I started here and it seemed like a good idea to finish here too. I'll be off tomorrow."

"Too bad. Where did you get to then? Weren't you going up the coast?"

I tell Ben about the coast, and while Lily wanders off to attend to a customer I tell him about Lookout Cottage and John Hinkley. I want to tell him that I might have met John, but I don't in case that sounds weird, which makes me feel sorry in myself because it's something I want to be able to share. But I can tell by the way Ben keeps his eyes directly on mine while he wipes his glassware that he is genuinely interested in the story. I compromise and tell him that I was able to imagine John Hinkley and his life in ways that were unexpected, and which felt natural and reliable.

"You know what?" I say to Ben. "Before I set out on this I would have laughed at the idea of Genetic Memory. It seemed like a crazy idea, that you might have memories that were made by other people. But when you find yourself imagining that sort of thing in a way that seems so real it surprises you. It seems to be coming from somewhere......well, it's like a memory, but I didn't put it there. How weird is that? It makes me wonder."

Ben nods slowly. "So you think you found that?"

"In a way, maybe. There was something helping me along." There's a moment of silence between us as Ben waits, sensing there's a bit more. "You know, I saw places, I could imagine the faces of people, and I quite often had a sense of their lives. Sometimes I wonder if I want to believe that just a bit too much, but yes, I think something was definitely helping me along, guiding my thoughts."

When Ben gets distracted by customers and his work behind the bar I leave him to it and take a table on my own. I have a glass before me, the yellow lights along the coast road outside the dark windows and the low sounds of the bar surround me. I'm sitting, sipping, flicking through the pages of my notebook, the jottings of days spent wandering the North East. I made a lot of notes as I went along, scribbles as I encountered unexpected feelings, memories and images. I'm flipping the pages and underlining sections in red, scribbling asterisks against lines.

I see a note about the photographs I saw on the wall of The Fishing Boat in Boulmer, old sepia prints, and I remember the figures I saw depicted there. Figures caught in a split second of time, a moment from which we seek to deduce their life.

I have photos myself. Not of John Hinkley, or the Beverages - they came too soon for the technology. But of Albert my grandfather, white haired, slim in baggy trousers holding his first grandchild, looking just like my father. And an old, cracked sepia print of James William when he's about 80 years old in a huge grey beard and a bath chair, centre-stage, surrounded by family. And I have photos of Harry, Gran Elliott and others, all treasured, all safe in a heavy cardboard chocolate box my mother gave to me after my father died. And one of George Elliott my great-grandfather who died in the pit, particularly special because when I look at it, I see myself in his eyes.

How often on this journey have I occupied the same space as those people, separated only by the passage of time? Lookout Cottage, the woodland at Cornsay Colliery, the streets of Grange Villa to name but a few. How often in these places has the blanket of the 21st century been stripped away and history revealed? What memories, what influence has enabled me to see those things? Was that the Genetic memory I've been looking out for? Or was it the product of a mind persuaded by a determination to see?

I don't think it was determination that invoked the connection I felt when my mind produced George before me at his graveside, or Albert in Grange Villa. There was something helping me along there. I don't know if Pete McCarthy ever found that. He never told us. But I thank him for the idea, because I think I did.

***

My eyes fall to a jotting I made in my notebook three weeks ago about Whitley Bay and Tynemouth, when I was sitting here in this bar. I had scribbled down "*Connected. Feel at home here. Do I belong?*" I underlined it then, and it holds my attention now. That word, "*home*".

I once met Paul Young in Marseilles airport. Not that he will remember. It was one of those "*Are you Paul Young the musician?*" moments while squashed together in an airport transfer bus. I always assumed celebrities like him travelled British Airways first class, but here he was slumming it on a budget airline like me. He was very friendly as I recall, and I find myself thinking about the song for which he is probably most famous, "*Wherever I lay my hat, that's my home*". To be honest, I don't buy that. When I was in my late teens I laid my hat under Bournemouth pier when the local Youth Hostel tumbled the fact that my pals and I were on a beer pilgrimage and wouldn't let us in. There was no sense of being at home as the tide came in, cold sand and grit filled our sleeping bags, and the local plod moved us on. So that's not it.

***

The evening has passed quickly. It's passed me by as I sat in my own world of jottings and the memories of the three weeks just past. Looking up from my notepad I notice that my glass is as empty as the bar. Ben and Lily are chatting behind the counter. I gather up my stuff from the table, and step up to take one of the high stools, and Ben takes my glass for a refill.

I'm sitting with both elbows on the bar, swiping photos on my phone as Ben and Lily peer over to see. The main door is quite a few yards away, across tables and past a couple of pillars, and when it opens in comes a small, elderly and slightly round figure in a coat, I'm delighted to see George Smiley again. The beaming face and the sparkle in the eyes betray the tradecraft of Brendan of the Camino Way. Brendan of the large Merlot and endless anecdote. Brendan with a limp, a big smile and a warm greeting. Brendan whose first words are "How's the book?" I have the feeling I probably talked about it too much last time.

We greet each other as if we have known each other for far longer that the three or four glasses we spent together the last time I was here. Brendan asks me how I've been, and where I've been, and we talk. We talk about all things Tyneside, all things Northumberland, and we talk about what this place means to us.

I ask him, "So, what is it about the North East? What makes you feel you belong here?"

"The people," he says without hesitation, "definitely the people."

Lily is standing next to Ben and listening to what I imagine she regards as the wandering philosophies of old men with too much Merlot inside them. I ask her, "What about you, Lily? What keeps you here?"

She thinks, and blinks like a semaphore lamp. "The beach," she says in soft, lyrical Geordie, with a giggle and a glossy pink smile. Then, "Oh all right," as if discarding a flippancy, "the people," she concedes.

"The landscape," says Ben. "Which means everything - the accent, the beach, Geordie girls, the city, the river, football. And yes, the people. Everything." We all nod. We understand. It is nothing without everything.

***

Brendan gets another Merlot. "Where's your home then? Did you find that out?" he asks me, taking a long pull at his glass.

"Where my heart is? Wherever I lay my hat? On the range?" which sounded a bit flippant because Brendan was being unusually serious.

"You know," he says, "when I walked all that way to Santiago, you meet people on the way, become friends. There was a great camaraderie about that whole trip, and when we got there we hung around together for a while, and I felt really at home there. I could have stayed for a lot longer, and maybe would have done if the others had stayed too. But when I got back here that's when I realised where home really is. It's right here."

***

This journey, this story that I have uncovered, has given me much more than I ever expected it to do. I have drawn out pictures of my childhood which have been hidden away for years. I have seen my parents in ways I had forgotten. I have acquired a richer understanding of my heritage than I could ever have done by research in books or front of a screen. I have engaged with what I perceive to have been the lives of my ancestors. I have made connections with them, with my childhood, and with the North East of England.

I have met people, been to places and experienced feelings that would otherwise have been lost to me. Many of them I didn't even know existed. I have had my existential radar adjusted to a wider spectrum.

I set out to inquire and explore what Pete McCarthy called "*a sense of belonging*". I have learned that that expression comprises a melting pot of feelings, memories, emotions and a mix of internal and external landscapes that is hard to disentangle. In the wide picture there's no doubt that all the places in which I have dwelled a while on this journey have made their own contributions, offered their own connections and given me a sense of belonging in one way or the other. That has been especially strong in Tynemouth and Whitley Bay. I feel Northern blood in my veins.

But I have felt I wanted to explore further than that, and on this journey I have found that I have distilled Pete's question to something I find more manageable, more reckonable. I have found myself wanting to know where I feel "*at home*", which I determine to be a different thing altogether.

Home, a place which is comfortably dependable in ways which are within the boundaries of reality. Home in the second decade of the 21st century, not home in the 1950s, the 1960s, or even the 1970s. What is home? Perhaps it is my wife, my house, my neighbours, my garden, my cat, the pub on the corner. Little John who grew up into a London City lawyer, produced a delightful niece for me, and is now in rotund retirement in Norwich; drinking buddy, best mate, soulmate, argumentative brother. Friends I love, friends I like, and friends who fall into neither category but are friends anyway. My mother, at the time of writing. My bookshelves, my wine rack, my drawing easel and all the stuff I have around me animal, vegetable or mineral.

Or perhaps not. A while ago I asked myself where I would belong if I stripped all that away and had the whole map to choose from. But the question is theoretical, hypothetical, rhetorical, academic, and actually just pointless. I can't strip it away, and I wouldn't if I could.

I once lived in Tyneside. I once had a home here and I belonged here. I feel the connection even now, and it's a strong, welcome connection. I have unexpectedly found that I speak the language, enjoy the landscape in the way that Ben meant it, and I have discovered deep memories. But my life has moved, lock, stock and baggage. I am mildly surprised to have discovered this, but I have a feeling of ease that I have done so. I feel validated. I am not somewhere I should not be. I don't need to be chasing dreams.

I wonder when on this journey that discovery came to me. The answer, I expect, is that I've always known it, but with my new radar I can see it more clearly.

Brendan places his empty glass on the bar counter and reaches for his coat. "Well," he says, "that's it for me." He grins and takes my hand. "Perhaps I'll see you again someday. You're off tomorrow? Going home?"

"Yes," I say, gripping his hand, "tomorrow I'll be going home."

****

Ancestral Tree

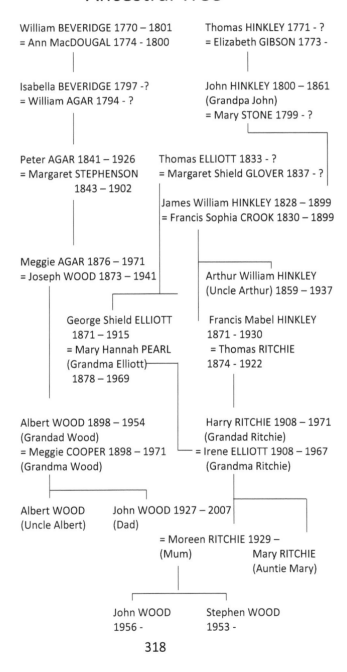

William BEVERIDGE 1770 – 1801
= Ann MacDOUGAL 1774 - 1800

Thomas HINKLEY 1771 - ?
= Elizabeth GIBSON 1773 -

Isabella BEVERIDGE 1797 -?
= William AGAR 1794 - ?

John HINKLEY 1800 – 1861
(Grandpa John)
= Mary STONE 1799 - ?

Peter AGAR 1841 – 1926
= Margaret STEPHENSON
1843 – 1902

Thomas ELLIOTT 1833 - ?
= Margaret Shield GLOVER 1837 - ?

James William HINKLEY 1828 – 1899
= Francis Sophia CROOK 1830 – 1899

Meggie AGAR 1876 – 1971
= Joseph WOOD 1873 – 1941

Arthur William HINKLEY
(Uncle Arthur) 1859 – 1937

George Shield ELLIOTT
1871 – 1915
= Mary Hannah PEARL
(Grandma Elliott)
1878 – 1969

Francis Mabel HINKLEY
1871 - 1930
= Thomas RITCHIE
1874 - 1922

Albert WOOD 1898 – 1954
(Grandad Wood)
= Meggie COOPER 1898 – 1971
(Grandma Wood)

Harry RITCHIE 1908 – 1971
(Grandad Ritchie)
= Irene ELLIOTT 1908 – 1967
(Grandma Ritchie)

Albert WOOD
(Uncle Albert)

John WOOD 1927 – 2007
(Dad)
= Moreen RITCHIE 1929 –
(Mum)

Mary RITCHIE
(Auntie Mary)

John WOOD
1956 -

Stephen WOOD
1953 -

AUTHOR'S NOTE

I made this journey over a period of about 4 weeks between November 2019 and March 2020. I arrived back home in Norfolk on 2nd March 2020 – very shortly before the Coronavirus pandemic caused the lockdown which, had I travelled only a little later, would have prevented me from completing it at all.

I haven't made anything up. Well, not much. I really did fall head over heels in Cornsay woods, I really did meet a man with no nose in Esh Winning, and I really did feel the presence of the past as I have described. I've often wondered, when reading other authors' travelogues, at the curious events and encounters they describe. I've wondered how much of it is make-believe, but now I know that, actually, stranger things really do happen when you set off on your own to explore.

I have tried to be accurate with historical fact. One place where I have taken licence is in the fictional chapter 9, concerning my grandfather Albert in the village of Grange Villa, and the character Morris. In 1953 the National Health Service had been established for a few years and Morris would have had free healthcare available to him. I wanted to show Albert as he would been in that year because that was when we knew each other for a few, short months. But I also wanted to depict the hardships that the community would have endured only a short time earlier, especially in things like healthcare. I have blended the two and in doing so I have created an historical inaccuracy, to which I put my hand up.

And things change quickly. I have written things as I saw them, but by the time this book is released who knows if the Tynemouth Lido will have received its funding and a complete restoration, or if the Rex Hotel has become the promised haven for the elderly. By the time this is published The Sage Gateshead may have been painted pink and the Northumbrian coastline littered with spas and resorts. It's as I saw it, and I make no apology for that.

Otherwise, if I have any dates or historical observation wrong, I am happy to be corrected.

At the time I write this the coronavirus situation is far from resolved and I don't think anyone has much idea how it will all turn out in the long-run. There is economic disturbance throughout the world, ethnic and cultural margins are at a height of division, and regional military and paramilitary activity continues to rumble on in many parts of the world. Political shenanigans threaten personal liberties and the big, global players square up to each other with ever more sabre-rattling belligerence. The changing course of history over the last two centuries that I have observed has yet a long way to go, and I can't help thinking that reflecting on the past has at least the benefit of certainty. Reflection on the future has no such comfort.

In terms of the journey and in addition to those I have thanked elsewhere, I must thank The National Trust, The Black Horse Hotel at Beamish and The Park Hotel in Tynemouth for their help in organising some of the logistics, and Francis Rossi in Seahouses for helping me fix my car. The Chester-le-Street Heritage Group, The National Coalmining Museum, Beamish Museum, The Admiralty Archivist and many others like them have assisted me greatly with my research.

About the Author

Stephen Wood was born on Tyneside and spent his childhood and adolescent years there surrounded by the business of shipbuilding (his father was a naval architect) and the seaside resort of Whitley Bay. He was educated at Barnard Castle School on the Durham/Yorkshire border, and at De Montford University, Leicester where he gained an Honours degree in law. His career took him to East Anglia where he eventually became a senior partner of a Norfolk law firm.

Outside of writing, Stephen enjoys painting, the fells of the Lake District and the wide landscape of Northumberland, exploring his heritage and reading. Playing golf was a favourite activity until the onset of arthritis and an increasingly obvious lack of talent consigned it to the receptacle of Things That Are Not Going To Happen Anymore.

Stephen enjoys many genres of writing, but is especially drawn to contemporary travel writers such as Michael Palin, Paul Theroux and Bill Bryson. Pete McCarthy, who so well blended the travelogue with internal connection to both people and places, introduced him to the concept of Genetic Memory and was a major influence on this book.

Stephen is now retired and lives in the city of Norwich with his wife. His brother, who features in this story as "Little John", is a close friend, sounding board and mentor.

"In Search of a Northern Soul" is Stephen's first book